THE
WAL

STI
An elusive
Killer" who murdered nine Californi-
ans in one year.

STILL AT LARGE
A Texas madman who claims human
heads as trophies of the hunt.

STILL AT LARGE
LA's "Southside Slayer," known for the
knife-torture of his fourteen victims
and his horrific pattern of overkill.

STILL AT LARGE
A west coast occult killer who has left a
trail of fifteen nude and unspeakably
abused corpses in his wake.

HUNTING HUMANS

VOLUME 2

Other Avon Books by
Michael Newton

HUNTING HUMANS, VOLUME 1

HUNTING HUMANS

VOLUME 2

MICHAEL NEWTON

AVON BOOKS ◆ NEW YORK

Hunting Humans originally appeared as a single hardcover volume by Michael Newton, published by Loompanics Unlimited in 1990.

AVON BOOKS
A division of
The Hearst Corporation
1350 Avenue of the Americas
New York, New York 10019

First Avon Books Printing: May 1993

AVON TRADEMARK REG. U.S. PAT. OFF. AND IN OTHER COUNTRIES, MARCA REGISTRADA, HECHO EN U.S.A.

Printed in the U.S.A.

RA 10 9 8 7 6 5 4 3 2 1

To Barbara Gowdy. More grist for the mill . . .

ACKNOWLEDGMENTS

I am indebted to the following individuals and institutions for their kind assistance in the preparation of this work. Geographically, they include:

ALABAMA: John Fay, Associate Executive Editor, Mobile *Press-Register;* Sgt. Wilbur Williams, Mobile Police Dept.

ALASKA: Brenda Files, Anchorage *Daily News;* Investigator Mark Stewart, Alaska State Troopers, Criminal Investigation Bureau

ARIZONA: Tucson *Citizen*

ARKANSAS: Lt. R.L. Jenkins, Little Rock Police Dept.; Lt. Doug Stephens, Arkansas State Police; Chief James Vandiver, Little Rock Police Dept.

CALIFORNIA: Robert Andrew, Librarian, Long Beach *Press-Telegram:* Lt. Ray Biondi, Sacramento County Sheriff's Dept.; David Cappoli, Librarian, Los Angeles *Herald Examiner;* Sgt. Garry Davis, Kern County Sheriff's Dept.; D.A. Dicaro, Librarian, Beale Memorial Library (Bakersfield); Joan Douglas, Librarian, Riverside *Press-Enterprise;* Capt. Robert Grimm, Los Angeles County Sheriff's Dept.; John Irby, the Bakersfield

Californian; Rhonda Kruse, Senior Librarian, San Diego Public Library; Sgt. A. Thurston, Kern County Sheriff's Dept.; Union-Tribune Publishing Co., San Diego

CANADA: Alberta—Patricia Garneau, Librarian, Edmonton *Journal;* British Columbia—Pacific Press Limited; the Vancouver *Sun;* Ontario—Deborah Jessop, Librarian, the Windsor *Star;* Quebec—the Montreal *Gazette;* Saskatchewan—Eric Jenkins, head librarian, Regina *Leader Post*

COLORADO: Eleanor Geheres, Manager, Denver Public Library; James Jordan, Senior Agent, Colorado Dept. of Public Safety

CONNECTICUT: Hartford *Courant;* Barbara White, Editor, Meriden *Record-Journal*

DELAWARE: Col. Daniel Simpson, Director, Delaware State Police

ENGLAND: Kevin Wilson

FLORIDA: Vernon Bradford, Florida Dept. of Corrections; Hernando County Library; J.E. McMillen, Jacksonville Sheriff's Dept.; Heath Meriwether, Editor, Miami *Herald;* Lt. Mark Schlein, Broward County Sheriff's Dept.; Arnold Summers, General Manager, Park Newspapers of Florida

GEORGIA: K. Wayne Ford, Staff Writer, Athens *Banner-Herald;* Starr Holland, Librarian, Albany *Herald;* Diane Hunter, Librarian, *Atlanta Journal;* E.P. Peters, Director, Georgia Bureau of Investigation

HAWAII Charles Memminger, Staff Writer, Honolulu *Star-Bulletin*

IDAHO: Jon Jensen, Staff Writer, Idaho Falls *Post-Register*

IOWA: Thomas R. Ruxlow, Director, Iowa Division of Criminal Investigation; Eugene Thomas, Editor, Nevada *Journal*

ILLINOIS: Bill Behrens, Investigator, Cook County Sheriff's Dept.; David L. Morse, Illinois State Library

INDIANA: Cecil Smith, Editor, Salem *Leader*

KANSAS: Jack H. Ford, Assistant Director, Kansas Bureau of Investigation; Ethel J. Hunt; Davis Merritt, Jr., Executive Director, Wichita *Eagle-Beacon;* Capt. Ken Pierce, Shawnee County Sheriff's Dept.; Lt. Tom Sargent, Shawnee County Sheriff's Dept.

KENTUCKY: Morgan T. Elkins, Commissioner, Kentucky State Police

LOUISIANA: Helen C. Hudson and Susan Parmer, Shreve Memorial Library; New Orleans Public Library; Gwen Pearce, Reference Librarian, Bossier Parish Library

MARYLAND: Susan E. Stetina, Deputy Clerk, Circuit Court of Cecil County; Sgt. Paul D. Waclawski, Baltimore County Police Dept.

MASSACHUSETTS: Worcester *Telegram & Gazette*

MICHIGAN: *The Detroit News;* P.W. Dukes, Librarian, Detroit *Free Press;* Vonda Jamrog, Dept. of Corrections; Kalamazoo *Gazette;* Jim Shanahan, Managing Editor, St. Joseph *Herald Palladium;* Maj. Lewis G. Smith, Michigan State Police; Lt. Paul H. Wood, Michigan State Police

MINNESOTA: Meredith R. Cook, Blue Earth Community Library

MISSISSIPPI: Cleveland *Bolivar Commercial;* Beverly Canerdy, Jackson *Clarion-Ledger;* Maj. Walter Tucker, Dept. of Public Safety

NEBRASKA: Capt. J.E. Burnett, Nebraska State Patrol; Sheriff David R. Schleve, Scotts Bluff County

NEVADA: Carroll Edward Cole; Las Vegas *Review-Journal;* Jenny Scarantino, Librarian, Las Vegas *Sun*

NEW JERSEY: Eloise Lehnert, Blairstown *Press;* Mary Ann McDade, Morristown Library; Howard A. McGinn, Prosecutor, Warren County

NEW YORK: Detective Al Sheppard, NYPD Intelligence Division

NORTH CAROLINA: Fayetteville *Observer;* Ken Reading, Public Library of Johnston County

NORTH DAKOTA: Dick Hickman, Special Agent, Bureau of Criminal Investigation

OHIO: J. Richard Abell, Cincinnati Public Library; James Bates, Assistant Prosecuting Attorney, Lucas County; Det. Donald Bradley, Cleveland Police Dept.; Lee McLaird, Reference Archivist, Bowling Green State University; Margaret Marten, Cleveland *Plain Dealer;* Medina County *Gazette;* J. Bradford Tillson, Editor, Dayton *Daily News*

OKLAHOMA: Ted Limke, Director, Oklahoma State Bureau of Investigation

OREGON: Capt. Robert J. Brickeen, Oregon State Police

PENNSYLVANIA: Marcia Morelli, New Castle Public Library; Scranton *Times;* Carol Thomas, Librarian, Wilkes-Barre *Times-Leader*

SOUTH CAROLINA: M.S. Crockett, Librarian, Charlotte *Evening Post*

TENNESSEE: Ellen Henry, Librarian, Jackson *Sun;* Nashville *Banner;* Steve O. Watson, Director, Tennessee Bureau of Investigation

TEXAS: Sheriff Larry R. Busby, Live Oak County; Opal Miller, Librarian, County of Live Oak; Robert Sadler, Associate Editor, Waco *Tribune-Herald;* Dennis Spies, Managing Editor, Amarillo *Globe-News;* Patricia Starr, Austin *American-Statesman;* Larry Todd, Public Information Officer, Dept. of Public Safety; Richard Veit, Librarian, Texas Collection, Baylor University

UTAH: Chief Swen C. Nielsen, Provo Police Dept.

VIRGINIA: Lucy Proctor, Senior Staff Writer, Christianburg *News Messenger;* Julian Pugh, Dept. of Corrections

WASHINGTON: Jeanne Engerman, Librarian, Washington State Library; Tacoma Public Library; Harold D. Wilson, Librarian, Seattle Public Library

WISCONSIN: La Crosse *Tribune;* Kate Lorenz, Jefferson Public Library; Milwaukee *Journal;* Newspapers, Inc., Milwaukee; the *Wisconsin State Journal*

WYOMING: Christopher A. Crofts, Director, Wyoming Division of Criminal Investigation; Bess Sheller, Director, Carbon County Library

With special thanks to my wife, Judy, for her assistance in the final preparation of the manuscript.

*"Society's had their chance.
I'm going hunting. Hunting humans."*

JAMES OLIVER HUBERTY, 1984

PREFACE

The face of modern homicide is changing. We are caught up in the midst of what one expert calls an "epidemic of homicidal mania," victimized by a new breed of "recreational killers" who slaughter their victims at random, for the sheer sport of killing. In the years since World War II, our annual solution rate for homicides has dropped from 90% to 76%, indicating that one in every four domestic murders goes unsolved. In human terms, that means 5,000 victims—13 each and every day—will be dispatched by murderers who walk away, scot free. According to the FBI's best estimate, at least 3,500 of those will be slain by "serial killers," a special breed of predator who kill repeatedly, without remorse, sometimes for years on end.

Initially, we run afoul of definitions. Self-proclaimed "authorities" butt heads in endless arguments about the mandatory body count and length of intervals between specific crimes that are presumed to qualify a "genuine" serial killer. Most such guidelines have been arbitrary and entirely artificial, stacking the odds in favor of this or that pet theory. In an effort to restore common sense to the subject, I have adopted the definition published in a 1988 report from the National Institute of Justice. The NIJ report defines serial murder as "a series of two or more murders, committed as separate events, usually, but not always, by one offender acting alone. The crimes may occur over a period of time ranging from hours to years. Quite often the motive is psychological, and the offender's behavior and the physical evidence observed at the crime scenes will reflect sadistic, sexual overtones."

Serial murder is the crime of the 1990s, but is it really new? The term is certainly of recent vintage, coined around 1980 to differentiate between "mass murderers"—who slaughter several victims in a single, frantic outburst—and the more insidious, methodical killers who spin out their crimes over time. New terminology, however, does not signify a new phenomenon. Criminologist Melvin Rheinhardt discussed the subject of "chain killers" as early as 1962, and the problem was already ancient. Gilles de Rais, the richest man in France and confidant to Joan of Arc, was executed in the 15th century for slaying upwards of 100 children. Several interesting cases were prosecuted under the Inquisition, cloaked in the theological trappings of witchcraft, vampirism, and lycanthropy. Elizabeth Bathory was convicted, in 1611, of personally killing some 650 young women, for the purpose of bathing herself in their blood. Joseph Phillipe slaughtered Parisian prostitutes in the 1860s, and Jack the Ripper carried the game to London twenty years later, inspiring a host of imitators over the next decade. In short, the problem seems to be as old as human history.

The work in hand confines itself, for practical reasons, to a survey of 20th-century serial killers.

Geographically, serial killers are found on every continent except Antarctica, with North America claiming 76% of the total and Europe running a distant second with 19%. Easily leading the field, the United States boasts 74% of the world total—and 97% of the North American gross—in serial murders. Europe's leaders are England (with 36%), Germany (with 29%), and

France (trailing with 11%). Communist nations contribute a mere 1.8% of the total, with ten cases recorded since 1917, a fact explained in equal parts by cultural differences and the tendency of state-owned media to "lose" bad news.

Who are the murderers among us? In America, 85% are male and 8% female; sex remains undetermined in another 7% of cases, where the killers are still at large. Ethnically, 82% of American serial killers are white, 15% are black, and 2.5% are Hispanic. (Native Americans and Orientals figure in one case each, with the Oriental killer serving as accomplice to a white man.) Few of them are legally insane, and all are cunning, indicated by the fact that some 18% of cases in this century remain unsolved.

In operational terms, 87% of American serial killers are loners, while only 10% hunt in pairs or packs. Of the "social" killers, 59% represent all-male groupings (ranging from two-man teams to gangs of a dozen or more), while 23 percent are male-female couples, and 18% include mixed groups of varying sizes.

Generalizations are dangerous, but serial killers may be loosely classified in terms of their hunting techniques. *Territorial* killers stake out a defined area—a city or county, sometimes a particular street or municipal park—and rarely deviate from their selected game preserve. An estimated 58% of American serial killers fall into this category, including 65% of all blacks and 44% of all female killers. *Nomadic* slayers travel widely in their search for prey, confounding authorities as they drift aimlessly from one jurisdiction to another. The nomad ranks include 34% of America's "recreational" killers, with 30% of black killers and 28% of lethal ladies falling into this category. *Stationary* killers crouch like spiders in a web, committing murders mainly in their homes or places of employment—clinics, nursing homes, and hospitals included. Only 8%

of America's serial killers belong in this category, including a bare 3% of black killers and a substantial 28% of female practitioners.

As defined above, the motives for serial murder are "quite often" psychological, with strong sado-sexual overtones and evidence of compulsive behavior. Coolly professional killers-for-hire are excluded from the definition, but that does not preclude a profit motive in serial crimes. Approximately 6% of cases here described are exercises in greed run amok, incorporating what psychologist Stanton Samenow has called a "double voltage"—that is, the amplified thrill of killing for profit *and* pleasure. (Significantly, 31% of female serial killers have murdered for gain, compared to 3% of their male counterparts.) Since 1969, a disturbing 8% of American serial cases have involved practitioners of Satanism or black magic, while another 5% involve members of the medical profession—doctors, dentists, nurses, nursing aides.

Ancient or otherwise, serial murder is clearly escalating in modern society. In the first half of this century, American police recorded an average of 1.2 serial cases per year. Since 1960, the figure has leaped to 12 cases per year, and by the 1980s new cases were capturing headlines at an average rate of two per month. While new police investigative methods and wider journalistic coverage clearly account for some of the phenomenal increase, it remains obvious that serial crimes *are* multiplying dramatically.

The work in hand suggests no ultimate solutions to our "murder epidemic." The FBI's Violent Criminal Apprehension Program (VICAP) is a long step in the right direction, coupled with early diagnosis of potential killers and referral of their cases for competent treatment. We have known for years that many future murderers display a tell-tale "triad" of symptoms—bedwetting, arson, and cruelty to animals—in their childhood years, but parents, teachers, and physicians must be trained to spot the warning signs. More recent evidence establishes that child abuse and early trauma to the brain may help to launch a killer on his way. At least four of the male killers considered here were subjected to identical childhood abuse, forced to dress in girl's clothing by sadistic relatives who sought to "teach them a lesson."

Prevention is essential, then ... but is it practical? Psychologists inform us that the human character is rather firmly set between years two and five—that is, before a child leaves home for public school. Once having killed, they are apparently immune to psychiatric therapy. Confined, they are a constant danger to their keepers, fellow prisoners, and to society at large, inevitably claiming further victims if they manage to escape or win parole. Such cases, sadly, are not rare, and the deliberate release of psychopathic killers to the street provides a telling argument for proponents of capital punishment.

If nothing else, our survey of the predators among us may assist potential victims in an effort to protect themselves, their families, and loved ones from the random killers who select their prey as "targets of opportunity." Depriving the sadistic hunters of their chosen game, while running them to earth with new technology, appears to be the last, best hope of wiping out the lethal epidemic in our midst.

CASE HISTORIES

Adorno, George

Born in 1959, the son of Puerto Rican immigrants, Adorno had his first close encounter with police at age four, after setting his sister on fire. He ran up an impressive record of sixteen arrests, all for theft, before he was charged—at age 15—with triple homicide. George confessed the slayings to a New York district attorney, in the presence of his sister. Adorno's mother spoke no English and had not been summoned for that reason, but her absence led a juvenile magistrate to throw out the confession, dismissing three counts of homicide. Convicted on a lesser charge of robbery, Adorno was sentenced to three years confinement, with his juvenile record sealed by court order, in compliance with state law.

Released after serving half his sentence, Adorno was free nineteen days before he killed again. The latest victim was Steven Robinson, a black law student working as a cab driver to pay his tuition. Adorno's guilty plea, entered on July 12, 1977, earned him a sentence of fifteen years to life. (Two accomplices—Mark Davis, 17, and Calvin Gaddy, 15—also pled guilty in Robinson's death, receiving identical sentences.) Under New York law, he became eligible for parole after serving half the lesser period. Justice Burton Roberts, in sentencing

Adorno, delivered a scathing attack on the American system of juvenile justice. "Nothing ever happened to Adorno," Roberts said. "He plays the courts like a concert player plays the piano. Is there ever a time when a red light goes on and you say, 'We have to control this person'?"

Alaska—Unsolved Murders

In January 1931, it was announced that the United States Attorney General's office was committing federal agents to the search for an elusive killer, blamed for fifteen murders and a string of unsolved disappearances in the territory of Alaska. All of the killings and disappearances were reported from the southeastern part of the territory, in the wilderness area between Fairbanks and the Gulf of Alaska. Hunters and fishermen lived in constant fear of the nameless slayer who struck without warning, trailing his victims to isolated killing grounds, leaving no trace of himself behind. In every case, it was reported that the killer "slipped away with ghost-like ease."

In fact, there *was* a trace, if anything could be determined from the meager evidence. The latest confirmed murder victim, fish buyer John Marshall, had been found a few miles outside Ketchikan on October 20, 1930. The victim was still on his anchored boat, laid out where he fell after crushing blows shattered his skull. Clutched in one stiff hand, for what they might be worth, were several strands of hair.

If Marshall was the last known victim, he was not the latest local resident to disappear, and terrified survivors counted every missing soul as victims of the killer. John Wickstrom had gone out trolling in a small boat, shortly before Marshall's murder and at the same spot, only to vanish without a trace. Since Marshall's death, at least three more locals had disappeared. Albert Anderson, hunting from his skiff, was named among the missing. More recently, Albert Farrow and L.C. Davis had disappeared from their small boat, found anchored in a lonely cove and partly swamped with water.

On January 18, 1931, a federal marshal was reportedly en route to an isolated part of Prince of Wales Island, tracking an unnamed suspect, but the progress of his search was never reported, and the case remains unsolved today.

Allen, Howard Arthur

A black serial killer with a taste for elderly victims, Howard Allen never strayed far from hometown Indianapolis in his search for prey. In August 1974, at age twenty-four, he invaded the home of 85-year-old Opal Cooper, beating her to death in the course of a petty robbery. Convicted on a reduced charge of manslaughter, Allen received a term of two to twenty-one years in state prison. Paroled in January 1985, he returned to Indianapolis and found work at a car wash, biding his time before he resumed the hunt.

On May 18, 1987, a 73-year-old Indianapolis woman narrowly escaped death when she was choked and beaten by a prowler in her home. Two days later, Laverne Hale, 87, was attacked in a similar fashion, dying of her injuries on May 29.

The raids continued, on June 2, when a burglar ransacked the home of an elderly man five blocks from the scene of Laverne Hale's murder. This time, the tenant was absent; the prowler vented his anger by setting the house on fire.

On July 14, Ernestine Griffin, age 73, was murdered in her Indianapolis home, stabbed eight times with a ten-inch butcher knife, a kitchen toaster smashed repeatedly against her skull. Grieving relatives estimated that the killer had escaped with fifteen dollars and a camera belonging to his victim.

The case broke on August 4, 1987, with Howard Allen's arrest on multiple charges. Witnesses linked him with the May 18 attack, leading to Allen's indictment on charges of battery, burglary, and unlawful confinement. He was also charged with arson and burglary (from the June 2 incident), as well as the murder of Ernestine Griffin.

Police were not finished with their suspect, however. As it happened, Laverne Hale had been a neighbor of Allen's, living directly behind his house, and he remains a suspect in her murder, based upon the killer's modus operandi. In early August, detectives announced that Allen was a prime suspect in eleven other cases, each involving robbery or assault of elderly victims in their homes around Indianapolis.

In the spring of 1988, Allen was convicted of burglary and felony battery in the May 18 assault, with an additional count of habitual criminal behavior. He was sentenced to 88 years on those charges, but the worst was yet to come. On June 11, 1988, he was convicted of murder and robbery in the slaying of Ernestine Griffin, with members of his jury recommending the death penalty.

"Astrological" Murders— California

Between December 1969 and November 1970, police in Northern California linked nine unsolved murders with a single perpetrator, still at large. A common bond is found in the disposal of the bodies, cast off in ravines, and in the killer's hypothetical obsession with astrology. Of nine acknowledged victims, seven died in fair proximity to a seasonal solstice or equinox, while two were slain on Friday the thirteenth. Additionally, it is possible the murders may have lasted through December 1973, with six more victims added to the body count.

The list begins, officially, with one Leona Roberts, found ten days before the winter solstice, in December 1969. Her death was treated as a homicide, although the cause is listed as "exposure" by the medical examiner.

The killer had a busy month in March of 1970, beginning with Cosette Ellison, found nude in a ravine seventeen days before the vernal equinox, the cause of death undetermined. Two days later, on March 5, Patricia King was strangled and discarded, naked, in a rural gully. Nurse Judith Hikari vanished on March 7, thirteen days before the equinox; she was discovered, nude and bludgeoned in an overgrown ravine, on April 26. On Friday, March 13, Marie Anstey was kidnapped in Vallejo, stunned by a blow to the head, and then drowned; her body was recovered in rural Lake County, on March 21, and an autopsy revealed traces of mescaline in her bloodstream. Celebrating the equinox itself, on March 20, the slayer clubbed Eva Blau to death and dumped her body in a roadside gully; once again, the medical examiner found drugs in the victim's system.

The seventh victim on official rosters is a nurse named Donna Lass, abducted from Lake Tahoe prior to the autumnal equinox, on September 26, 1970. Her body has never been found. Nancy Bennallack appeared to break the killer's pattern, dying with her throat cut in a Sacramento flat October 26, but she remains on the official roster. Number nine was Carol Hilburn, a Sacramento X-ray technician, found beaten to death in a ravine on Friday, November 13. She had been stripped except for one boot and the panties that her killer left around her knees.

The tally might end there, but author Robert Graysmith, ever seeking victims in his search for the elusive "Zodiac," reports at least six other homicides that seem to fit the general pattern. Betty Cloer, 21, was shot and beaten by her killer during June 1971, her body discovered two days before the summer solstice. Linda Ohlig, age 19, was found beaten to death at Half Moon Bay on March 28, 1972—six days after the vernal equinox. Eighteen days before the autumnal equinox, in September 1972, Alexandra Clery was beaten to death in Oakland, her nude body discarded like a broken rag doll. Susan McLaughlin, 19, was stabbed to death and left without a stitch of clothing in March 1973, eighteen days before the vernal equinox. And finally, nineteen days before the winter solstice, in December 1973, Michael Shane and Cathy Fechtel were shot and dumped beside a road in Livermore.

Coincidence? Police are confident of a connection in at least the first nine cases, hedging on the other six described by Graysmith. Is the "Zodiac" responsible for these and more than twenty other unsolved murders, in addition to his six known homicides? The answer to that question, like the killer's true identity, remains a mystery. (See also: "Occult" Murders; "Zodiac," Vol. 1)

Ax Murders—Alabama

Between November 1919 and October 1923, residents of Birmingham, Alabama, were terrorized by a series of brutal assaults, committed by ax-wielding blacks, which claimed the lives of at least fifteen victims, leaving others gravely injured. In most cases, the targets were immigrant merchants in outlying parts of the city, wounded or killed in their shops by assailants who afterward robbed them of money or merchandise.

It is impossible to verify the final body-count in Alabama's four-year reign of terror. After Charles Graffeo's murder, on May 28, 1923, local journalists described him as the nineteenth murder victim, with another seventeen survivors adding up to thirty-six casualties in twenty-eight attacks. Seven months later, with the arrest of five suspects, the *New York Times* referred to twenty-four fatalities in forty-four attacks. At the same time, Birmingham reporters actually reduced their estimate of casualties, with published lists of fifteen dead and thirteen wounded since the raids began.

However that may be, the crimes were indisputably initiated on November 28, 1919, with the death of merchant G.T. Ary. Slain on Christmas Eve, John Belser was the second victim, and his death appeared to satisfy the killers for a time. No further raids were publicly recorded until March 5, 1921, when unidentified attackers wounded J.J. Whittle in his shop.

Another four months passed before the next attack, which wounded Charles Baldone, his wife and daughter, on July 13. Another survivor, H.I. Dorsky, was wounded on August 17. Three weeks later, on September 6, the killers scored another near-miss with Mrs. Sam Zideman, mistaking her for dead as they looted her shop.

The Christmas season was obscured by tragedy that year, in Birmingham, as unidentified assailants murdered Joseph Mantione and his wife, December 21. The same attacker, or a copy-cat, moved on to Titusville that afternoon, and there dispatched Mose Parker, adding a black to the growing list of dead.

The new year offered no relief from carnage, with Clem Crawford and his wife slaughtered on January 11. Two weeks later, Tony and Rosa Lomio were attacked in their shop, but both survived their injuries. Three members of the Lucia family were wounded—one of them fatally—on June 3, 1922. Survivor J.H. Seay was hospitalized on September 30, while Abraham Levine died on November 6, in an attack that also injured his wife.

Police seemed baffled as the crimes continued into 1923. Joseph Klein was killed, his daughter wounded, on January 10. Two weeks later, Luigi and Josephine Vitellaro were hacked to death in their store. A welcome respite followed the Graffeo homicide, in May, but the killers returned with a vengeance on October 22, slaughtering Elizabeth Romeo and Juliet Vigilant.

On January 6, 1924, police in Birmingham announced that five black suspects—Peyton Johnson, O'Delle Jackson, Pearl Jackson, John Reed, and Fred Glover—had confessed to eight of the unsolved murders. Confessions had first been obtained through the use of a "truth serum," scopolamine, and later confirmed without drugs. Petty robbery was listed as the motive, with members of a local "syndicate" drawing straws for the honor of committing the next murder. The founding father of the gang, a black named Garfield, was reported dead of natural causes during 1922. Solicitor James Davis reported that three other members of the group, including its unnamed ringleader, were still at large, hiding somewhere in central Alabama.

Ax Murders— Louisiana and Texas

Between January 1911 and April 1912, an unidentified killer (or killers) slaughtered 49 victims in the states of Louisiana and Texas, leaving police baffled. In each case, the dead were mulattoes or black members of families with mulatto children. The killers were supposed, by blacks and law enforcement officers alike, to be dark-skinned Negroes, selecting victims on the basis of their mixed—or "tainted"—blood.

The first attack took place in early January 1911, at Rayne, Louisiana, when a mother and her three children were hacked to death in their beds. The following month, at Crowley, Louisiana—ten miles from Rayne—three members of the Byers family were dispatched in identical fashion. Two weeks later, the scene shifted to Lafayette, where a family of four was massacred in the small hours of the morning.

Texas endured the killer's first visit in April 1911, when five members of the Cassaway family were axed to death at their home in San Antonio. As in preceding cases, the victims died in their sleep, with no evidence of robbery or any other "rational" motive.

On the last Sunday of November 1911, the action shifted back to Lafayette, Louisiana. Six members of the Norbert Randall family were butchered in their beds, each killed with a single blow behind the right ear. This time, police arrested a black woman, Clementine Bernabet, on suspicion of involvement in the crime. She would be held in custody through spring of 1912, but her incarceration would not halt the carnage. On January 19, 1912, a woman and her three children were hacked to death as they slept in Crowley, Louisiana. Two days later, at Lake Charles, Felix Broussard, his wife and three children were killed in their beds, each with a single blow near the right ear. This time, the killer left a note behind. It read: "When He maketh the Inquisition for Blood, He forgetteth not the cry of the humble—human five."

Stirred by the quasi-Biblical implications, police made several arrests, including two members of the miniscule "Sacrifice Church." Rev. King Harris, leader of the sect, had addressed a meeting in Lafayette on the night of the Randall massacre, and informants reported links between the "Sacrifice Church" and certain voodoo cults in New Orleans. Try as they might, police could find no evidence against their several suspects, and all were soon released.

On February 19, 1912, a Mulatto woman and her three children were axed in their sleep at Beaumont, Texas. Seven weeks later, on March 27, another mulatto mother, her four children, and a male overnight guest were slaughtered in Glidden, Texas.

Police began to notice a geographical pattern in the crimes. Since November 1911, the killer(s) had been moving west, striking at stops on the Southern Pacific Railroad line. The next murders, likewise, would occur further westward on that line, at San Antonio.

Meanwhile, in early April 1912, Clementine Bernabet surprised authorities with a confession to the early crimes. While she admitted sitting in on meetings of the "Sacrifice Church," Bernabet insisted that the slayings were related to a voodoo charm—*candja*—purchased from a local witch doctor. The charm reportedly insured Bernabet and her friends that "we could do as we pleased and we would never be detected." For no apparent reason, they had chosen to test the magic by committing a series of ax murders. Police were ultimately dubious, and Bernabet was never sent to trial.

On the night of April 11-12, five members of the William Burton family were hacked to death in their beds, in San Antonio. Two nights later, at Hempstead, the ax-wielding prowlers claimed three more mulatto victims, thereafter lapsing into a four-month hiatus.

The lull was broken in San Antonio, at 4 a.m. on August 16, 1912, when the wife of mulatto James Dashiell woke to the pain of an ax shearing through her arm. The killer had missed his target for the first time, and he took to his heels as anguished screams roused the sleeping family. His shaken victim glimpsed only one prowler, but she could offer no coherent description to police.

The bungled raid in San Antonio wrote *finis* to the murder spree, and left police without a single solid piece of evidence. Defectors from the "Sacrifice Church" referred authorities to a text from the New Testament Book of Matthew—"Every tree that bringeth not forth good fruit is hewn down, and cast into the fire"—but detectives never managed to identify a valid suspect in the case.

Ax Murders—New York City

On May 25, 1985, Janet Scott, age 85, was found dead in her New York hotel room. An autopsy determined that death was caused by repeated blows to the head with a heavy, sharp instrument similar to an ax or hatchet. Following the murder, splintered pieces of the victim's skull and scalp were removed and placed near the body, in a pattern bearing some apparent significance to the killer.

Five days later, friends of 58-year-old Ruth Potdevin became concerned when she failed to arrive at a business luncheon convened in another downtown hotel. A friend was sent to check her room and found the door ajar. Inside, Potdevin lay dead on the floor, her skull crushed by more than forty blows with an ax-like instrument. Once more, selected fragments of the skull and scalp had been arranged to form a cryptic pattern on the floor.

The day after Potdevin's murder, two blacks were arrested for trying to purchase a radio with one of her stolen credit cards, but police were unable to link them with the actual murder. On June 10, 1985, authorities announced there were sufficient similarities between the recent homicides to link them with a single murderer—

and there the matter rests. Thus far, there have apparently been no new murders in the series, and the case remains unsolved.

Baldi, Joseph

Between September 1970 and June 1972, residents of Queens, New York, were terrified by the activities of a nocturnal prowler who invaded homes at random, striking on the weekends, slashing women in their beds. The first fatality occurred September 20, 1970, when Areti Koularmanis was killed in her home. Eighteen months elapsed, with four non-lethal attacks, before the stalker killed again on March 19, 1972. His victim was Camille Perniola, age 17, stabbed to death while she slept in her parents' home, in Queens.

The unknown attacker was picking up his pace. On April 13, 1972, he killed 21-year-old Clara Toriello in her bed. On June 13, he reached through an open bedroom window to slash the face of a sleeping teenager, who survived her wounds. Two days later, in the pre-dawn hours of June 15, another resident of Queens woke to find an armed man climbing through her bedroom window, saved by the screams that put him to flight. On June 17, in Jamaica, Queens, 16-year-old Deborah Januszko was less fortunate; she slept through the intruder's entry and was stabbed to death.

While there were no reports of any victims being raped, police regarded the attacks as sex crimes. Several times, the prowler made a point of slicing his victim's brassiere, once pausing to slash a bra hanging outside, on a clothesline.

At 1 a.m. on June 21, police arrested Joseph Baldi, 31, and charged him with the murder of Deborah Januszko. The hulking suspect—6 foot 4, 200 pounds—had a ten-year record of commitment to mental institutions, including several terms at the Creedmore State Hospital in Queens. Five knives, a pistol, and a stack of porno magazines were found when homicide detectives searched his rented room, no more than fifty feet from the Januszko home.

Nine months earlier, on September 5, 1971, Baldi had fired shots at policemen who surprised him during the burglary of a woman's home in Queens. Committed for psychiatric observation on October 19, he had been transferred to Creedmore on November 30 and then released, "by mistake," on January 21, 1972. The doctor who signed his release papers "didn't know" that Baldi was charged with attempted murder of a police officer. Examination of the suspect's hospital records revealed that Baldi was free on the nights when each of the ten attacks took place in Queens. On June 23, 1972, police spokesmen announced that all four homicides in the series were considered solved with Baldi's arrest.

Bankston, Clinton, Jr.

In sheer ferocity, the crimes were something new to residents of Athens, Georgia. On the night of August 15, 1987, three women—63-year-old Ann Morris, her 59-year-old sister, Sally Nicholson, and Sally's daughter Helen, 22—were hacked to death in a home in suburban Carr's Hill. The murder weapon was believed to be a hatchet, recovered at the scene, but mutilations were so extensive that verification and identification of the victims came only through post mortem testing.

On August 16, patrolmen spotted a stolen car, owned by one of the victims, outside the home where Clinton Bankston lived with his half-brother, Curtis Johnson. Arrested on three counts of murder, Bankston watched the charges multiply the next day, when he was charged with the April 1987 stabbing deaths of Glenn and Rachel Sutton.

The product of a broken home, Bankston was living with his mother when his father died in a fire, during May 1982. Associates and relatives professed no knowledge of his violent tendencies, but Clinton readily confessed participation in the murders, blaming most of the violence on an elusive accomplice named "Chris." As months slipped past, authorities could find no trace of Chris, and they believe that Bankston made him up in an attempt to shift the blame for his atrocious crimes.

On May 12, 1988—his seventeenth birthday—Bankston pled guilty, but mentally ill on five counts of first-degree murder. Rescued from death row by a state law forbidding execution of killers 16 or younger at the time of their offense, he was sentenced to five terms of life imprisonment.

Beck, Dieter

A handsome, charming man, Beck never lacked for girlfriends in his native town of Rehme, West Germany, but there was viciousness behind that winning smile. For sport, he preyed on women less attractive than his usual dates, the sort who yearned for more than average male attention and affection. During 1961, he raped and strangled Ingrid Kanike, repeating the performance with Ursula Fritz in 1965, and with Anneliese Herschel in 1968. At Beck's trial, in June 1969, a string of girlfriends testified on his behalf, as character witnesses, but under cross-examination several suddenly remembered how he liked to slip his hands around their throats while having intercourse. Convicted on three counts of murder, Beck was consigned to prison for life.

Becker, Marie Alexander

Born in 1877, Marie Becker spent most of her adult life as a housewife in Liege, Belgium. In 1932, when she was 55 years old, she entered into a tempestuous affair with Lambert Beyer, a local lothario several years her junior. Soon after their first meeting, in a local grocery market, Becker poisoned her husband with digitalis and began spending all her time with her lover. Romance paled as Beyer failed to keep up with her pace, and Marie soon dispatched him, as well.

Bent on recapturing lost youth, Becker became a fixture in the local nightclubs, performing wild dances with men half her age, bribing a series of young lovers to share her bed. It all cost money she could ill afford, and soon Marie opened a modest dress shop in Liege, supplementing her income by robbing and poisoning elderly patrons. Before her sideline was discovered, it is estimated that she murdered ten, at least, obtaining minor sums of cash from each.

A female friend was Becker's undoing, running to Marie with complaints about her husband, declaring that she wished the no-good rascal dead. Marie suggested digitalis, offering a sample from her own supply, and after several days of cooling off, her friend reported the discussion to the police. Marie was arrested in October 1936, with tests revealing poison in the bodies of her husband, Lambert Beyer, and a number of her female customers. At trial, she gloated over details of the several deaths and drew a term of life imprisonment. She died in jail, while World War II was underway.

Bernard, Norman

A black drifter from Fayetteville, North Carolina, Bernard attempted his first murder there on August 15, 1983. Accosting a drunken migrant worker, 58-year-old Manuel Diaz, Bernard shot him once in the head with a small-caliber pistol, afterward severing the victim's penis for good measure. Believing Diaz to be dead, Bernard fled across country, winding up in Los Angeles, where he quickly resumed his activities.

On October 13, 1983, Anthony Cody, a 34-year-old transient, was shot and killed in L.A. with a small-caliber weapon. Precisely one month later, an elderly "John Doe" victim was killed on Skid Row with the same gun. The following day, November 14, 52-year-old Milton Regzarrie was shot twice in the head, but he managed to survive his wounds. On November 20, Bobby Joe Jones, 45, was killed in the gunman's final attack.

Arrested on November 21, the 32-year-old suspect led police on a tour of the shooting scenes, describing his crimes "in a matter-of-fact tone." Bernard professed a desire "to help" homeless men, stating that he was "doing them a favor" by putting them out of their misery. Surprised to learn that Manuel Diaz had lived through the attack in Fayetteville, Bernard confessed that crime on November 28. Three months later, on March 7, 1984, he pled guilty to three counts of murder "with special circumstances" in Los Angeles and was sentenced to a term of life without parole.

Bird, Jake

A rootless drifter, big Jake Bird would tell authorities that he was born December 14, 1901, "somewhere out in Louisiana where they ain't no post office." He started roaming in his nineteenth year and never settled anywhere for long, spending much of his time as a manual laborer and "gandy dancer" on various railroads. It was back-breaking work, but it built up Jake's strength and kept him in motion, trolling for human targets. By the time of his arrest in 1947, he would claim a body-count approaching one victim for each year of his life.

On October 30, 1947, Bird was prowling through Tacoma, Washington, when he stopped at the home occupied by Bertha Kludt, 52, and her teenage daughter Beverly. Finding an ax in the woodshed, Bird reportedly stripped off his clothes before breaking into the house and hacking both victims to death. Their dying screams alerted neighbors, and police were just arriving on the scene as Bird emerged from the backyard, shoes in hand. Violently resisting arrest, he slashed two officers with a knife before he was finally beaten into submission and dragged off to the county hospital for treatment of various injuries.

In custody, Bird first pled innocence, then dropped his pose when blood and brain tissue were found on his trousers. Sentenced to die for the slayings, he stalled execution for nearly two years, regaling police with his intimate knowledge of 44 deaths nationwide. At least eleven crimes were solved through Bird's confessions, starting with the ax murders of two women at Evanston, Illinois, in 1942. Other victims were confirmed in Louisville, Kentucky; Omaha, Nebraska; Kansas City, Kansas; Sioux Falls, South Dakota; Cleveland, Ohio; Orlando, Florida; and Portage, Wisconsin. Police in Houston suspected Bird of murdering Mrs. Harry Richardson there, and Chicago authorities were curious about a weighted body retrieved from Lake Michigan, five miles south of Kenosha. Los Angeles detectives had their eyes on Jake for murdering a black youth and a Jewish grocer, while in New York City he was tentatively linked to the robbery and murder of a delicatessen owner.

Psychiatrists examined Bird in jail and labeled him a psychopath, deriving satisfaction from the sight of women cowering in terror. In the verified cases, most of his victims were female, most were white, and the majority had been killed with hatchets or axes in their homes. (Bird also put a "hex" on several enemies from prison, journalists reporting that some half a dozen of them subsequently died.) Inevitably, Jake ran out of stories, and he climbed the gallows on July 15, 1949, in the Washington state prison at Walla Walla.

"Black Doodler, The"

Ten years before the first discovery of AIDS, the gay community in San Francisco was confronted with another lethal menace, wrought in human form. Between January 1974 and September 1975, the faceless stalker was responsible for seventeen attacks, with fourteen deaths, that baffled homicide investigators in the city by the bay.

Initially, considering discrepancies in choice of victims, the police believed they had *three* manic killers on the prowl. Five of the victims were Tenderloin drag queens, mutilated by a slasher who apparently despised transvestites. Six others were selected from the sadomasochistic world of "leather bars"—the dives with names like Ramrod, Fe-Be's, Folsom Prison—and dispatched with hacking knife wounds. (One, attorney George Gilbert, was slaughtered at his home in San Francisco's poshest high-rise.) The last six were middle-class businessmen, stabbed by an assailant who picked them up in Castro Village bars, wooing his victims with cartoon portraits and pausing for sex before wielding his knife.

Three of the latter victims survived their ordeal, providing police with descriptions of the killer, although they would ultimately refuse to testify in court. The slasher's taste for comic art provided newsmen with a handle on the case, and so the "Black Doodler" was born.

In time, as leads were run down and eliminated, homicide investigators realized that they were searching for a single killer in their string of unsolved homicides. In 1976, suspicion focused on a particular suspect, described by police as a mental patient with a history of treatment of sex-related problems. Questioned repeatedly, the suspect spoke freely with police, but always stopped short of a confession. Meanwhile, the surviving victims stubbornly refused to make a positive I.D., afraid of ruining their lives by "coming out" with an admission of their homosexuality.

On July 8, 1977, frustrated authorities announced that an unnamed suspect had been linked with fourteen deaths and three assaults in San Francisco during 1974 and '75. Indictment was impossible, they said, without cooperation from survivors of the "Doodler's" attacks. At this writing, the case remains a stalemate, officially unsolved, with the suspect subject to continuing police surveillance.

Bladel, Rudy

The rage that snuffed out seven lives in fifteen years began for Rudy Bladel as an economic twist of fate. The son of a Chicago railroad fireman, Rudy loved the trains from childhood, never seriously entertaining the idea of any other occupation. In Korea, during 1950, he was posted on a military train and saw his share of action from the rails. Returning to civilian life, he signed on with his father's line, the old Rock Island and

Pacific, settling in Niles, a suburb of Chicago. During 1959, the railroad's base of operations moved to Elkhart, Indiana. Protests from employees based in Niles were unavailing; Rudy Bladel was among those who were fired. He found another railroad job, with Indiana's Harbor Belt line, but his bitterness remained, to fester over time and finally explode in lethal violence.

He claimed his first two victims on the third of August, 1963, at Hammond, Indiana. Engineer Roy Bottorf and his fireman, Paul Overstreet, were found dead on that date, in the cab of their train, in the Harbor Belt rail yards. Each man had been hit by two rounds from a .22-caliber weapon. The crime remained unsolved, and ultimately passed into the realm of rail yard legend. It had nearly been forgotten five years later, when the killer struck a second time.

A shotgun ambush, on the sixth of August, 1968, claimed engineer John Marshall as he climbed aboard his train in Elkhart, Indiana. Witnesses described a hulking stranger, glimpsed in silhouette, who waddled from the murder scene with a distinctive, almost ape-like stride. Again, police were left without a suspect or substantial clues.

Their break came three years later, once again in Elkhart, after Rudy Bladel drew a pistol in the railroad yard and shot another engineer. Though wounded, Rudy's victim managed to disarm him, wounding Bladel with a bullet from his own .357 magnum. Rudy filed a guilty plea to aggravated battery and drew a prison term of one to five years. He served eighteen months, and was paroled in 1973. His bitterness increased when Harbor Belt executives refused to reinstate him in his old position with the line.

On April 5, 1976, James McCrory was seated in his locomotive, in the yard at Elkhart, when a shotgun slug crashed through the window, shattering his skull and killing him on impact. This time, Bladel was an instant suspect, and police secured permission for surveillance. In January 1978, he was arrested as he left a South Bend gun shop, carrying a brand-new magnum. Ownership of firearms is forbidden for convicted felons, and he served eleven months on weapons charges, but police could not connect him with the string of murders spanning thirteen years.

So far, he had been relatively lucky, but the heat in Indiana got on Rudy's nerves, provoking him to shift his hunting ground. On New Year's Eve, 1978, he carried a shotgun into the rail yards at Jackson, Michigan, surprising flagman Robert Blake and William Gulak, a conductor, in the depot. They were waiting for a train when Bladel cut them down with close-range blasts of buckshot. Moving to the outer platform, Rudy shot and killed Charles Burton, railroad fireman, as he came to work. The depot's ticket manager, responding to the sound of shots, described the gunman for police.

The canny change of scene secured Bladel a reprieve, but time was running short. An engineer in Hammond, Indiana, who had shared a cab with Rudy in the old days, told police about the fireman who had seemed obsessed with graphic reenactments of the early shootings. Briefly held for questioning about the Jackson massacre, Bladel was soon released for lack of solid evidence. Three months elapsed before a group of hikers found his shotgun in a park outside of Jackson. Serial numbers traced the weapon to Rudy, and a test-fire linked the firing pin to cartridges recovered at the murder scene. Bladel was booked for triple murder on March 22, 1979, confessing to the Jackson crimes. He changed his story at his trial, in August, but to no avail. Convicted in the face of his contention that he sold the shotgun to an unknown individual before the murders, Bladel drew three consecutive life terms in prison.

But the railway sniper's story was not finished, yet. In 1985, the Michigan Supreme Court overturned the verdict in his murder trial, on grounds that Bladel had confessed without a lawyer present to advise him of his rights. The ruling was upheld by the United States Supreme Court on April Fool's Day, 1986. A second trial was held in June of 1987, Rudy clinging to his story of the shotgun's sale. The prosecution countered with results of microscopic fiber tests, which placed the gun in Rudy's suitcase just before it was discarded. Bladel was convicted once again, on June 19th. This time, the terms of life imprisonment were made consecutive, insuring he would never walk the streets—or haunt the railroad yards—again.

Bolber-Petrillo Murder Ring, The

America's most prolific team of killers-for-profit were active in Philadelphia during the 1930s, claiming an estimated 30 to 50 victims before the ring's various members were apprehended. Students of the case, in retrospect, are prone to cite the gang's activities as evidence that modern homicide statistics may be woefully inaccurate. If 20,000 murders are reported in a given year, they say, it is entirely possible that 20,000 more go unreported, overlooked by the authorities.

The basic murder method was conceived in 1932, by Dr. Morris Bolber and his good friend, Paul Petrillo. After one of Bolber's female patients aired complaints about her husband's infidelity, the doctor and Petrillo planned for Paul to woo the lonely lady, gaining her cooperation in a plan to kill her wayward spouse and split $10,000 in insurance benefits. The victim, Anthony Giscobbe, was a heavy drinker, and it proved a simple matter for his wife to strip him as he lay unconscious, leaving him beside an open window in the dead of winter while he caught his death of cold. The grieving widow split her cash with Bolber and Petrillo, whereupon her "lover" promptly went in search of other restless, greedy wives.

It soon became apparent that Italian husbands, caught up in the middle of the Great Depression, carried little life insurance on their own. Petrillo called upon his cousin Herman, an accomplished local actor, to impersonate potential victims and apply for heavy policies. Once several payments had been made, the husbands were eliminated swiftly and efficiently through "accidents" or "natural causes." Dr. Bolber's favorite methods included poison and blows to the head with a sandbag, producing cerebral hemorrhage, but methods were varied according to victims. One target, a roofer named Lorenzo, was hurled to his death from an eight-story building, the Petrillo cousins first handing him some French post cards to explain his careless distraction.

After roughly a dozen murders, the gang recruited faith healer Carino Favato, known as the Witch in her home neighborhood. Favato had dispatched three of her own husbands before going into business fulltime as a "marriage consultant," poisoning unwanted husbands for a fee. Impressed by Dr. Bolber's explanation of the life insurance scam, Favato came on board and brought the gang a list of her prospective clients. By the latter part of 1937, Bolber's ring polished off 50 victims, at least 30 of which were fairly well documented by subsequent investigation.

The roof fell in when an ex-convict approached Herman Petrillo, pushing a new get-rich scheme. Unimpressed, Petrillo countered with a pitch for his acquaintance to secure potential murder victims, and the felon panicked, running to police. As members of the gang were rounded up, they "squealed" on one another in the hope of finding leniency, their clients chiming in as ripples spread throughout a stunned community. While several wives were sent to prison, most escaped by testifying for the state. The two Petrillos were condemned and put to death, while Bolber and Favato each drew terms of life imprisonment.

Bonin, William George: See "Freeway Murders"

Boost, Werner

A child of post-war Germany, Werner Boost began stealing at age six, spending several years in a home for delinquents near Magdeburg. Released for military service near the end of World War II, he had a fleeting taste of action prior to being captured by the British. Cease-fire brought no change in Werner's attitude, and during 1951 he was incarcerated for stealing scrap metal from cemetery vaults.

Behind the larcenous exterior lurked darker passions. Boost acquired a friend, Franz Lohrbach, who would later tell police that Werner "hypnotized" him and compelled him to participate in heinous crimes against his will. In the beginning, they were merely chums who went out target shooting, graduating to the robbery of couples found in isolated trysting spots. Boost managed to concoct a drug, with which he rendered victims senseless, stealing from the men and raping their companions, "forcing" Lohrbach to participate.

One night, in early 1956, Boost and Lohrbach encountered one Dr. Serve, a Dusseldorf businessman, parked on the banks of the Rhine with a young male companion. Werner drew a gun and killed the doctor, ordering his sidekick to eliminate the boy, but Lohrbach panicked, merely knocking out the witness.

Police had a description of their suspects by the time Boost struck again, shooting a young man to death and injecting his date with cyanide. Their bodies were discovered in the ashes of a straw pile, torched in an attempt to wipe out evidence. Boost chose another courting couple for his third attack, clubbing both unconscious in their car before he sank it in a nearby pond and watched them drown.

On June 6, 1956, a forester near Dusseldorf observed an armed man spying on a couple from the trees. He tackled the voyeur and held him for police, who soon identified the prisoner as Werner Boost. In custody, Boost stubbornly denied the lover's lane attacks and said he merely hoped to frighten off the latest couple, since public displays of affection made him "see red." Self-righteously, the killer rapist told his jailers, "These sex horrors are the curse of Germany."

When news of Boost's arrest was published, Lohrbach voluntarily surrendered to authorities and launched into a marathon confession. On the night of Dr. Serve's murder, he explained, Boost was experimenting with a plan to gas his victims, using toy balloons and cyanide. Ballistics tests revealed that Werner's pistol killed Serve, and old investigations were reopened in a series of murders around Helmstedt, in Lower Saxony, during 1945. Boost had been living in the area when several refugees were shot and killed, attempting to cross the border between Russian and British zones of occupation.

The case of Werner Boost dragged on for years, producing one of the longest indictments in German history. Upon conviction, Boost was sentenced to a term of life imprisonment, the maximum allowable in postwar German law.

Boyle, Benjamin Herbert

Gail Smith, age 20, had been working as a waitress at a topless bar in Ft. Worth, Texas, but with salary and tips together, she had still not saved the money that she needed for a car. Accordingly, when she decided it was time to see her mother in Lake Meredith, 300 miles away, Gail chose her spot along the highway, stuck her thumb out, waiting for a ride.

She never made it.

On October 14, 1985, police in Amarillo got a call from an excited trucker, who had stopped along the highway, north of town, to answer nature's call. Discarded in the brush, he found a woman's naked, lifeless body, bound in silver duct tape, with a man's tie knotted tight around her throat. An autopsy discovered evidence of beating prior to death. A fingerprint comparison identified the victim as Gail Smith.

A friend of Gail's had seen her off when she departed from Ft. Worth, remembering her first lift as a big, red semi trailer, Peterbilt; its trailer bore the legend "Ruger Freight." Detectives traced the firm to Mangum, Oklahoma, two days later, and examination of the schedules on file revealed that Herbert Boyle had been the only driver in the area. Detectives noted that he also matched the general description of the trucker that Gail's friend had managed to provide.

By sheer coincidence, Boyle had secured a load that morning, bound for Diboll, Texas, sixty miles due north of Houston. Stopped en route for questioning, Boyle readily identified a snapshot of the victim, claiming he had dropped her off, alive, in Wichita Falls, near the Texas-Oklahoma border. If she died near Amarillo, surely someone else must be responsible.

A search of Boyle's belongings netted officers a roll of silver duct tape, several sheets and blankets. Fibers from the latter were dispatched to Washington, D.C., where FBI analysis described them as identical with fibers found on Gail Smith's body. Boyle's wife recalled that she had seen some bloody sheets inside the truck, a short time earlier. Stray hairs recovered from the corpse was also matched to Boyle, and fingerprints, recovered from the duct tape used to bind Gail Smith, completed the array of damning evidence.

A background check on Boyle revealed that he was forty-two years old. He had completed three years military service during August 1963, thereafter moving on to Colorado, where he lived and ran an auto body shop from 1969 to February 1980. Boyle was next employed at a Las Vegas body shop, returning to his native Oklahoma in November 1981. He had been driving long-haul trucks since then, on routes that took him all throughout the country.

Working a variety of jobs had not prevented Boyle from stalking female victims on his leisure time. He had attempted to abduct a 28-year-old in Colorado Springs, November 20, 1979, but she produced a knife and stabbed him several times in self-defense. Boyle's guilty plea to an attempted kidnap charge had earned him five years on probation, but he failed to learn his lesson. At the time of his arrest in Texas, Boyle was also being sought for rape, in Canyon City, Colorado, where the victim had identified his photograph.

Review of Boyle's extensive travels linked him with a second homicide, near Truckee, California, where a "Jane Doe" victim was discovered on June 21, 1985. Her naked body had been stuffed inside a cardboard box, her hands and feet bound up with bandages and several kinds of tape. A wad of bedding had been left beside the corpse, and FBI reports said fibers taken from the body matched a blanket found inside Boyle's Oklahoma residence.

Boyle went to trial for Gail Smith's murder in October 1986. It took a jury three short hours to convict him on October 29. The sentence: Death.

Brisbon, Henry

The first two victims credited to Henry Brisbon were James Schmidt, a Chicago businessman, and his fiancee, Dorothy Cerny, both 25. While traveling on Highway 57, in Cook County, on the night of June 3, 1973, Schmidt and Cerny were stopped by a gang of four men, dragged from their vehicle and forced to lie down on the grassy shoulder of the road. Brisbon was identified as the triggerman who killed them both with close-range shotgun blasts as they lay helpless on the ground.

Conviction on a charge of double murder earned Brisbon a sentence of 1,000 to 3,000 years, but the prison term was less impressive than it sounded. Actually, Brisbon could have been paroled in just eleven years, but he was not content to wait. On October 19, 1978, he used a sharpened soup ladle to stab inmate Ronald Morgan at the Statesville penitentiary, striking without apparent motive. While awaiting trial for that murder, Brisbon took part in a 1979 riot and was transferred to the maximum security lockup at Menard.

Brisbon was convicted of Morgan's murder on January 22, 1982, and a month later he was sentenced to die. Leaving the courtroom after pronouncement of sentence, Brisbon told his guards, "You'll never get me. I'll kill again. Then you'll have another long trial. And then I'll do it again." As good as his word, Brisbon tried it again on February 15, 1983. Slipping out of handcuffs and breaking away from a guard on death row, he used a piece of sharpened heavy-gauge wire to stab convicted killers William Jones and John Wayne Gacy. (Neither man was seriously injured.) At this writing, Brisbon is awaiting execution—and, undoubtedly, preparing for his next attempt at homicide.

Brogsdale, Rickey

For seven weeks, between September and October 1987, Washington, D.C. was haunted by the specter of a prowling, voyeuristic gunman who apparently derived sadistic pleasure from attacking women or young couples in their homes. Lurking in darkness, the sniper selected his victims by peering through windows, blasting away with a .22-caliber weapon once suitable targets were found.

The first of Washington's "Peeping Tom" shootings occurred on September 5, 1987, but police withheld warnings until the fifth attack wounded an off-duty policewoman on October 15. The eighth attack, on October 17, also resulted in the first fatality, as 35-year-old Yvonne Watts was killed by a shot fired through her bedroom window.

Several hours later, officers arrested Rickey Brogsdale, 26, a few blocks from the murder scene; a .22-caliber gun was found hidden nearby. In custody, Brogsdale—paroled five months earlier on a conviction for carrying an unlicensed pistol—confessed to all the "Peeping Tom" attacks, along with three more slayings that police had not connected to the series. Helpful to a fault, the suspect even led detectives to the scene of a shooting that had never been reported.

Rickey Brogsdale had been in and out of trouble since the time of his parole. In June, he had been charged with violation of parole. In June, he had been charged with violation of parole following an arrest for indecent exposure, but authorities refused to send him back to prison, arbitrarily deciding that he posed no threat to the community. A week before his ultimate arrest on murder charges, Brogsdale was accused of molesting a neighbor's ten-year-old daughter and paying the girl five dollars to insure her silence.

According to Brogsdale's confession, his first murder took place along the Suitland Parkway on September 5, the same day the "Peeping Tom" shootings began. The male victim, Myers Jackson, was accused of trying to rape Brogsdale's mother during 1976, in a crime still unsolved by police. On September 6, Brogsdale turned up at the address where his sister resided prior to her beating death in April 1985. Inside the apartment, he shot and killed 28-year-old Steven Wilson, also wounding Wilson's girlfriend as they slept. Revenge was once again the motive, Brogsdale blaming Wilson for his sister's unsolved murder.

The final victim linked to Brogsdale's murder spree was Angela Shaw, a teenage part-time prostitute, found dead September 20 beside a local bike path. Shaw's attacker had choked her unconscious and raped her before shooting her to death with a .22-caliber weapon. An anonymous caller directed police to the body, and someone also left a ghoulish note at the home of a friend. It read: "I raped and killed your friend, Angela Shaw. You can find her on the bike path behind Marbury Plaza." Brogsdale told police that he witnessed the murder but did not participate, a claim that failed to impress detectives under the circumstances. On October 18, he was charged with first-degree murder in the deaths of Steven Wilson and Yvonne Watts, ending the capital's "Peeping Tom" nightmare.

Brooks, John

First arrested in February 1982, at age fifteen, for molesting an eight-year-old girl, within five years John Brooks was named by homicide detectives as "the largest one-man crime ring in recent New Orleans history." Arrested December 29, 1986, on two counts of murder, within two weeks his rap sheet listed four more homicides, two counts of attempted murder, nine armed robberies, plus individual counts of kidnapping, rape, and attempted robbery. It was an impressive tally for a 20-year-old, but police remained convinced that they had only glimpsed "the tip of the iceberg."

According to the charges filed against him, Brooks began his solitary crime wave with an armed robbery on June 14, 1986, waiting over a month before pulling his second on July 27. Foiled in an attempted robbery on August 23, he rebounded the same afternoon by shooting Wilbert Johnson, age 50, and leaving him dead on the street.

More robberies followed, on September 1 and 27, October 18 and 19. In the predawn hours of November 1, 51-year-old James Williams was shot to death without apparent motive on a dark New Orleans street, his heavy-set assailant seen by several witnesses. On November 27, taxi driver Artis Thompson was killed by a stranger who approached his cab, demanded money, and then shot Thompson several times before stealing a purse from his terrified passenger. Another robbery on November 29 kept Brooks in spending money, but his thirst for blood had not been quenched.

Things heated up as the Christmas season approached, with another robbery on December 12. Two days later, Zachary Turnell was parked on the street with a woman companion when he was shot and killed by a stranger, his pockets rifled for cash. Turnell's killer then kidnapped the woman, driving her to a downtown motel, where she was brutally raped. On December 20, Terry Young was gunned down without motive while leaving a New Orleans tavern.

Brooks celebrated Christmas morning with another random shooting, killing Diane Gipson as she sat in her boyfriend's car, on Lakeshore Drive. Her companion, Tyrone Wilkinson, was shot in the stomach but survived. Three days later, 18-year-old Darren Mercadel was slain on the street while exchanging gifts with a female acquaintance. Ballistics tests showed that the same gun was used to kill victims Young, Gipson, and Mercadel over a period of eight days.

Brooks was finally identified after his fingerprints were matched with some recovered from Tyrone Wilkinson's car. His name was already familiar to homicide investigators, as Brooks had claimed to be a witness in an unsolved double murder—that of Thomas Morris and Cabrini Jareau, shot in a parked car October 23, 1986. Charged in the murders of victims Johnson, Williams, Thompson, Young, Gipson and Mercadel, Brooks also remains a prime suspect in the slayings of Turnell, Morris and Jareau.

Brown, Kim S.

On June 12, 1987, three weeks after graduating from a local high school, Angela Fay Hackl disappeared from her hometown of Lone Rock, Wisconsin. Search parties scoured a two-county area after her car was recovered near Sauk City, twenty miles away, and her body was found on June 15, in the woods six miles west of Sauk City. Chained by her neck to a tree, the young woman had been shot repeatedly at point-blank range, leaving final identification to dental records.

A month later, on July 9, schoolteacher Barbara Blackstone vanished from her home in nearby Lyndon Station, leaving her purse behind, her keys in the ignition of a car parked just outside. Her nude and decomposing body was retrieved on August 4 from Lafayette County, sixty miles due south of the Wisconsin Dells that had become a madman's hunting ground.

On July 24, police logged reports of burglary and arson at a home in Oxford, Wisconsin. No one had been home to greet the prowler, but the family dog was stabbed to death, discarded in a bedroom, after which a braided rug was draped across the stove, the burners on and liquor poured around the kitchen to accelerate the blaze. Reported stolen were a .357 magnum revolver, a black holster, and a distinctive "butterfly" knife, so called after its two-piece folding grip.

Four days later, on July 28, housewife Linda Nachreiner was reported missing from her home in Dell Prairie, six miles from the site of the burglary and twenty miles removed from the home of murder victim Barbara Blackstone. A visiting neighbor found Nachreiner's two small children unattended, a basket of wet laundry fresh from the washer, and police were summoned. Officers identified fresh stains of semen and saliva on a bedroom comforter, retrieving panties and a single stocking from the floor.

The missing woman was found next morning, four miles from her home. She had been stripped by her assailant, with her blue jeans pulled over her head, hands bound behind her back. She had been raped and tortured before a single bullet was fired through her head. Tire tracks discovered at the scene matched others found outside the victim's home; a slug recovered by detectives matched bullets fired by the .357 stolen July 24.

By this time, local homicide investigators were deluged by tips from nervous residents of the Wisconsin Dells. Kim Brown was one of those suggested as a suspect, and detectives learned that Brown knew Linda Nachreiner's husband from working together on various jobs. Brown also lived within half a mile of the burglarized dwelling in Oxford, a short seven miles from the Nachreiner home. A review of Brown's work record showed that he had called in sick on July 24 and clocked out after working for less than two hours July 28.

Police interviewed Brown on September 2, observing that tires on his car closely resembled their casts from the Nachreiner home and the scene of her murder. Brown claimed that he stayed home all day on July 24 and accompanied his wife on shopping errands four days later; his wife, meanwhile, recalled that Brown had worked a full shift on both days in question. Searching the trunk of Brown's car, with the suspect's permission, police found the stolen revolver and "butterfly" knife, together with a quantity of .357 ammunition and two spent cartridges. A second knife, found in the glove compartment, bore animal hairs matching those of the dog stabbed to death on July 24.

In custody, Brown first told detectives that the stolen weapons belonged to "a friend," later changing his story to claim that he "found" them. Samples of the suspect's blood and saliva matched those from the Nachreiner home, and casts of his tires provided further confirmation. On September 4, 1987, Kim Brown was charged with arson, burglary, and the murder of Linda Nachreiner. No further charges have been filed, although authorities consider him responsible for all three local slayings, and the string of crimes stopped short with Brown's arrest.

Brown, Raymond Eugene

In October 1960, 14-year-old Raymond Brown had his mind on sports. Specifically, he wanted football shoes, but he was short on cash. Instead of looking for a part-time job around his home, in Clay County, Alabama, he opted for burglary, selecting the home jointly occupied by his grandmother, great-grandmother, and great-aunt as his target.

Entering under cover of darkness, Brown moved bare-foot through the house, searching for cash. Despite his stealth, a sound roused his great-grandmother from sleep, and she went to investigate. Fearing exposure, Brown picked up a butcher knife, killed the old woman, and went on to murder his other two relatives. Detectives counted 123 stab wounds in the three victims, but Brown had forgotten his quest in the heat of the moment. A purse, containing forty dollars, had been left untouched.

It took three weeks, but bloody footprints put investigators on Brown's trail, and he was locked away for thirteen years, using his prison time to learn auto mechanics. Paroled in 1973, he found work in a garage at Ashland, Alabama, and rented a small apartment nearby. Soon after his release, Brown tried to rape the manager of his apartment building, choking her when she resisted, leaving her for dead. This time, his victim lived, and Brown was carted back to prison, his parole revoked.

Another thirteen years elapsed, and Brown was once again paroled, in June of 1986. Working as a mechanic in Phoenix City, he met divorcee Linda LeMonte, 32, and they began dating. Brown became familiar to LeMonte's neighbors, dropping in for dinner, spending evenings with LeMonte and her ten-year-old daughter, Sheila.

On August 10, 1987, Linda and Sheila LeMonte were found dead in their home, each stabbed numerous times, as if in a frenzy of rage. Detectives speculated that the slayer had assaulted Sheila first, attempting rape, and had been interrupted by her mother in the act. A neighbor told police that Raymond Brown had parked his car outside the night before, and Sherlock Holmes was not required to make the obvious connection.

Taking to the woods, Brown managed to elude a sweeping manhunt until August 12, when he emerged to buy a soda and was run to earth by deputies. With double murder charges and another count of violating his parole, it seems unlikely Raymond Brown will ever qualify for leniency again.

Bryan, Joseph Francis, Jr.

A native of Camden, New Jersey, Joseph Bryan first ran afoul of the law in 1958, at age nineteen, when he abducted two small boys, tied them to a tree, and sexually molested them. Committed to a Camden County mental hospital, Bryan was diagnosed as schizophrenic, once informing doctors that he liked to see little boys "tied up and screaming." Upon release from the hospital, Bryan enlisted in the navy, but was discharged after further psychiatric tests and treatment. Convicted of burglary and auto theft in Nevada, he served time in the state prison and was paroled on January 20, 1964. By that time, Bryan's twisted sexual desires had blossomed into something dark and dangerous.

On February 27, John Robinson, age seven, disappeared in Mount Pleasant, South Carolina, while riding his bicycle near home. FBI agents discovered that Joe Bryan had spent the night in a local motel, and they looked up his record of crimes against children. Two farmers reported pulling a car from a mud hole on the morning of February 28; the driver had been traveling with a boy and the license number was traced back to Bryan. The clincher was John Robinson's abandoned bike, discovered in some weeds not far from where the car bogged down.

On March 23, 1964, seven-year-old Lewis Wilson, Jr., vanished from his school in St. Petersburg, Florida. Searchers were beating the bushes, in vain, when three youths on vacation discovered the remains of a child in a marsh near Hallandale. Stripped clean, except for shoes and socks, the skeletal remains were finally identified by reference to the footwear. The search for Johnny Robinson was over.

A fugitive from charges of kidnapping and murder, Joseph Bryan was declared a federal fugitive from justice. On April 14, 1964, his name was added to the FBI's "Most Wanted" list, with photographs displayed from coast to coast.

By that time, David Wulff, age eight, was missing from his home in Willingboro, New Jersey. Snatched on April 4, his fate was still a mystery when eight-year-old Dennis Burke disappeared from Humboldt, Tennessee, on April 23.

Five days later, a pair of off-duty FBI agents spotted Bryan's car—a distinctive white Cadillac—outside a shopping mall in New Orleans. They staked out the vehicle, pouncing when Bryan emerged from the mall with Dennis Burke in tow. Held on $150,000 bond, Bryan denied kidnapping anyone. Asked how he came to be traveling with a child, he seemed bewildered. "I don't know how it happened," he said. "I don't know." Dennis Burke, for his part, described Bryan as "a nice man" who fed him well and rented comfortable motel rooms during their three days together. Indicted on federal kidnapping charges in Tennessee, on January 12, 1965, Bryan pled guilty and was sentenced to a term of life imprisonment.

Butler, Eugene

"Eccentric" Eugene Butler had been dead a full two years before his crimes were finally exposed, discovery of skeletal remains beneath his rural home outside Niagara, North Dakota, writing *finis* to an eerie chapter in the region's local history.

A paranoid and recluse, Butler lived southeast of town, avoiding contact with his fellow man for years, until he was declared insane and sent to an asylum, at Jamestown, in 1906. He died there in 1913, but two years elapsed before routine excavation at his home revealed six skeletons, lined up in shallow graves beneath the floor. According to the coroner, Butler's victims—all male—included five adults and one young man between the ages of fifteen and eighteen years. Each had been killed by crushing blows to the skull, then lowered through a hidden trap-door in the floorboards, buried in a crawlspace underneath the house. The homicides apparently had spanned a period of four or five years prior to Butler's ultimate incarceration.

Without a living suspect or a known identity for any of the victims, the authorities were left to theorize on motive, speculating that the hermit may have thought his transient farm hands planned to rob him, striking first, before they had a chance to carry out their schemes. In light of other cases—such as those of Northcott, Corll, and Gacy—it would seem that violent homosexuality may be another likely motive for the North Dakota murders.

Cannibal Murders—China

On March 29, 1986, police in Xidan, China—a district of Peking—arrested a 42-year-old restaurant owner on charges of murdering three teenagers, cooking their flesh, and serving it to other members of his own family as "pork." No principals in the case were named, but the slayer's victims were described as two boys and a girl. The suspect's wife and two children were briefly held for questioning, then released upon convincing authorities of their innocence. Police declined to speculate on any further victims or the possibility that human flesh was offered in the killer's restaurant. At this writing, no disposition of the case has been announced.

Carignan, Harvey Louis

By all rights, Harvey Carignan should never have become a serial killer. Sentenced in Alaska to be hanged for murdering a woman during 1949, the hulking killer might have been eliminated early on had not the system intervened. An over-zealous sheriff had elicited confessions from the suspect with assurances that Carignan would not be executed, a condition that appeals courts found disturbing. Carignan's death sentence was reversed in 1951, and after serving nine more years on a conviction for attempted rape, he was paroled in 1960. There would be more arrests, for burglary, assault, and other crimes; in 1965, Carignan was sentenced to a term of fifteen years in Washington, but with time off for good behavior, he would hit the streets again in 1969, consumed with an abiding rage against society in general and women in particular.

Harvey married a Seattle widow shortly after his parole, but their relationship was doomed from the beginning. Sullen, uncommunicative, Carignan would frequently get up at night and drive long distances, "to be alone and think." When he refused to share his thoughts or name his destinations on the long nocturnal drives, the marriage fell apart. Remarrying another widow in 1972, Carignan showed no improvement. His lascivious attentions to a teenaged step-daughter finally forced the girl to run away from home, and he was faced with yet another failing marriage in the spring of 1973.

That May, young Kathy Miller answered Harvey's advertisement for employees at a service station that he leased. The girl was missing for a month before two boys discovered her remains while hiking on an Indian reservation north of Everett, Washington. Nude and bundled in a sheet of plastic, Kathy had been bludgeoned with a hammer, knocking holes the size of nickels in her skull.

Detectives in Seattle were aware of Harvey's record, and they hounded him with such intensity that he departed from their city shortly after Kathy Miller's body was retrieved. A speeding ticket from Solano County, California, on June 20 placed Carignan in the vicinity where half a dozen women had been murdered in the past two years, but there was nothing solid to connect him with the crimes, and he was on his way cross-country, seeking sanctuary in his old, familiar haunts of Minneapolis.

On June 28, Marlys Townsend was assaulted at a bus stop in that city, clubbed unconscious from behind. She woke in Harvey's car, still groggy from the blow, but when he tried to make her masturbate him, she found strength enough to save herself by leaping from the speeding vehicle. Police made no connection with the human time-bomb ticking in their midst.

September 9, Jewry Billings, age thirteen, was hitching rides in Minneapolis to reach her boyfriend's house, when Carignan pulled up and offered her a ride. Inside the car, he threatened Jewry with a hammer, forced her to fellate him while he rammed the hammer's handle in and out of her vagina. When he finished with her, Carignan released his battered captive, but the incident was so humiliating that the girl maintained it as a closely-guarded secret for a period of several months.

A year would pass before detectives witnessed Harvey's handiwork again. On September 8, 1974, he picked up Lisa King and June Lynch, both sixteen, while they were hitching rides in Minneapolis. He offered money if the girls would help him fetch another car that had been stranded in a rural area. Once out of town, however, Harvey stopped the car and started beating June about the head and face. When Lisa ran for help, he sped away and left his latest victim bleeding on the roadside.

A month before, on August 10, another romance had collapsed for Harvey, ending no less tragically for his intended. Eileen Hunley was a woman of the church, who looked for good in others. She had looked for good in Harvey Carignan, when they began to date, but there was nothing to be found. She had informed her friends of her intent to terminate the sour relationship, but Eileen Hunley disappeared on August 10. When she was found in Sherbourne County five weeks later, she would be a rotting corpse, her skull imploded by the force of savage hammer blows.

An engine failure on September 14 almost cost Gwen Burton her life. When Harvey Carignan appeared to offer her a ride, she had no inkling that the trip would turn into an endless nightmare. Once alone, he ripped her clothing, choked her into semi-consciousness, and raped her with the handle of his hammer, finally slamming her across the skull with brutal force before he dumped her in a field to die. Miraculously, she survived and crawled until she reached a local highway, where a passing motorist arrived in time to save her life.

On September 18—the day Eileen Hunley's body was recovered—Harvey picked up Sally Versoi and Diane Flynn. He used the old ruse about fetching a car, then began to make lewd propositions, assaulting both girls when they failed to respond on command. They escaped when he ran short of fuel and was forced to stop at a rural service station.

Two days later, eighteen-year-old Kathy Schultz did not return on schedule from her college classes, and a missing persons bulletin was issued by police. Her corpse was found next day, by hunters, in a corn field forty miles from Minneapolis. As in the other cases, Kathy's skull had been destroyed by crushing hammer blows.

Police in Minneapolis were talking to their counterparts in Washington by now, and within days, survivors started picking Harvey out of lineups as the man who had abducted and assaulted them throughout the past two years. A search of his possessions turned up maps with some 181 red circles drawn in isolated areas of the United States and Canada. Some of the circles yielded nothing, indicating points where Harvey had applied for jobs or purchased vehicles, but others seemed to link him with a string of unsolved homicides and other crimes involving women. One such cryptic circle marked the point where Laura Brock had disappeared, near Coupeville, Washington. Another, at Medora, North Dakota, coincided with discovery of a murdered girl in April 1973. Yet another had been drawn around the very intersection in Vancouver where a woman, waiting for the city bus, had been assaulted from behind and beaten with a hammer.

An ill-conceived insanity defense involving messages from God did not impress the jury at Carignan's trial for attempted murder (of Gwen Burton) in March 1975. He was convicted and received the maximum of forty years in prison. Since no criminal in Minnesota may be sentenced to a term exceeding forty years, the other trials and sentences were merely window dressing: 30 years for the assault on Jewry Billings; 40 years for Eileen Hunley's murder; 40 years for killing Kathy Schultz. One hundred fifty years in all, of which the killer may be forced to serve no more than forty, with the usual time off for "good behavior."

Catoe, Jarvis R.

At 6 a.m. on August 4, 1941, Evelyn Anderson, age 26, left her home in the Bronx, walking to her job as a waitress in a nearby restaurant. She never punched the clock that day, and it was 9 p.m. before her lifeless body was discovered in an alley off Jerome Avenue. She had been strangled by a powerful assailant, marks of fingernails imbedded in her throat, but she had not been sexually abused.

A few days later, Anderson's watch was recovered from a New York pawn shop, hocked by one Charles Woolfolk. Under questioning, Woolfolk swore that he received the watch from a lady friend, Hazel Johnson, who in turn pointed an accusing finger at suspect Mandy Reid. Hauled in for interrogation, Reid said she got Anderson's handbag—containing the watch—from her friend, Jarvis Catoe, a resident of Washington, D.C.

Catoe, a 36-year-old black man, was arrested by authorities in Washington. On August 29, he confessed to the murders of seven women in Washington and one in New York City; four others had been raped but left alive, and he reportedly had failed in efforts to abduct two more. Another slaying in the District of Columbia was added on September 1. Corroborating his confession, Catoe told police where they could find one victim's lost umbrella, and he knew that twenty dollars had been stolen in another case—a fact known only to detectives, members of the victim's family, and her killer.

Catoe named Evelyn Anderson as his New York victim, but the rampage had started years earlier, in Washington. Florence Darcy was the first to die, raped and strangled in 1935, but the case had been "closed" a year later, with the conviction of an innocent suspect. Josephine Robinson was next, murdered on December 1, 1939. Lucy Kidwell and Mattie Steward were killed two months apart, in September and November 1940. Ada Puller was the first victim of 1941, murdered on January 2.

Things started heating up for Washington police six weeks later, when Catoe shifted to Caucasian victims for the first time. Rose Abramovitz, a bride of one month, hired the strangler to wax some floors on March 8 and was murdered for her trouble, sprawled across her bed, while Catoe scooped up twenty dollars and escaped.

It rained in Washington on June 15, and Jesse Strieff, a pretty secretary at the War Department, was relieved when Catoe stopped to offer her a lift. Mistaking his car for a taxi, she climbed in and was driven to a nearby garage, where Catoe raped and strangled her, hiding her umbrella, stuffing her clothes in a trash bin. Strieff's nude body was discarded in another garage, ten blocks away, her death provoking congressional investigations and a personnel shake-up in the Washington police department. Still, the case remained unsolved until Catoe got careless in New York.

At once, police from several eastern jurisdictions sought to question Catoe in a string of unsolved murders. Officers from Lynn, Massachusetts, suspected a connection with a homicide recorded in July of 1941, and detectives from Garden City, Long Island, were curious about the death of a patrolman in 1940. Authorities from Hamilton Township, New Jersey, questioned Catoe about a series of shotgun murders, between 1938 and 1940, that were later cleared with the arrest of Clarence Hill. Spokesmen for NYPD requested that Catoe be questioned about the February 1940 strangulation death of Helen Foster. For all the circus atmosphere, the final tally stands, as far as anyone can tell, at nine.

Brought to trial in late October 1941, for killing Rose Abramovitz, Catoe sought to recant his confessions, claiming that police had tortured him while he was "sick and weak." A jury failed to buy the act, deliberating only eighteen minutes before returning its verdict of guilty, with a recommendation of death.

Chapman, George:
See Klosovski, Severin

Chicago—Unsolved Murders

Initially billed as the murders of six black "businessmen," Chicago's unsolved homicides of 1971 and '72 had several things in common: all the victims were black males; each was shot in the back of the head, execution-style; and all were discarded, like refuse, in the muddy South Branch of the Chicago River.

Lee Wilson was the first to die, in September 1971. Employed as a laborer in a meat packing plant, Wilson worked a shift from 4 a.m. to midnight. Dropping a coworker off around 1 a.m. on September 2, he started for home but never arrived. Wilson's car was recovered later that day; his body, hands bound, a bullet in his brain, was fished from the river on September 6. Robbery was suggested as a motive, though Wilson had carried no more than three dollars on the night of his death.

William Thomas, a baggage handler at O'Hare Airport, habitually traveled with two or three hundred dollars in his pocket, in case of "emergencies." On the night of November 4, 1971, he called home and told his wife not to hold dinner, as he would be late on the job. Around 9:30 p.m., he picked up an employee's airline pass to Florida—and disappeared. The pass was in his car, discovered three days later. Thomas, bound and shot like Wilson, was retrieved from the Chicago River on December 12.

Meanwhile, the elusive slayer had selected victim number three. The owner of his own taxi, 47-year-old Albert Shorter was off duty and cruising the bars when he vanished on November 17. The victim's Cadillac was found next day; his lifeless body was recovered on November 21.

Vernell Lollar, although unemployed, was flush with $900 from an insurance settlement when he vanished on November 26. His body, sans cash, was pulled from the river on December 13.

Lieutenant Scott (his name, not a military rank) was the first victim to qualify as a businessman. A partner in a snack shop, he withdrew $2,000 from a pension fund on the afternoon of December 13, 1971, and vanished that same evening. His car was found the next day, Scott's body hauled ashore on New Year's Eve.

The final victim in the murder series, Richard Stean, was twenty-eight years old, a partner in a television sales and service business. He left home around midnight on January 2, 1972, carrying $2,000 earmarked for a building contractor the next morning. Stean missed his appointment, and his car was recovered on January 6, after witnesses saw four passengers enter the infamous Cabrini-Green housing projects. On February 5, Stean's body was found in the river, but FBI agents were already working the case, tracking anonymous callers who demanded an $11,000 ransom from Stean's father. The drop was made on schedule, but no one ever came to get the cash.

A special task force was created in a bid to crack the case, but officers were getting nowhere fast. With half a dozen victims on their hands, no suspects, and a dearth of clues, police could only say, "The trail is cold."

Child Murders—Illinois

Between October 1955 and August 1957, six Chicago teenagers were slaughtered in a grisly string of homicides which have remained unsolved for more than thirty years. No positive connection in the cases was deduced, but they have entered modern folklore as a series and are so considered here. The evidence required to prove—or disprove—a connection, like the killer, has remained elusive.

On October 16, 1955, John Schuessler, age 13, went bowling at a North Side alley with his brother Anton, age 11, and a neighbor, Robert Peterson, 14. They never made it home for supper, and a search was launched, resulting in a grim discovery two days later. Hikers found the naked, battered bodies in a ditch near the Des Plaines River, in the Robinson Woods Forest Preserve. An autopsy showed that the three boys were strangled, but police had no other clues. More than forty confessions were logged in the case, but they all came from cranks with a yen for attention.

Fourteen months later, on December 28, 1956, Barbara Grimes, 15, and her sister Patricia, 13, failed to come home from a neighborhood theater. Reminded of the triple murder, still unsolved, Chicago panicked. Elvis Presley, star of the last movie seen by the sisters, made a public appeal for the girls to go home and be "good Presley fans." Columnist Ann Landers received an anonymous letter, allegedly written by a girl who had seen the Grimes sisters forced into a car by a young man. A partial license number of the car led nowhere, and the author of the note was not identified.

On January 22, 1957, a motorist in Du Page County spotted the victims in a roadside ditch, their naked, frozen bodies laid out side by side. Both sisters had been raped and beaten, but the coroner reported that their deaths resulted from exposure to the freezing January weather. Homicide detectives stubbornly refused to comment on reports that Barbara and Patricia had been mutilated, with the lips of one girl sliced away.

On August 15, 1957, Judith Anderson, 15, went missing on the one-mile walk between a friend's house and her home. There was no doubt about mutilation a week later, when her dismembered remains surfaced in two 55-gallon drums, floating in Montrose Harbor. One barrel contained the girl's head, with four .32-caliber slugs in the brain. Police discovered that the victim had been threatened by a man or boy who phoned her on the job, at a local modeling agency, but there the trail ran cold.

A short time later, homicide detectives picked up Barry Cook, a youth suspected in the strangulation death of Margaret Gallagher, a middle-aged victim, on Foster Beach. The evidence was marginal, at best, and Cook was cleared of murder charges at his trial. He subsequently went to prison for eleven years upon conviction in an unrelated case, on charges of aggravated assault and attempted rape.

Years after the fact, "psychic" Peter Hurkos fondled snapshots of the victims in Chicago, searching for "vibrations" from their killer, but he came no closer to an ultimate solution than police who had pursued the case from the beginning. The Chicago killer(s) who selected teens as victims in the 1950s is, presumably, at large today.

Child Murders—Montreal

Between November 1984 and June 1985, parents in Montreal, Canada, were terrorized by the specter of an anonymous child-killer stalking their city, selecting his victims at random, brutalizing and sexually abusing his male victims before discarding their bodies like so much rubbish. Although police made every normal effort to detect the killer, he remains at large, his case unsolved.

The first to die were Wilton Lubin, 12, and his playmate, eight-year-old Sebastien Metivier, reported missing on November 1, 1984. Lubin was found in the St. Lawrence River a month later, his throat slashed, but Sebastien Metivier is still among the missing. On December 2, four-year-old Maurice Viens was reported missing from home; discovered in a vacant house five days later, the child had been sexually abused, then killed by heavy blows to the back of his head. Twelve-year-old Michel Ethier disappeared on Christmas Day 1984, turning up in the St. Lawrence, a reported drowning victim. Denis Roux-Bergevin, age five, had been missing for three days when strollers found his bludgeoned, violated body on the shoulder of a highway, twelve miles east of town.

Based on the existing evidence, authorities acknowledged a connection only in the Viens and Roux-Bergevin murders, but the frightened residents of Montreal were not convinced. Gary Rosenfelt—who lost a step-son in the Clifford Olson murder spree—told newsmen, "Everything indicates that there is a serial killer in Montreal, and the police there do not seem to even acknowledge it."

Speaking for his department, Detective Sgt. Gilles Boyer informed the media that all sixteen members of the Montreal homicide squad were involved in the manhunt. "We are looking all over—in sewers, everywhere," he said. "The kids are not that big. They are easy to get rid of."

Christiansen, Thor Nis

In late 1976 and early 1977, female students at the University of California in Santa Barbara were terrorized by a grim series of "look-alike" murders, so-called because the victims closely resembled one another. The first to die was co-ed Jacqueline Rook, 21, abducted from a bus stop in the Santa Barbara suburb of Goleta on December 6, 1976. A Goleta waitress, Mary Sarris, disappeared the same day, and both were still missing on January 18, when 21-year-old Patricia Laney vanished from another local bus stop. Laney's corpse was discovered next day, in nearby Refugio Canyon, and police recognized the sinister pattern when Jacqueline Rook was found dead, in the same area, on January 20. Each had been killed by one shot to the head, fired from a small-caliber pistol.

Thor Christiansen first came to the attention of police in February 1977, as one of several hundred persons questioned in the case. Cited as a minor in possession of alcohol, he was not considered a suspect at the time, although authorities confiscated a .22-caliber pistol from his car. No one remembered Christiansen on May 22, when the skeletal remains of Mary Sarris were discovered in Drum Canyon, north of Santa Barbara. Homicide investigators wrote him off as one more teen-aged punk, picked up with liquor on his breath.

Linda Preston, age 24, was thumbing rides in Hollywood on April 18, 1979, when Christiansen picked her up, traveling several blocks before he drew a gun and pumped a bullet into her left ear. Bleeding profusely, the young woman managed to leap from his car and save herself, escaping on foot to find medical aid. Three months later, on July 11, Preston spotted her assailant in a Hollywood tavern and summoned sheriff's deputies, who booked him on a charge of felonious assault. Police in Santa Barbara noted similarities between the crimes; they also learned that Thor had been arrested on a drunken driving charge July 7, another .22-caliber handgun removed from his car. On July 27, Christiansen was formally charged with three counts of first-degree murder in Santa Barbara, held over for trial without bond.

Christofi, Styllou

A native of Cyprus, born in 1900, Styllou Christofi was tried, in 1925, on a charge of murdering her mother-in-law by ramming a lighted torch down the old woman's throat. She persuaded a jury of her innocence and was released, but her problems with in-laws were not at an end.

In 1953, Christofi went to live with her son and his German wife of fifteen years in Hampstead, England. The women failed to hit it off, and things became so tense around the house that Hella Christofi announced her intention of taking the children to Germany for a holiday in July 1954. She let her husband understand that she did not expect to find his mother in the house when she returned.

On the night of July 28, Styllou ambushed her daughter-in-law in the bathroom, knocking her unconscious with an ash plate lifted from the stove. Dragging Hella into the kitchen, she strangled the younger woman with a scarf and tried to hide the evidence by pouring paraffin over the body, setting it on fire. In moments, the flames leaped out of control, threatening to consume the house and her grandchildren, sleeping upstairs.

At 1 a.m., a married couple parked near Hampstead station were approached by Christofi, babbling in broken English about a fire at her home. Returning with her to the scene, they doused the flames and found a woman's body, charred in places, with the livid mark of strangulation still visible on her throat. Police were summoned, and a neighbor came forward to describe Christofi stirring the flames around a prostrate "tailor's dummy."

Prison doctors found Styllou Christofi insane, but she refused to permit an insanity defense at her trial. Convicted and sentenced to death in October 1954, her subsequent appeals were dismissed and she was executed after three doctors pronounced her sane. Her son did not attend the hanging.

Cincinnati—Unsolved Murders

Suburban Cumminsville is normally a peaceful place, but in the six-year period from 1904 to 1910 it earned the grisly reputation of a "murder zone," where women walked in fear and dreaded riding street cars after nightfall. A ferocious "mad killer" was on the loose, claiming five victims within a mile of the point where Spring Grove Avenue meets Winton Road, eluding the police and neighborhood patrols to leave a nagging legacy of doubt and mystery behind.

Mary McDonald, 31, had "been around" before she met her killer in the predawn hours of May 4, 1904. An ill-fated affair with her late sister's husband had left her to find solace in whiskey, but things were looking up that spring, with her engagement to be married. Shortly after 1:30 a.m., she left a local tavern in company with her fiancee, and he saw her safely aboard an "owl car," homeward bound. Near daybreak, the switchman on a train near Ludlow Avenue spied Mary's body by the tracks and help was summoned. She was still alive but incoherent, with a fractured skull and one leg severed, dying hours later from her injuries. Police initially dismissed her death as "accidental," later shifting to the view that she was beaten and pushed in front of a train in a deliberate act of murder.

Louise Mueller, 21, was the next to die, leaving home for a stroll on October 1, 1904. She never returned, and her body was found next morning, the skull battered to pulp, in a gully beside some disused railroad tracks. Her killer had scooped a shallow grave from the soft earth nearby, but the corpse lay above ground, as if some passerby had disturbed the hasty burial.

At 9 p.m. on November 2, 18-year-old Alma Steinigewig left her job as an operator at the local telephone exchange, vanishing before she reached her home. The next morning, a street car conductor spotted her corpse in a nearby vacant lot, her skull crushed by savage blows. The victim's clothes were muddy after being dragged across the lot, and officers discovered suspect footprints that would ultimately lead them nowhere. Clutched in Alma's hand, they found a street car transfer punched at 9:40 p.m. on the day of her death.

An ugly pattern had begun to form, and homicide investigators hauled in suspects by the dozens, forced to free them all for lack of evidence. One who eluded them, a stocky man remembered for his heavy beard, had turned up at the Mueller crime scene, wringing his hands and crying out, "It was an accident!" Other witnesses placed him at the scene of Alma Steinigewig's death, but he was never identified, his link—if any—with the case remaining open to conjecture.

Six years passed before the killer struck again, claiming 43-year-old Anna Lloyd on December 31, 1909. Employed as a secretary at a local lumber yard, the victim worked until 5:30 p.m. that New Year's Eve, her body found hours later, a short distance from the office. She had been gagged with a cheap black muffler, her skull crushed, her throat slashed, leaving signs of a fierce struggle behind. A single strand of black hair was clutched in her fist, but primitive forensics tests of the day rendered it worthless as evidence. Police initially called the slaying a contract murder, but no suspect or motive was ever identified.

The stalker claimed his final victim on October 25, 1910, when 26-year-old Mary Hackney was found in her cottage on Dane Street, her skull fractured and throat slashed. Suspicion focused briefly on her husband, but police discovered Mary was alive when he reported to his job. A spate of letters, signed with the initials "S.D.M.," were mailed by someone claiming knowledge of the crimes, but homicide investigators finally dismissed them as a hoax.

The fading memories of murder were revived in December 1913, by investigators of the Burns Detective Agency, assigned to check out unsolved acts of violence in a recent street car strike. Detectives told the mayor they had discovered an "indefinite" solution in the case of Anna Lloyd, pointing the finger of suspicion at a onetime conductor, now confined to a sanitarium as hopelessly insane. A search of his lodgings had turned up a threatening letter, addressed to persons "who saw him in the act of Dec. 31," and authorities leaped to a theoretical connection with the three-year-old murder. Ultimately fruitless, the investigation petered out a few days later, and the crimes in Cumminsville remain unsolved.

Clarey, Richard N., Jr.

Raised in West Germany by American parents working abroad, Clarey was the product of a troubled childhood exacerbated by the use of drugs. In 1977, at age sixteen, he left Wiesbaden for the United States, living briefly with an aunt in Oregon. The relationship didn't work out, and Clarey spent the next two years drifting aimlessly through the western half of the country, living off the proceeds of burglaries, armed robberies, and drug sales before he settled in Kalamazoo, Michigan, during 1979.

By the spring of 1984, he craved a change of scene. On April 15, he killed 35-year-old Robert Baranski in Kalamazoo, dumping his victim in Lake Michigan and stealing Baranski's car for the trip across country. Clarey made it as far as New Buffalo, 50 miles to the southwest, before piling his stolen vehicle into a ditch on April 17. Approached by tourists from a nearby rest stop, he shot Floyd Holmes and Dean Bultema, killing both men before he slipped across the Indiana border. Arrested later that day, while hiding in a garage at La Porte, Clarey was returned to Michigan for trial on murder charges.

Defense attorneys blamed the killer's crimes on nightmares generated by his childhood. Clarey was obsessed, they claimed, by dreams of German Nazis who demanded that he kill Americans. He wore a swastika tattoo upon his chest, together with the likeness of a German helmet on his arm, committing himself to do "as much damage as he could" to blacks and other minorities in his cross-country ramblings. Ignoring the psychological argument, a jury in Berrien County deliberated one hour before convicting Clarey of dual murder charges on December 20, 1984, imposing the mandatory sentence of life without parole.

In February 1985, Clarey sat for interviews with a psychologist, Dr. Leonard Donk, who diagnosed the subject as a schizophrenic sociopath. In the course of those interviews, Clarey confessed to numerous slayings—"more than 100 but less than 150"—dating back to the age of fifteen. He recalled feeling "excited and detached" during the murders, but details on most of the cases remained vague. Donk explained that it was "very difficult to tell" where fantasy left off and stark reality began for Richard Clarey. "I suspect he's killed more people than he's been charged with," Donk said. "How many more, I wouldn't even want to speculate on." (Authorities were able to rule out at least one case: the victim, named by Clarey, was alive and well.)

On February 12, 1985, in the midst of his second murder trial, Clarey pled guilty, but mentally ill in the slaying of Robert Baranski, facing another maximum term of life imprisonment. In October 1986, he joined another inmate in a foiled escape attempt, commandeering a truck and crashing it into a fence at the prison near Ann Arbor. Clarey's bid for freedom was foiled when the fence held and the truck's engine stalled. He remains in custody today.

Clements, Robert George

A British physician and practicing "bluebeard," Dr. Clements was charged with killing his fourth wife and strongly suspected of slaying her three predecessors, as well. His first two brides were described, respectively, as victims of "sleeping sickness" and "endocarditis," with Clements signing the death certificate in each case. Wife number three seemed perfectly fit when Clements began predicting her imminent death, in 1939, but doctor knew best. After she collapsed and died in Southport, a physician friend of Clements persuaded police to order an autopsy—but the remains had already been cremated, on orders from the grieving husband. Once again, Clements was on hand to sign the certificate of death by natural causes.

The merry widower acquired his fourth wife that same year, in London. She lasted until May 27, 1947, but this time there was a discrepancy concerning cause of death. A Lancashire pathologist, Dr. James Houston, accepted Clements's word in listing the cause as myeloid leukemia, but an independent examiner noted signs of morphine poisoning. Police learned, from neighbors, that Dr. Clements seemed to have strange advance knowledge of his wife's "dizzy spells," and further investigation revealed that Clements had prescribed large doses of morphine for a patient who never received the injections. A second autopsy revealed traces of morphine, and warrants were issued for Clements's arrest.

Calling on Clements and Dr. Houston in turn, detectives found both men dead in an apparent double suicide. Clements had relied on morphine, leaving a note which read: "To whom it may concern ... I can no longer tolerate the diabolical insults to which I have recently been exposed." Dr. Houston, taking his own life with cyanide, left a more plaintive message: "I have for some time been aware that I have been making mistakes. I have not profited from experience."

Coddington, Herbert James

On May 16, 1987, two teenaged models and their elderly female chaperones were reported missing after they failed to return from a trip to Lake Tahoe, on the California-Nevada border, for production of an anti-drug video program. Missing were: Maybelle Martin, 69, operator of the Showcase Finishing and Modeling School in Reno, Nevada; her friend Dorothy Walsh, 67; model Alecia Thoma, 14, of Reno; and model Monica Berge, age 12, from nearby Sparks. A three-day search by fifty law enforcement officers, including agents of the FBI, centered on Lake Tahoe, where local girls had complained of a "weird" man who tried to recruit them for anti-drug video projects. One of the girls was suspicious enough to record the man's license plate number, a detail which led investigators to the rural home of Herbert Coddington.

The name was a familiar one to officers throughout Nevada. Coddington had worked at two casinos in Las Vegas during 1980, and a warrant filed in Douglas County charged him with a cheating scam in April 1984. Arrested in Las Vegas, he had been released on $500 bail and the case was still pending.

On May 18, 1987, federal agents armed with warrants raided Coddington's mobile home, freeing Thoma and Berge from a boarded-up bedroom where they were held captive. The bodies of Maybelle Martin and Dorothy Walsh were found in an adjoining room, bound up in plastic garbage bags. On May 20, Coddington was arraigned on two counts of murder, with five other counts charging rape and acts of deviate sexual abuse against the teenaged victims.

With their man in custody, authorities began to search his background, and they soon discovered links with yet another crime. In August 1981, 12-year-old Sheila Keister had been kidnapped, raped and strangled in Las Vegas, her body discarded beside an unpaved road on Sunrise Mountain, east of town. Upon examination, prosecutors charged that dental casts obtained from Coddington matched bite marks on the dead girl's body, and another charge of homicide was filed on July 22, 1987.

Code, Nathaniel Robert, Jr.

A native of Shreveport, Louisiana, bisexual Nathaniel Code was convicted of aggravated rape in March 1976, sentenced to fifteen years imprisonment. Paroled for "good behavior" during January 1984, he returned home and was married two years later. From all appearances, he was reformed, a pleasant family man, but dark compulsions lurked beneath the surface, driving him to savage acts of violence in his own community.

Before his ultimate arrest, he would dispatch at least twelve victims in a three-year period, and homicide investigators feel his crimes may span the 1970s as well, with victims yet unknown.

The first official casualty was Debra Ford, stabbed to death in her home—a block from Code's residence—on August 31, 1984. Ford had been bound before she died, and there were no signs of forced entry at the scene, suggesting that she knew her killer and invited him inside.

Ten months later, circumstances were nearly identical in the stabbing death of 48-year-old Wes Burks, a Shreveport homosexual. Burks' home was fitted with a set of burglar bars, and again there was no sign of forced entry, leading police to surmise that his death had resulted from a "date" gone wrong.

On July 18, 1985, Monica Barnum, age 20, was found tied up in her apartment, strangled with a wire coat hanger. The next morning, Shreveport police were called out to the scene of a grisly massacre, four victims bound with electric cord, listed as dead on arrival. Vivian Chaney, 34, had been strangled and drowned in her own bathtub, while other members of her family—including her common-law husband, her brother, and a teenaged daughter—had been killed in different rooms, two of them shot in the head, one with a slashed throat. Two younger daughters, nine and ten, had saved themselves by hiding in a closet while the killer ran amok. They offered vague descriptions of a husky black man, but police were still no closer to a suspect in the case.

On February 21, 1986, Johnny Jenkins was bound and stabbed to death in his home, while victim Jake Mills met an identical fate on December 12 of that year. Murder struck closer to home on August 5, 1987, claiming 73-year-old William Code and his two "adopted grandsons"—brothers Eric Williams, age eight, and Joe Robinson, Jr., age 10—in the house where Nathaniel Code was raised. Police picked Code up the next morning, confiscating several weapons in the process, and by August 7 they were tentatively closing down a dozen unsolved cases.

There were problems along the way—witnesses refused to identify Code as the perpetrator of the Chaney massacre—but his palm print was matched to a print from the bathtub where Vivian Chaney was murdered. Indicted on five counts of first-degree murder, including that of Debra Ford, Code was held over for trial on capital charges. Investigation in seven other slayings was eventually suspended on grounds of insufficient evidence.

Cook, William

Born in 1929 near Joplin, Missouri, William Cook was one of eight children fathered by an alcoholic miner. When his mother died, Cook's father moved the family into an abandoned mine shaft, where they lived like animals until the old man finally deserted them entirely. Welfare workers placed Cook's siblings in foster homes, but little William was repeatedly rejected due to a congenital deformity which prevented his right eye from closing completely. The resulting "sinister" look unnerved prospective foster parents, and Cook found placement only when the court agreed to pay his room and board.

Unfortunately, Cook's appointed foster mother was more interested in earning money from the boy than raising him correctly. Two years running, Cook was given bicycles for Christmas, and they were immediately repossessed for lack of payment. As he entered adolescence, Cook began to run the streets at night and practice petty theft; upon his first arrest, he told the court he would prefer reform school to his foster home.

Released a few months later, Cook immediately robbed a cab driver of eleven dollars, earning a five-year stretch in the reformatory. Violent outbursts there resulted in a transfer to state prison, where he earned a reputation as a brawler. Once, Cook nearly killed a fellow inmate with a baseball bat, the incident resulting from a joke about his droopy eyelid.

Finally released in 1950, at the age of 22, Cook stopped in Joplin long enough for a reunion with his drunken father, moving west from there with the expressed intent to "live by the gun and roam." He picked up the gun—a .32 pistol—in El Paso, Texas, traveling as far as California before he doubled back, wandering aimlessly across country. The words "Hard Luck," tattooed across the fingers of his left hand, foretold the fate of hapless strangers who would cross his path.

In Lubbock, Texas, on December 30, 1950, Cook abducted a motorist at gunpoint, pushing north toward Joplin. His hostage escaped in Oklahoma, and Cook ran out of gas on Highway 66, between Tulsa and Claremore, on New Year's Eve. Carl Mosser, his wife and three children were bound for New Mexico when they stopped to help another motorist in trouble, and their trip became a nightmare from the moment they laid eyes on William Cook.

Flashing his pistol, Cook ordered Mosser to "drive him around." Stopping for gas and food in Wichita Falls, Texas, Mosser tried to disarm his captor, but Cook was quicker and stronger, firing several shots at a grocery clerk who tried to intervene. Over the next two days, Mosser drove Cook through New Mexico, Texas, and Arkansas, winding up in the gunman's old stamping grounds, around Joplin. There, Cook massacred the family (and their dog), dumping the bodies down an abandoned mine shaft before continuing his odyssey.

His bloodstained car broke down in Osage County, Oklahoma, and Cook flagged down a deputy sheriff, disarming the officer, whom he left in a roadside ditch, his hands bound. Driving the stolen patrol car, Cook stopped a traveling salesman, Robert Dewey, and changed vehicles again, forcing Dewey to head for California. On arrival, Cook dispatched his hostage execution-style, the corpse and car alerting lawmen to his presence on the coast.

Pushing south, Cook crossed the border at Tijuana, picking up two more male hostages en route. On January 15, 1951, he was recognized by the police chief in Santa Rosaria and disarmed without a struggle. Returned to California for trial, on murder charges, Cook was convicted and sentenced to die. He was executed in San Quentin's gas chamber on December 12, 1952.

Cooke, Eric Edgar

Ostracized in childhood for his harelip and cleft palate, Eric Cooke grew up an angry, brooding loner in the neighborhood of Perth, Australia. As a young man, he was prone to accidents, suffering repeated mishaps on the job. His injuries included several traumas to the head, and it remains unclear to what extent brain damage may have charted Eric's future course of violence.

Sexually, Cooke preferred the non-participating role of a voyeur. He also had a flair for burglary and arson, serving eighteen months in jail for burning down a church where he had lately been rejected in a choir audition. Later, Eric torched a theater, apparently for spite. He was accelerating toward a mental detonation which would rock Australia with its violence, confounding homicide investigators with a scarcity of clues.

On February 2, 1959, Pnena Berkman was attacked while sleeping in her Perth apartment, stabbed repeatedly and fatally before she had a chance to struggle with her killer. The police discounted sex and robbery as motives; she had not been raped, and nothing had been stolen.

Ten months later, on December 20, Jillian Brewster, age 22, was found in bed at home, another murder victim. Jillian's killer had employed a knife and hatchet, hacking at her face before (or after) he delivered lethal stab wounds. She had died sometime between midnight, December 19, when her fiancee left the house, and 9:00 a.m. the next morning, when her body was discovered. Once again, there was no rape, no sign of robbery.

Fifteen months elapsed without a break in the disturbing homicides. The citizens of Perth were happy to forget until, on April 17, 1961, a deaf mute held in jail on unrelated charges suddenly confessed the Brewster killing. He possessed an iron-clad alibi for Pnena Berkman's murder, and in August, at his trial, he would recant the earlier confession, but in vain. Convicted on a murder charge, he was condemned to hang.

On April 7, 1961, a middle-aged businessman parked with a young barmaid in the Perth suburb of Cottesloe. Distracted by each other, they were unaware of the approaching gunman as he stood beside their car, took aim, squeezed off a single shot. His bullet drilled the woman's hand and pierced her male companion's neck. Both wounds were superficial, and they managed to provide police with a description of the young man they saw running from the scene. By that time, though, the sniper had already struck again.

Within the hour, Perth authorities were notified that local resident George Walmsley had been killed by one shot through the forehead, murdered in the act of answering the doorbell which had roused him out of bed at 4:00 a.m. Nearby, a landlady awakened by sirens of police cruisers rushing to Walmsley's house stopped in to tell her roomer there was unaccustomed action in the neighborhood. She found John Sturkey, age 19, a student, lying on the open balcony outside his room, a bullet in his head. He died a short time later, at the hospital.

It seemed the grisly night would never end. At 8:10 in the morning, officers were told that yet another victim had been found. The latest human target, an accountant, 29, had been shot down sometime within the past six hours. Surgeons saved his life, although he lingered for a time in critical condition. Like the other victims of the shooting spree, he had been wounded by a .22-caliber weapon.

On August 10, a married couple coming home at 2 a.m. discovered babysitter Shirley McLeod, age 19, lying dead in their Dalkeith home. The single bullet which had pierced her skull was, once again, a .22.

On August 17, an elderly couple gathering wildflowers near the Canning River found a rifle lying in the brush and called police. Ballistics tests confirmed it was the weapon used to kill the babysitter one week earlier. The rifle was impounded, replaced with a look-alike, and detectives staked out the scene. They waited fifteen days before a man arrived to claim the weapon, and they took him into custody without a struggle.

Suspect Eric Cooke was 32 years old, married, the father of seven. Family life, apparently, had failed to calm him down from youthful days of burglary and arson. He confessed to killing Shirley McLeod, and when ballistics tests revealed the captured rifle had not been employed on January 27, he led homicide detectives to the place where a second gun was fished out of the Swan River, near Perth. This time, ballistics matched across the board.

Interrogation of the killer failed to yield a motive, Cooke insisting that he shot six people, killing three, because he "just wanted to hurt somebody." Convicted on a triple murder count in late November 1963, Eric Cooke was hanged October 24, 1964. At execution

time, police considered him their prime—and only—
suspect in the hacking deaths from 1959.

Cota, Fernando Velazco

It should have been a routine traffic stop. Two officers of the California Highway Patrol noticed the white
van around 8:00 p.m. on October 14, 1984, weaving er-
ratically in the fast lane of Highway 101, some fifteen
miles north of San Jose. Suspecting alcohol at work,
they stopped the van and left their cruiser, moving in on
foot. The driver seemed more nervous than intoxicated.
When they asked to look inside the van, their suspect
suddenly erupted from the driver's seat, a pistol in his
hand.

Incredibly, the gunman started shouting, "Kill me!
Kill me! I'm very sick. If you don't kill me, I'll kill
myself!" With that, he jammed the barrel of his gun inside his open mouth and fired a single shot, producing
almost instant death.

Inside the van, a wooden box resembling a coffin
held the body of a young, dead woman. She was nude
except for panties and a pair of stockings; chains and
rope secured her hands. She had been raped and strangled. Subsequent investigation named the victim as
Kim Dunham, 21, reported missing one day earlier. The
driver of the van—and Kim's apparent murderer—was
local resident Fernando Cota. An examination of the
dead man's record showed a rape conviction from El
Paso, Texas, during 1975. Cota had attacked a nurse,
and two days later mailed a note which read: "Sorry
about the argument we had. Still loving you." The "argument" earned Cota twenty years in prison, eight of
which he served before parole released him in September 1983. His wife had left him, with their children,
while Fernando did his time, and on release he moved

to California, settling in San Jose. A young woman and her daughter moved in with Cota in May 1984, but they soon departed, citing his behavior as "too weird."

Kim Dunham's murder, and the killer's wild "confession," prompted local homicide investigators to review the other open cases in their files. Immediately, they began to see a common thread in other recent sex-related murders.

On September 10, a co-ed, Kelly Ralston, 21, was stabbed to death by an intruder in her San Jose apartment. One day later, housewife Gwendolyn Hoffman, 57, disappeared from her home in Campbell, a San Jose suburb; on September 13, her strangled body was recovered from the trunk of her own car, two miles from her home. Tania Zack disappeared on September 15, when her car ran out of gas near Los Gatos. Her body was recovered on October 5, discarded in a roadside ditch; she had been raped and bludgeoned, rope burns on her wrists suggesting she was held alive for some time after her abduction.

Lori Miller, 20, was the manager of a cafe in San Jose. She was reported missing by her live-in boyfriend on September 26, when he came home from work to find their phone off the hook, eggs burning on the stove, the smoke alarm buzzing in an empty house. That afternoon, he told detectives, someone posing as a plumber had come knocking at their door, but Lori, learning that her landlord had no knowledge of the visit, told the man to leave. Her semi-naked corpse was found October 6, in a ravine a few miles south of San Jose. She had been bound and tortured, strangled, raped. With hindsight and a suspect's address fresh in hand, detectives realized Fernando Cota had resided in a block of apartments directly behind Miller's home.

And there were other victims, tentatively added to

the list. Joan Leslie, 28, a transient, had been stabbed to death, her corpse recovered in a subdivision near Aptos, fifteen miles due south of San Jose. In San Jose itself, September 30, a group of children had reported rancid odors emanating from an empty house, within two blocks of Lori Miller's home. Inside, police discovered the remains of 29-year-old Teresa Sunder, first reported missing two weeks earlier. She had been raped and beaten brutally by her assailant.

Fernando Cota, having spared the residents of California an expensive trial, is definitely linked with only one of eight crimes in the five-week murder rampage. Still, detectives are convinced, by the proximity of time and place, that Cota was responsible for all the homicides in question.

Cummins, Gordon Frederick

Born in 1914, Cummins was the well-educated son of a good British family, but his breeding somehow failed to take. Married at age 22, he was dismissed from a series of jobs for being unreliable and dishonest. Affecting an Oxford accent and posing as the illegitimate son of a British lord, Cummins was derided as "the Duke" by friends who saw through his disguise. When World War II erupted, Cummins joined the RAF as a cadet, residing in North London with his wife.

On February 9, 1942, Evelyn Hamilton, a 40-year-old teacher, was found strangled in a London air raid shelter. Although her purse was missing, she had not been raped or otherwise abused.

On February 10, Evelyn Oatley, 35, was found dead in her flat, stretched out nude on the bed. Her throat was slashed, her lower body mutilated with a can opener. Fingerprints were recovered from the weapon and a bedroom mirror, but without a suspect they were useless.

The following day, Margaret Lowe, age 43, was murdered in her London flat and mutilated with a razor blade, her wounds essentially identical to Oatley's. She would not be found for three more days, by which time London's "Blackout Ripper" had already claimed another victim.

Doris Jouannet was last seen alive around ten o'clock on the evening of February 13. She was already dead—strangled with a stocking, her body mutilated with a razor—by the time her husband, a hotel night manager, came home the next morning. Police were still swarming over the scene when their suspect struck again, in another part of London.

Approaching his prospective victim in a pub, the young airman followed her into the street and choked her unconscious, disturbed by passersby before he could complete the kill. In flight, he dropped a gas mask with his service number stenciled on it, but he either failed to notice or was too far gone to care. Immediately after that assault, another woman picked him up and took him home, where he attacked her and attempted strangulation. Frightened by the volume of her screams, he bolted from the flat and left his belt behind.

Swiftly identified by his service number, Cummins was arrested on return to his billet, twelve hours after the last incident. His fingerprints matched those from the Oatley murder scene, and Cummins confessed going home with another prostitute on February 10, sparing her life when he learned she had no money. Sentenced to die for his crimes, he was hanged on June 25, 1942. Ironically, his execution was accomplished in the middle of an air raid.

Dalton, Lawrence

On April 22, 1979, FBI spokesmen announced their search for 34-year-old Lawrence Dalton, sought on murder charges after a woman's corpse was unearthed near Kenosha, Wisconsin, in front of a house which Dalton had occupied from March 1977 through February 1978. The victim was identified as Blanchie Penna, 23, missing from Racine, Wisconsin, and Dalton was also sought in connection with the murder of 12-year-old Lisa Slusser, slain in Waukegan, Illinois, during 1977.

The fugitive had earlier been charged with rape, deviate sexual assault and taking indecent liberties with a child, following an incident in Brooklyn, where a 14-year-old girl accused Dalton of holding her hostage over a period of four months. Dalton's wife, Karen, and a female acquaintance named Barbara Filipski were also arrested in that case, charged with sexually abusing the girl.

On April 23, Dalton was arrested in Cleveland and held for questioning on two counts of murder. (Further inquiries concerned a "Jane Doe" victim found in Lake County, Illinois, in the summer of 1978.) Formally charged with the Penna murder on the day of his arrest, Dalton waived extradition to Waukegan, where authorities placed the number of his homicides at four and counting.

Daughtrey, Earl Llewellyn, Jr.

One of the South's most intriguing murder mysteries revolves around this native of Berrien County, Georgia, born in 1949. While Daughtrey's long history of crimes against women does not include a murder conviction—so far—agents of the FBI and state authorities have publicly declared him a suspect in at least three Serial slayings, and their investigation is continuing with an eye toward prosecution. On the side, the husband of his first suspected murder victim—twice convicted for the crime himself—has filed a multi-million dollar lawsuit against Daughtrey, charging the Georgia suspect with wrongful death. At this writing, the lawsuit remains unresolved.

Earl Daughtrey's problems with violence are traceable to high school, in the late 1960s, when a female classmate accused him of trying to choke her on campus. No charges were filed, and he dropped out of school in his senior year to find work. Married in March 1971, Daughtrey moved to Anniston, Alabama, where he was hired by a local construction crew. Three months later, Daughtrey's team was landscaping the home of Harvie and Betty Renfroe, at nearby Lincoln, when Harvie found his wife dead in their kitchen, partially clothed and strangled, one of his own shirts double-knotted around her neck.

Convicted of murder on the testimony of a local sheriff—later impeached and removed from office for embezzlement and violent, irrational behavior—Harvie Renfroe won his appeal for a new trial in 1972. Twelve years later, a report from state investigators named Earl Daughtrey as a "possible suspect" in the slaying, but prosecutors suppressed the document and Renfroe was convicted again in 1980, of first-degree manslaughter, ultimately serving 17 months of a five-year prison term. He emerged from the lockup embittered and determined to clear his name.

Daughtrey, meanwhile, had moved back to Ray City, Georgia, in September 1971. That same month, he was charged with assault after choking Jo Ann Peters in her Ray City home, the assault interrupted when her parents arrived and chased Daughtrey away. In lieu of criminal prosecution, Earl was sent to the state hospital at

Milledgeville, where he was diagnosed as an hysterical neurotic with a "good" prognosis for recovery. He was released as "cured" on April 19, 1972.

On August 3, 1973, 27-year-old Emma Rogers was forced off the road and shot six times while driving through Madison County, Florida, just over the Georgia state line. Nine months pregnant at the time, Rogers survived to provide a description of the man who shot her and then stole her purse from the car. Earl Daughtrey was named as a suspect, but no charges were filed at the time.

Four months later, in Cook County, Georgia, Doris Register was chased down in her car and wounded by a shotgun blast to the head. She, too, would survive after facing the gunman who peered through a window and laughed in her face. More to the point, she saw his license number, traceable to Earl Daughtrey, and paint samples from his car matched specimens recovered in the Rogers case. Conviction for attempted murder earned Daughtrey a life sentence in Florida, plus fifteen years for robbery and aggravated assault with intent to kill. A second trial, in Georgia, added ten more years, to run consecutively with the time Earl owed to Florida. Confined in the Sunshine State from September 16, 1974, through February 19, 1980, he was then delivered to Georgia authorities. Three and a half years later, Daughtrey was released by a parole board that "honestly believed he had gotten his act together."

His act looked much the same on January 7, 1984, when police found him trying to strangle 34-year-old Brenda Debruhal at a public park, in Tift County, Georgia. Captured after ramming two patrol cars in a high-speed chase, Daughtrey was charged with aggravated assault, reckless driving, and attempting to evade arrest. He failed to notify his parole officer of the case, and so his parole was revoked on January 23, landing Earl back behind bars until his ultimate release on February 24, 1985. (While still in prison, he was convicted of simple assault in the Tift case, receiving a one-year term of probation.)

On October 29, 1985, Cheryl Fletcher was found dead in her home at Ocilla, Georgia, northeast of Tifton; she had been strangled with a lamp cord, tied with double knots around her neck. Investigators learned that she had advertised some articles for sale through a local newspaper, the *Tiftarea Shopper,* receiving at least one call from an unidentified male "customer." And there, for the moment, the trail went cold.

A second "want-ad" murder was recorded on March 12, 1987, when Beverly Kaster was killed in her Lenox, Georgia, home, strangled with a blouse double-knotted around her neck. Again, the victim had placed ads in the *Shopper,* receiving several calls from an unidentified man who expressed interest in visiting her home.

Two months later, Louise Spotanski grew suspicious of the man who phoned in response to her *Shopper* ad offering a pair of recliner chairs for sale. She alerted the sheriff, then invited the "buyer" to drop by on May 13, 1987. Officers arrived to find Earl Daughtrey advancing on the woman in menacing fashion, a towel wrapped around his fists, and he compounded the problem by giving them an alias when asked his name. Sentenced to thirty days for making false statements to police, Daughtrey served a week in jail before he was released. Meanwhile, state authorities had taken a look at his telephone records, discovering a call from Daughtrey's phone to Cheryl Fletcher's number on October 22, 1985—a week before she died.

The double knots employed in three known murders rang a bell, and in November 1987 state investigators sought a warrant to search Daughtrey's home, filing an affidavit that read in part: "Careful analysis by Special Agents of the FBI Behavioral Science Unit and the Georgia Bureau of Investigation of crimes known and suspected to have been committed by Earl L. Daughtrey, Jr., strongly suggest that Daughtrey exhibits the behavioral traits and tendencies of a serial killer." One incident cited had taken place since the Kaster slaying in March. The female organist at a Tift County church service had turned around to find Daughtrey standing behind her, grinning, his hands curled in a "choking posture." As she turned to face him, Daughtrey backed away and said, "I could have killed you easy."

A search of Daughtrey's home revealed no solid evidence, but the investigation is continuing. Meanwhile, in December 1987, Harvie Renfroe filed suit against Daughtrey for the wrongful death of Betty Renfroe, seeking $32.5 million in punitive damages. Daughtrey responded with a countersuit in January 1988, asserting that Alabama's statute of limitations had run out on the charge, denouncing Renfroe's suit as a "frivolous" example of harassment. At this writing, both lawsuits are still before the courts.

Davis, Bruce A.

Born in 1948 at Toledo, Ohio, and raised in rural, Fayette County, Davis dropped out of high school in the mid-1960s and moved to Manhattan, in hopes of pursuing a singing career. He earned a diploma from night school, in 1968, but success in show business eluded him, leaving the young man embittered, struggling to make ends meet. A sexual assault at age thirteen left Davis hating homosexuals, and when his cash ran short he hatched a plan to prey upon his childhood enemies, seducing gays and robbing them of cash and other valuables.

In February 1972, Davis was arrested in Washington, D.C., and charged with the murder of a local businessman, James Earl Hammer. Convicted of manslaughter, he drew a sentence of five to fifteen years imprisonment before Illinois authorities linked him with the strangulation of Rev. Carlo Barlassina, murdered in a Chicago hotel on June 29, 1971. Extradited to Chicago in December 1972, Davis was convicted of murder, his 25-to-45-year prison term consecutive with his existing sentence.

Serving his federal time first, Davis logged eight and a half years in the lockup at Terre Haute, Indiana, with side trips to the prison hospital at Springfield, Missouri. In 1979, he was transferred to the Illinois state prison at Menard, where he remained until October 1982. On the afternoon of October 24, Davis armed himself with an ax, fatally wounding Joe Cushman, a guard, before fleeing in Cushman's car. The vehicle was recovered next day, near Christopher, Illinois, but Davis remained at large until Halloween, when deputies picked him up for attempted auto theft in Smithers, West Virginia.

Back in custody, the homicidal drifter launched into rambling confessions, claiming 32 murders between 1969 and 1971. With a few exceptions, his victims were described as wealthy professional men, seduced with promises of sex, then killed for profit and amusement. The body-count included eight victims in Washington, D.C. and more in the suburbs, five in New York, with others in Baltimore, Boston, Fort Lauderdale, Reno, Las Vegas, New Orleans, Los Angeles, and San Juan, Puerto Rico. Authorities in Illinois confirmed at least four slayings, based on Davis's intimate knowledge of the crime scenes, and New York police "feel certain" of his guilt in the May 1970 strangulation of voice teacher Eric Tcherkezian. Returned to Illinois in mid-November 1982, Davis was convicted of Joe Cushman's murder ten months later and sentenced to life.

Davis, Frank

On June 3, 1971, 13-year-old Duane Bush was reported missing from his home in Union Mills, Indiana. Suspected as a runaway, in light of recent confrontations with the local juvenile authorities, Duane had actually been kidnapped, sodomized, and strangled. Three months elapsed before a hunter found his scattered skeletal remains on wooded ground, five miles northeast of town. The dead boy was identified from dental charts.

The terror had begun, but it was quickly interrupted. Shortly after Duane Bush died, Frank Davis was convicted on a charge of burglary and sentenced to a term of one to ten years in the penitentiary. Three months after his release, he joined a friend in sticking up a grocery store for forty dollars. Once again, the sentence bore a ten-year maximum. Davis escaped briefly, in 1975, but was swiftly recaptured. Parole put him back on the street in 1982, and he was hunting even as the prison gates swung shut behind him.

On January 10, 1983, a 15-year-old victim was assaulted in Laporte, Indiana, ten miles northeast of Union Mills. Choked semi-conscious and clubbed with a pistol, the boy survived his injuries and staggered to the police station, where he filed a report of the incident.

On June 16, young Darrin Reed, 14, abruptly vanished on the short walk to his girlfriend's house. His body, sodomized and strangled, was recovered three days later, in the afternoon. By that time, other victims had been added to the list.

On June 18, Jeff Lopez, age 15, had set up camp with friends at Kingsbury Fish and Wildlife Park, between LaPorte and Union Mills. That afternoon, a man who called himself Frank Davis offered Lopez and another boy free motorcycle rides. A friend recalled that Jeff had briefly bogged the cycle down in mud, but Davis did not seem to mind. He was a friendly sort, all smiles.

At 3:00 a.m. on June 19, the "friendly" man abducted Lopez from his camp and dragged him through the woods until they reached a clearing where the boy was sodomized, then murdered in an ax-and-knife assault which left him nearly headless. Doubling back, the killer seized a sleeping friend of Jeff's, repeating the assault and leaving victim number two for dead. The boy was still alive, however, when a team of searchers found him in the afternoon and rushed him to a local hospital. Upon regaining consciousness, he offered homicide detectives a description of the killer— and he offered them a name, as well.

The body of Jeff Lopez was recovered on June 21, and officers arrested Davis later in the day. The murder weapon was an ax belonging to the dead boy's father, picked up at the camp site at the time of the abduction. Tests revealed no fingerprints, but they would not be necessary. From his cell, Frank Davis made a full confession in the deaths of Lopez, Reed, and Bush, along with two counts of attempted murder for the victims who survived.

Scheduled for trial in January 1984, Davis opted for a guilty plea on two counts of felony murder (Reed and Lopez) and two counts of attempted murder. The latter charges earned him prison terms of fifty years apiece; on the murder charges, Davis was condemned to die.

Davis, Gregory

The son of a Baptist minister, born in Jackson, Mississippi, during 1966, Davis had developed a sexual fixation on older women by the time he reached his teens. His special hangout was the Jackson public library, where he would sit by the hour, staring at women, sometimes reaching through the stacks to fondle unsuspecting victims as they browsed for books. In January 1985, librarians called police on a patron's complaint that Davis was crawling around on the floor, peeking up her skirt and touching her legs. Arrested for disorderly conduct, he was also carrying two stolen credit cards when police checked his pockets for weapons.

The Jackson charges added up to misdemeanor time, but it was still humiliating, and Davis was packed off to Georgia shortly after his arrest, enrolling in the Job Corps program at Albany. The change of scene made no apparent difference, and Davis was soon up to his old tricks, dropping his pencil in class as an excuse to wriggle under desks and fondle women's legs. On at least one occasion, he reportedly exposed himself in the classroom, and Albany police later accused Job Corps leaders of covering up his escapades, in order to spare themselves embarrassment.

On October 17, 1986, 59-year-old Lucy Spillers was killed in her Albany home, one block from the warehouse occupied by Job Corps trainees. On discovery, Spillers was tied to the foot of her bed with a rope tight around her neck. She had been sexually mutilated with a butcher knife.

By November 1986, Davis was back home in Jackson, and the murders followed him like a brooding shadow. On November 18, 81-year-old Mary Dewitt was sexually assaulted and beaten to death in her home. Bertha Tanner, 83, met a similar fate on December 11, and 80-year-old Addie Reid joined the list on March 31, 1987. A 74-year-old survivor, attacked on March 25, provided police with a vague description of the suspect, but another month would pass before they ran him down.

On April 17, 1987, Davis got careless with a home burglary, leaving behind evidence that led to his arrest three days later. By May 1, he was facing three counts of murder and one of assault in his native Jackson, with police from Albany preparing further charges in the Spillers case. Conviction, when it came, would take him off the streets for life.

Day, William Scott

An habitual criminal and three-time escapee from the Michigan state prison at Jackson, by autumn 1986, at age 35, Day was serving a seven-year term for attempted rape and prison escape. Transferred from Jackson to Ypsilanti's Center for Forensic Psychiatry in November, Day befriended Thomas Fortunato, a prison guard with fourteen years of service and a perfect record on the job. A short time later, Day asked Fortunato to assist him in escaping from the penitentiary; the guard, for reasons still unclear, agreed.

On December 3, 1986, Fortunato smuggled Day out of prison in a laundry cart, withdrawing $5,000 from his personal bank account and driving the fugitive to Louisville, Kentucky, for a wild night of touring singles bars and porno shops. The odd couple checked into a Louisville motel on the night of December 5, and Fortunato woke next morning to find Day missing, along with all but fifty dollars of his money. The bewildered officer turned himself in on December 12, and five months later pled guilty to aiding escape, receiving a sentence of two to seven years in prison.

William Day, meanwhile, was living on the highway, stopping only long enough to rob and kill. On December 9, elderly Mary Strobel, matriarch of a prominent Nashville, Tennessee family, was found dead in the trunk of her car, outside the local bus depot. She had been strangled, with her throat slit for good measure.

Day rolled on across country, leaving a trail of bodies behind him. On December 23, Robert Arzabalo-

Alcoser, a Mexican national, was beaten to death near the bus station in Tucson, Arizona. Ten days later, in Marianna, Florida, 55-year-old Evans Johnson was killed in his jewelry store, his throat cut from ear to ear. Fort Stockton, Texas, was the scene of mayhem on January 6, with tavern owner Billie Taylor murdered north of town; she was stabbed in the back, one side of her skull crushed by heavy blows.

On January 12, 1987, Day was stopped for speeding near Van Horn, Texas. Driving a pickup truck registered to Stanley Robertson, of nearby Valentine, the fugitive carried Robertson's I.D. but gave his name as "Thomas Wilkins," of Portland, Oregon. Jailed on suspicion of auto theft, "Wilkins" saw the charges revised after officers visited Robertson's home and discovered his corpse, his throat slashed, skull crushed with a claw hammer found at the scene. Confronted with the evidence, Day finally confessed his true identity, regaling officers with a recital of his crimes and tacking on a murder in New Orleans, for a final score of six dead in as many weeks.

Formally charged with Robertson's murder on January 14, Day was held in lieu of $200,000 bond. Eight days later, he was formally indicted in the Taylor case, while Nashville officers reported that a speeding ticket, written on December 9, linked Day with victim Mary Strobel. Physical evidence and eyewitness testimony also confirmed Day's connection with the murders in Arizona and Florida, while investigation continues in New Orleans.

Decapitation Murders—Texas

Residents of Houston, Texas, are accustomed to reports of violent death, but nothing in their past experience prepared them for the string of crimes which dominated headlines in the latter part of 1979. Between the last week of July and first week of October, four lives were extinguished by a killer who seemed bent on claiming human heads as trophies of the hunt. Despite sensational publicity surrounding the attacks, the case remains unsolved today.

The first attack took place in southwest Houston, with a female victim cornered and beheaded in her own apartment, on the twenty-seventh of July. Investigators had not found her head by August 10, when yet another victim was discovered, spared complete decapitation when her killer was disturbed and frightened off.

Five blocks away, the residents around Freed Park were roused from sleep by screams and gunshots in the late-night hours of October 3. Police responded to the call but found no evidence of any crime in progress. Daylight on October 4 would lead them to the body of 16-year-old Joann Huffman, shot to death and dumped beside a picnic table with her jeans unzipped. Nearby, her boyfriend's car was found abandoned on a used-car lot, the headless body of its driver—18-year-old Robert Spangenberger—locked inside the trunk.

To date, no trace of either missing head has been discovered, and police in Houston hesitate to link the several homicides, despite the geographic and forensic similarities. The killer's motive and identity remain unknown.

Delage, Richard Tobias

Described by defense attorneys as a man at war with himself, Richard Delage committed his first murder in 1960, two weeks shy of his fifteenth birthday. His victim, slain on July 29 of that year, was Carole Segretta, a 23-year-old schoolteacher from Poughkeepsie, New York, found shot to death in her car, in Westchester

County. Her killer used rare Swedish ammunition in his .32-caliber pistol, but police had no other leads, and the case was still open when Delage claimed his second victim nine years later.

On November 15, 1969, the corpse of 23-year-old Paget Weatherley, a recent graduate from the University of Connecticut, was found in a wooded culvert near Bolton. She had been shot three times in the chest, with the same pistol and rare ammunition used to kill Carole Segretta in 1960. The cases were obviously connected, but police still had no suspects, nothing in the way of solid evidence.

Delage may have waited six years for his next victim, selecting a female hitchhiker near Mansfield, Connecticut, on October 3, 1975. In that case, however, the young woman talked her way out of the trap and was set free, unharmed, while Delage drove to Norwich and signed himself into a mental hospital. He was still at the admission desk, held up by paperwork, when officers arrived and took him into custody on kidnapping charges. Two months later, on December 10, he was formally charged with the murders of Carole Segretta and Paget Weatherly, while police in Massachusetts and Pennsylvania compared his technique to their own unsolved cases. One likely "possible" involved two student nurses, dumped beside a lonely road in Fulton County, Pennsylvania, in November 1970, but no charges were filed in that case.

Delage initially pled innocent to killing Paget Weatherly, but changed his mind on September 9, 1976, entering a negotiated guilty plea to manslaughter, receiving a sentence of 14 to 15 years in prison. A second guilty plea, on charges of kidnapping the hitchhiker, earned him a concurrent term of 10 to 20 years.

"De Mau Mau" Murders

Four years after San Francisco had been terrorized by random "Zebra" murders, residents of the Chicago area were confronted with a similar nightmare. In a four-month period of 1978, at least ten persons were shot and killed in random, racially-motivated attacks. As in San Francisco, all the victims were white, their killers black. Unlike the "Zebra" case, however, the attackers claimed no trappings of religion. Chosen from the ranks of bitter, disaffected military veterans, they called themselves De Mau Mau—after terrorists who slaughtered whites in Kenya, during 1952–56—and racism alone was ample motive for their crimes.

The gang's first victim was 19-year-old Michael Gerschenson, a college student, shot in Highland Park on May 3, 1978. On June 20, Kathleen Fiene, 16, was murdered by gunmen who invaded her Chicago home. The invasion technique was repeated on August 4, in Barrington Hills, where gunmen massacred Paul Corbett, his wife and daughter, and an elderly houseguest. One of the weapons used in Barrington Hills, a .30-caliber carbine, had also killed Michael Gerschenson on May 3.

William Richter, a soldier home on leave, was sitting in a pickup truck, in Highland Park, when several blacks attacked him on the evening of September 2. Wounded with two separate pistols—including the same weapon used to kill Kathleen Fiene—Richter lived long enough to describe his assailants for police. James Davis, a truck driver, was fired on the same night, also in Highland Park, but managed to escape unharmed.

The killers moved south on September 3, invading the home of Stephen Hawtree and family, at Monee, in Will County. As in the Barrington Hills massacre, Hawtree, his wife and teenaged son were herded into one room, then shot execution-style. One of the weapons employed was the same .25-caliber pistol used on Kathleen Fiene and William Richter.

Working through informants, homicide detectives had their suspects in the bag by mid-October. Several members of De Mau Mau had defected as the group progressed from angry rhetoric to violence, and now they spoke freely about the group's original intent "to combat racial persecution." In addition to the ten Illinois murders, authorities speculated on possible connections with a home invasion at Grand Island, Nebraska, which left two victims dead and one wounded on September 9.

Confined and charged with homicides in Illinois were eight reputed Mau Maus: Nathaniel Burse, 23; Michael Clark, 21; Garland Jackson, 22; Edward Moran, Jr., 23; Darrell Patry, 20; Donald Taylor, 21; his brother Reuben Taylor, 22; and Robert Wilson, age 18. The Taylor brothers, Burse, and Clark all boasted records of arrests for auto theft, assault, armed robbery and weapons charges in Chicago. Burse and Moran were found strangled by persons unknown in their Lake County jail cells, on June 13, 1979. Conviction on outstanding charges sent the other Mau Mau trigger men to prison for life. (See also: "Zebra" Murders, Vol. 1)

Detroit—Unsolved Murders

Detroit has seen its share of violence, from the bootleg wars of Prohibition to the catastrophic riots of the latter 1960s, fueled by street gangs, racist groups and drug rings, yet by any estimation 1980 was a "special" year. From January through December, eighteen women were dispatched in brutal fashion, twelve of them strangled, all but one discarded outdoors, with little or no effort made to conceal their remains. Their murders spanned Detroit, without apparent pattern, but when plotted on a map they formed a narrow corridor of death, running northwest from the Detroit River at Belle Isle to Eight Mile Road, then westward to the city limits. Despite the arrest of two separate suspects—and the ultimate conviction of one—at least thirteen of the slayings remain unsolved today.

Lois Johnson, a 31-year-old alcoholic barmaid, was the first to die, on January 12. Her frozen body was discovered by a trucker in the early morning hours, torn by a total of 26 stab wounds in the neck, chest, and abdomen. An autopsy proved she was falling-down drunk when she died.

A month later, on February 16, 26-year-old Patricia Real joined the list. A known prostitute and heroin addict, she had been shot to death on the street, her death scarcely causing a ripple in greater Detroit. Helen Conniff was a different story. At age 23, she was a devout "born-again" Christian and a student at Oakland University, determined to succeed on her own terms. On the night of March 10, she left her class early to visit her boyfriend, but Helen never arrived. When the man's roommate arrived home at 10:30 p.m., he spotted Conniff's body hanging from a nearby fence, strangled with a dog leash.

Twenty-year-old Cecilia Jacobs was next, found strangled in a Detroit alley, fully clothed, with no apparent effort made at sexual assault. The same lack of motive was evident on March 31, when 26-year-old Denise Dunmore was strangled in the parking lot of her apartment complex with no sign of rape, her expensive jewelry undisturbed. Arlette McQueen, 21, had been working the night shift at an Oak Park supermarket over four months, but April 9 marked the first night she had taken the bus home. Her strangled body was found the next morning, dumped between houses a block from her destination.

A known prostitute, Jeanette Woods was twice hospitalized by beatings in the months before she met her killer. Nothing kept her off the streets, but she would sometimes take a break from "business," and on April 18 she was scheduled to meet her boyfriend around nine o'clock. She failed to keep the rendezvous, and it was 1:30 a.m. before a pedestrian found her body—battered, raped and strangled, with her throat slashed in an ugly *coup de grace*.

Two weeks later, 20-year-old Etta Frazier was discovered in an old garage behind a burned-out house. Nude, bound hand and foot, she had been beaten about the face, tortured with lit cigarettes, and sexually abused before she was finally strangled to death. While not a prostitute, the victim had a record of arrests for disorderly conduct and neglecting her young son.

Rosemary Frazier was no relation to Etta, but the 28-year-old's death bore striking similarities to that of her immediate predecessor. An epileptic and long-time mental patient, Frazier was found nude, battered and strangled on a grassy slope near the Rosedale Park Community House. In the wake of her death, relatives staunchly denied police reports characterizing Rosemary as a streetwalker.

On May 31, Linda Monteiro was murdered four blocks from the Conniff crime scene, in almost identical style, strangled in her own driveway as she returned home from a nightclub. Two weeks later, Diane Burks made the list, found with hands tied behind her back, nude but for panties and slacks that had been lowered to her knees. The 22-year-old prostitute and drug addict had been strangled to death with an intertwined chain and telephone wire.

Cassandra Johnson was the victim for July, described by police as a 17-year-old prostitute; her bludgeoned body was discovered shortly before noon on July 2. Another working girl, 23-year-old Delores Willis, was last seen with a "trick" on the night of August 26, found strangled the next morning, her scalp laid open to the bone.

On September 29, 19-year-old Paulette Woodward phoned her mother from business school, around five o'clock, to say she was on her way home. Anxious relatives were still waiting the next morning, when police reported the discovery of Paulette's body. Beaten and strangled to death, she had not been sexually assaulted by her killer.

Betty Rembert, age 26, was found beneath a hedge October 8, her legs protruding toward the sidewalk. Cause of death would be a toss-up, with a stab wound in the victim's neck and crushing injuries inflicted to her skull. Two months later, on December 17, 30-year-old prostitute Diane Carter rounded off the list. Last seen around 3 a.m., she was found eight hours later, lying in some bushes on a vacant lot, a single bullet wound in the base of her skull.

By that time, police had two suspects in custody, charged with a total of five homicides. David Payton, age 23, was locally famous for high school athletics, employed since graduation from college as a girl's basketball coach. Arrested on November 17, he was grilled by police for 84 hours prior to arraignment, ultimately signing confessions in four of the slayings. According to Payton's statements, he had murdered Jeanette Woods, Rosemary Frazier, Diane Burks, and Betty Rembert in arguments over the price of oral sex, beating, strangling, or slashing each in turn as they rejected his paltry offers.

It appeared to be a solid case, but problems soon developed. On December 15, homicide detectives bagged another suspect, Donald Murphy, charged with murdering two Detroit prostitutes in October and November. Confessing those crimes, Murphy *also* copped to the slayings of Woods, Burks, and Rembert, providing enough details that several investigators found themselves "absolutely convinced" of his guilt.

Despite the flagrant contradicting evidence, prosecution continued in both cases, Payton charged in four murders, Murphy facing trial on the original two. On March 20, 1981, a judge dismissed the murder charges in Payton's case, finding that a previous magistrate had "abused judicial discretion" by admitting Payton's confessions as evidence. (Payton still faced charges of rape and armed robbery in unrelated cases.) Prosecutors vowed to appeal the decision, but some authorities seemed quietly relieved. A source close to the investigation told newsmen that police were "convinced Payton was the wrong guy after Murphy came along," using the recent dismissal as a means of "saving face." Advised of the reports, Prosecutor William Cahalan replied, "That's interesting. All I can say is we have the right man (Payton) charged with the right crimes."

However that may be, Dave Payton never went to trial for any of the murders in Detroit, while Donald Murphy was convicted only in the two originally charged. Assuming Murphy's guilt in other crimes that he confessed, we find ourselves with thirteen victims unaccounted for, their killer(s) still at large. (See also: Murphy, Donald)

Diaz, Robert R.

One of thirteen children, born and raised in the Midwest, Robert Diaz was frequently ill during childhood, completing only ten years of formal education. He joined the Marine Corps at age eighteen, then went AWOL for six weeks and was discharged soon after his return to duty. Married in Jacksonville, Florida, during 1961, he was divorced in 1972. By that time, Diaz had decided to act on his long-standing desire for a medical career, and after the divorce he enrolled in a school for vocational nurses. At family gatherings thereafter, he insisted that the children introduce him to their friends as "Dr. Diaz."

By early 1981, Diaz was working his way through a series of temporary nursing jobs in several Southern California hospitals. Coincidentally administrators noted that their older patients had begun to die in record numbers; by the end of April, there were 30 suspicious deaths on file in Los Angeles County, with an equal number spread over Riverside and San Bernardino Counties. Autopsies revealed high levels of lidocaine—a drug used to control irregular heartbeats—in most of the corpses. While normal readings should have indicated 50 to 100 milligrams of lidocaine, the recent dead showed levels of 1,000 milligrams and more—enough to bring on cardiac arrests instead of saving lives.

A search for common links between the victims demonstrated that a single nurse—Diaz—had worked at each and every institution where abnormal death rates were recorded. Attention focused on Diaz after the death of Estel Jones, age 62, at Chino Community Hospital. First ascribed to "natural causes," her death was later ruled a homicide, and officers began examining the high mortality rate on Diaz's graveyard shift. A search of the suspect's home turned up bottles of lidocaine, but charges of illegal drug possession were later dismissed. Diaz fired back with multimillion-dollar lawsuits charging defamation of character and civil rights violations, but skeptical judges dismissed each in turn.

The investigation rolled on, detectives examining fifty deaths, finally narrowing their sights to a dozen where evidence seemed incontrovertible. On November 24, 1981, Robert Diaz was arrested on twelve counts of first-degree murder: eleven victims, ranging in age from 52 to 89, were killed at Community Hospital of the Valleys, in Perris, California, between March 30 and April 22, 1981; the twelfth, a 79-year-old man, died of a lidocaine overdose at San Gorgonio Pass Memorial Hospital, in Banning, on April 25.

Diaz entered his formal plea, innocent on all counts, at the end of September 1982. His trial was scheduled to open in March 1983, but various postponements delayed the event until Halloween. Waiving his right to a jury trial, Diaz placed his fate in the hands of a judge, who convicted him on all counts on March 29, 1984. Two weeks later, on April 11, Diaz was sentenced to die in the gas chamber at San Quentin.

Doss, Nanny Hazel

A daughter of Dixie, born in 1905, Nanny Doss had been molested by a string of local men before she reached her middle teens. At age 16, she married Charles Braggs, bearing him four children in rapid succession. Braggs was mystified when two of them died suddenly, a few months apart, but Nanny could offer no explanation. Each child had seemed healthy when Charles left for work, but they cried at his leaving and died in convulsions not long after breakfast.

Small insurance payments eased the pain, but Braggs became increasingly suspicious of his wife. One afternoon, he took their oldest living child and struck off for parts unknown, leaving Nanny behind with their daughter, Florine. Packing up their meager belongings, Nanny moved to Cedar Town, Georgia, where she met and subsequently married Frank Harrelson. Florine was barely two years old when Harrelson and Nanny hit the road, leaving the child alone in their abandoned house. Neighbors managed to track down Charles Braggs and he came for the child, but Nanny would not see her daughter again for nine years.

Their reunion evidently smoothed things over, and by 1945, Florine now married—felt secure enough to leave her infant son at Nanny's home in Jacksonville, Alabama, while Florine took off to see her father. Baby Lee survived three days in Nanny's care, his death producing anguished speculation that he accidentally "got hold of some rat poison." Three months later, Frank Harrelson fell suddenly ill and died within the week. Nanny used the insurance money to buy ten acres of land and build a small house for herself outside Jacksonville.

The early 1950s were a lethal time for Nanny's relatives. Her third husband, Arlie Lanning, died at Lexington, North Carolina, in 1952. A few months later, in January 1953, her mother died while Nanny nursed the woman for a broken hip. Two of her sisters died the same year, in different towns; each collapsed while Nanny was visiting, each with the same mysterious symptoms of stomach cramps and convulsions. In 1953, it was husband number four—Richard Morton—laid to rest at Emporia, Kansas.

Nanny married her fifth and last husband, Samuel Doss, in Tulsa, Oklahoma, during July 1954. He died a month later, and the obligatory autopsy revealed enough arsenic to kill twenty men. Confronted with the evidence of guilt, Nanny Doss issued confessions spanning three decades and at least ten murders, drawing a term of life imprisonment for the Tulsa case in 1955. She served ten years before succumbing to leukemia in 1965.

Throughout her various confessions and the years in jail, Nanny insisted that money played no significant role in her crimes. Despite various insurance payments, her murders were actually motivated by marital boredom, a dream of discovering the ideal husband, as described in her favorite "True Romance" magazines. "That's about it," Nanny told her interrogators. "I was searching for the perfect mate, the real romance of life."

Dowler, David A.

Raised in Albuquerque, New Mexico, the son of an Air Force colonel and his Japanese wife, David Dowler seemed to be a well-adjusted child. In school, he maintained a B-average while holding up his end on the wrestling team, dabbling in electronics and operating a ham radio. He spent three years in college without graduating, and picked up a black belt in karate along the way. Moving to Odessa, Texas, in 1981, he quickly found work as a sales representative for a local oil company.

Beneath the polished surface, though, there was another side to David Dowler. He regaled selected friends with tales of contract killings, posing as a former secret agent who had "taken out six guys" on various assignments for the government. Acquaintances took Dowler's stories with a grain of salt, but there was no denying that he seemed to have a sixth sense for predicting danger.

On the morning of August 16, 1983, Dowler telephoned the father of Lisa Krieg, a 26-year-old co-worker, to say that Lisa was late for work. Dowler was worried, and he could think of no one else to call. Stopping by his daughter's flat, the man found Lisa dead, stretched out across her bed and partially undressed. Her death was attributed to long-standing anorexia nervosa, but Dowler had a different story for his intimates, involving spies who had, for no apparent reason, tried to kill the woman several times before. In Dowler's version of events, *he* found the victim nude and partly dressed the corpse, to make her death "look natural," before he called her father to investigate.

Dowler had his next premonition of doom on February 12, 1986. It concerned Juan Casillas, Dowler's partner in a one-hour photo developing service, and he called Leza Chandler, Casillas' ex-wife, to say he was "worried about Juan." Stopping by her ex-husband's apartment, Chandler found him dead on the kitchen floor. An autopsy revealed traces of drugs in his system, but they were not identified.

Leza Chandler, herself, was the target of Dowler's next "premonition," on June 28, 1987. Phoning up another female friend, he asked if she would check on Chandler, "just in case." The woman found Leza dead in bed, her infant daughter crawling aimlessly around her mother's body on the mattress. Medical examiners ascribed her death to acute chloroform poisoning, and the search for a killer began.

By this time, friends and homicide investigators were becoming curious about Dowler's "sixth sense." His lady friend agreed to wear a microphone to several meetings with the suspect, in July, taping hours of conversation on espionage, assassination . . . and the various uses of chloroform. Dowler was arrested for Leza Chandler's murder on August 20, a search of his apartment netting chloroform bottles, a .22-caliber pistol, and two homemade silencers. Held in lieu of $100,000 bond, he was formally indicted on September 8.

While Dowler cooled his heels in jail, renewed forensic tests on Lisa Krieg and Juan Casillas turned up lethal dosages of cyanide in both. Dowler was indicted for their murders in December 1987, while police examined circumstances in the death of Dorothy Nesbitt, another Dowler acquaintance who died mysteriously in November 1986. (No charges have been filed in Nesbitt's death.)

At trial, in January 1988, the prosecutor described Dowler as someone who "likes to be the power that snuffs out life. He likes that supreme power." The jury agreed, convicting Dowler of first-degree murder on January 27. With two trials pending, he was sentenced to a term of life imprisonment.

Duffy, John Francis

The case of London's "Railway Murderer" began on December 29, 1985, when 19-year-old Alison Day disappeared en route to visit her fiancee, in Upminster. Discovered on January 15, 1986, the young woman had been raped and strangled to death with a piece of her own blouse, twisted around a four-inch piece of wood to form a crude garrote.

Three months later, on April 19, police discovered the remains of 15-year-old Maartje Tamboezer at West Horsley, near Guilford, in Surrey. Missing for two days, she had been raped and beaten with a heavy weapon, finally strangled and her body set on fire. A commuter recalled seeing a disheveled man board the train at East Horsley, the day of the murder, and police published sketches of the suspect, described as 18 to 25 years old, of slender build, with long, unkempt hair worn in a "perm."

Victim number three, 29-year-old Ann Lock, disappeared from the Potters Bar railway station, in Hertfordshire, during May. By the time her remains were discovered, concealed in nearby undergrowth, police had leaked the news that they were looking at connections in a string of twenty-seven rapes, many of them committed in or around railway depots.

Detained by police on November 27, 1986, suspect John Duffy, age 30, was initially charged with the Tamboezer slaying, plus three rapes of teenaged girls committed between February 1985 and October 1986. Two more counts of murder and four additional counts of rape were added to the list December 2. A former railroad carpenter, Duffy pled not guilty to all charges when his trial opened on January 13, 1988. On February 10, a magistrate directed jurors to acquit Duffy of killing Ann Lock, based on lack of evidence. Two weeks later, convicted of murdering Alison Day and

Maartje Tamboezer plus assorted rape charges, Duffy was sentenced to seven terms of life imprisonment.

Dufour, Donald William

A postman's working days in middle-class Orlando, Florida, are normally as uneventful as a man could hope for. There is seldom any major deviation from routine. A snapping dog, perhaps, but nothing that a can of Mace won't cure. Except, that is, for murder.

On the afternoon of July 15, 1982, the postman working Henry Balch Drive noted that deliveries of mail at Edward Wise's home had not been taken in for several days. The circumstance was curious, but not disturbing. Not until the carrier became aware of rancid odors emanating from the house itself.

Police were summoned, and they forced the door. Inside, patrolmen found Ed Wise, age 47, and his live-in lover, 44-year-old John Stinson, shot and stabbed to death. The medical examiner declared they had been dead at least a week, perhaps ten days. Though gay, the men had not been known as "cruisers," and police did not initially suspect them of inviting home "rough trade."

September 6. A young man riding his motorcycle through an Orlando citrus grove was startled to discover a corpse, partially covered by an orange blanket, lying beside the dirt road. The victim, a male, had been shot twice—in the head and back—with a .25-caliber pistol. A gasoline receipt, recovered from his pocket, identified him as Zack Miller, of Boston, Georgia, reported missing by his family two days earlier. Discovery of Miller's car, September 7, gave detectives in Orlando hope the killer might still be within their jurisdiction.

On October 10, three gunmen tried to rob a local fast

food restaurant, and one of them was captured near the scene. The clumsy stick-up artist named the "brains" behind the job as Don Dufour, a cocky thief who boasted a recent murder in an orange grove, with the victim robbed of jewelry. In fact, the would-be robber told detectives, Don had bragged of killing something like a dozen people, altogether.

Homicide investigators searching for Dufour were startled by the news of his arrest, in Jackson, Mississippi, four days after the attempted robbery. He had been charged with double murder in the stabbing deaths of Danny King, age 32, and 34-year-old Earl Peeples. Both men had been slain in the apartment occupied by Peeples and, again, there were persuasive indications that the victims might be gay.

Forensic evidence proved more persuasive to a Jackson jury than the suspect's feeble plea of innocence. Convicted of the Peeples homicide on March 31, 1983, Dufour was sentenced to die in Mississippi's electric chair. Unmoved by published interviews suggesting that their prisoner was "scared to death of electricity," prosecutors expressed their intention to try him again, for Danny King's murder. Meanwhile, in Florida, first-degree murder indictments were returned against Dufour in January 1983, on Wise and Stinson, and in September, for the Miller homicide.

Dyer, Albert

The slayer of three Los Angeles children during 1938, Dyer lured his victims to a secluded ravine, there molesting and murdering each in turn. After each killing, Dyer ritually cleaned the bodies, tidied up his victim's clothing, and lingered at the scene to pray over the corpse. Captured during an attempt to carry off his fourth victim, Dyer confessed the series of crimes and was ultimately put to death.

Edwards, Mack Ray

A native of Arkansas, born in 1919, Edwards moved to Los Angeles in 1941, logging one arrest for vagrancy that April, prior to finding work as a heavy-equipment operator. In that role, he helped build the freeways that made L.A. famous, and by early 1970 he was a veteran on the job, married and a father of two, the very model of blue-collar propriety. If anyone suspected his involvement in a string of brutal murders spanning sixteen years, they kept the secret to themselves.

On March 5, 1970, three girls, ages 12 to 14, were abducted by burglars from their home in Sylmar, a Los Angeles suburb. Two escaped from their captors, but one was still missing the next day, when Mack Edwards entered a Los Angeles police station, surrendering a loaded revolver as he informed the duty officer, "I have a guilt complex." Edwards named his teenage accomplice in the kidnapping, and directed police to the Angeles National Forest, where the missing girl was found, unharmed. Before authorities could take his statement down, the prisoner informed them there were "other matters" to discuss.

As homicide detectives listened, dumb-struck, Edwards voluntarily confessed to half a dozen murders, dating from the early 1950s. Stella Nolan, eight years old, had been the first to die, in June of 1953. Abducted from her home in Compton, she had never been recovered, and her fate remained a mystery for sixteen years, until a killer's conscience led him to confess. Mack's second crime had been a double-header, claiming 13-year-old Don Baker and 11-year-old Brenda Howell, in Azusa, on August 6, 1956. Once again, the bodies were missing, no solution in sight before Edwards surrendered himself to police.

According to the killer's statement, he had sworn off murder for a dozen years, returning with a vengeance in the fall of 1968. Gary Rochet, age 16, had been shot to his death at his home in Granada Hills, on November 26, and Roger Madison, also 16, had vanished in Sylmar three weeks later. The last to go was 13-year-old Donald Todd, reported missing in Pacoima on May 16, 1969.

On March 7, 1970, Edwards led officers into the San Gabriel Mountains, seeking the graves of two victims, but altered terrain foiled the search. He had better luck four days later, directing his keepers to a section of the Santa Ana Freeway, where the skeletal remains of Stella Nolan were unearthed from an eight-foot-deep grave. Edwards maintained that Roger Madison was buried beneath the Ventura Freeway, but authorities declined to plow the highway up in search of clues. The crimes, Mack said, had all been motivated by an urge for sex.

With Edwards safely under lock and key, police voiced skepticism at the 12-year gap in his "career," suggesting that there might be other victims unaccounted for—a body-count of 22, in all. Responding from his cell, the killer adamantly stuck by his confession. "Six is all there is," he told reporters. "There's not any more. That's all there is." Before his trial, he twice attempted suicide, slashing his stomach with a razor blade on March 30, and gulping an overdose of tranquilizers on May 7.

Charged in three of his six confessed crimes, Edwards was convicted and sentenced to die after telling the jury, "I want the chair; that's what I've always wanted." Immediate execution was his goal. As Edwards told the court, "My lawyer told me there are a hundred men waiting to die in the chair. I'm asking the judge if I can have the first man's place. He's sitting there sweating right now. I'm not sweating. I'm ready for it."

Ready or not, Edwards was faced with the prospect of mandatory appeals, conscious of the fact that no California inmate had been executed since 1967. On October 30, 1971, he cut the process short, using an electric cord to hang himself in his death row cell at San Quentin.

Enriqueta, Marti

A self-styled witch, who made her living through the sale of charms and potions, Enriqueta was arrested by police in Barcelona, during March of 1912, on charges of abducting local children. Her most recent victim, a young girl named Angelita, was rescued alive from the witch's lair, appalling police with a tale of murder and cannibalism. According to the girl, she had been forced by Enriqueta to partake of human flesh. Her "meal" had been the pitiful remains of yet another child, abducted by the murderess a short time earlier.

As ultimately pieced together by authorities, the local crimes of Enriqueta had already claimed at least six victims. After murdering the children, she would boil their bodies down to use as prime ingredients in her expensive "love potions." Convicted on the basis of her own confession, coupled with the testimony of her sole surviving victim, Marti Enriqueta was condemned to death and executed for her crimes.

Erskine, Kenneth

At age 24, Kenneth Erskine was diagnosed by court psychiatrists as possessing "a mental age of eleven." A persistent loner, abandoned by his English mother and

Antiguan father, he drifted through a milieu of special schools and flophouses, compiling a record of arrests for burglary in London, living on the proceeds of his thefts. Business was good enough for Erskine to open ten separate accounts for his stolen loot, but money isn't everything. Somewhere along the way, the simple-minded youth picked up a taste for homicide.

Eileen Emms, 78, was the first to die, strangled in her home during the first week of April 1987. A month later, Janet Crockett, age 67, was killed in identical fashion. The killer rebounded with a double-header on June 28, claiming 84-year-old Valentine Gleime and 94-year-old Zbigniew Stabrawa in separate incidents. William Carmen, age 84, was strangled in early July. Two weeks later, William Downes, 74, and Florence Tisdall, 80, were discovered on successive mornings.

By then, police were working overtime to find the "Stockwell Strangler," so-called after the southwest London neighborhood where five of his victims were slain. There had been petty theft in several cases, with a television stolen from Crockett's apartment and roughly $900 missing from Carmen's home, but robbery did not appear to be the driving motive. All of the victims were strangled manually, left on their beds with the sheets pulled up to their chins. Five had been sexually molested, but authorities could not determine whether the acts were committed before or after death.

Kenneth Erskine was arrested on July 28, at a social security office, for trying to conceal one of his numerous savings accounts. In custody, his palm print matched one lifted from a Stockwell murder scene, and he was picked up from a lineup by victim Frederick Prentice, 74, who had survived an attempted strangulation on June 27. Under questioning, Erskine seemed to plead amnesia. "I don't remember killing anyone," he told police. "I could have done it without knowing it. I am not sure if I did."

The court had little difficulty sorting out the problem. Charged with seven counts of murder and one count of attempted murder, Erskine was convicted across the board on January 28, 1988. (Two additional murders, dating from 1986, were eliminated from the list on grounds of insufficient evidence.) The presiding judge sentenced Erskine to seven life terms with an additional twelve years for attempted murder, recommending that the killer serve a minimum of 40 years before he is considered for parole.

Figueroa, Danny

Mentally, young Danny Figueroa never came of age. At 26, he liked to hang around with adolescent boys, but there was nothing sexual about his interest in the youths. Instead, he seemed to be in search of playmates, youngsters who would share his fantasies of high adventure and the paramilitary games he liked to play around his home in Perris, California, south of Riverside. He taught the boys to camp and hunt small game with BB guns, but when he went out hunting on his own, the young man leaned toward other weapons, other prey.

On May 13, 1986, Reynold Johnson was shot and killed at his home in Hemet, California, ten miles east of Perris. The single round, which struck him in the chest, had been fired from a high-powered rifle. Witnesses recalled a stranger in the neighborhood, attired in military green, but the police were left without a motive or a suspect in the crime.

May 29. Ray Webber, age 19, was working on his brother's ranch, in Riverside County, when the sniper struck again. Coworkers found him slumped over the steering wheel of his pickup truck in San Timoteo Canyon, skull shattered by the shotgun blast that took his life. Again, the victim had no enemies; there seemed to be no motive for his murder.

Five days later, an illegal alien was crossing a lettuce field in Imperial County, bound for El Centro and friends who would drive him to Los Angeles, when he was suddenly confronted by a man in uniform. He mistook the tall man for an agent of the Border Patrol, but instead of arresting the Mexican, his assailant raised a gun and shot him where he stood, leaving the victim for dead. He crawled to the highway, where a passing motorist stopped and drove him to a hospital in El Centro. Recovering, he offered sheriff's deputies a fair description of the gunman.

Officers patrolling the vicinity found Danny Figueroa, dressed in camouflage fatigues and carrying a rifle. They disarmed him and recorded his denial of the shooting, skeptical of Figueroa's claim that he was merely a survivalist, rehearsing field maneuvers in anticipation of society's collapse. Surprisingly, their witness hedged at naming Danny as the gunman, and their suspect was eventually released for lack of evidence.

June 8. At Indio, some forty-five miles east of Perris, Robert Jimenez was shot three times while barbecuing in his own back yard. A fourth shot struck him as he crawled back toward the house, to call police. By now, it was apparent to authorities in Southern California that they had a random sniper on their hands, and he was not afraid to kill.

June 17. In Redlands, twenty-five miles north of Perris, Mary Langerich, 72, was reported missing by her husband when she failed to return after taking their dog for its morning constitutional. Three hours later, searchers found her body in the brush beside a gravel road, shot five times in the back with a small-caliber weapon. Witnesses reported sightings of a young man, dressed in paramilitary garb, close by the murder scene, and officers stopped by the Figueroa home to question

Danny on June 21. His family reported that he had been "camping" in the desert for the past few days; they had no firm idea of when he might return.

Around the neighborhood, detectives turned up several boys who had accompanied Figueroa on his forays to the desert. All thought highly of the murder suspect, reporting that he "wore jungle stuff like Rambo and acted real cool." It was apparent that their suspect knew the territory, and the search became a week-long siege, complete with roadblocks, tracking dogs, and helicopters sporting infrared scopes, designed for seeking body heat on foreign battlefields. At every turn, the fugitive confounded his pursuers.

Figueroa's luck ran out June 28, when hikers spotted him in Reche Canyon, barely two miles from his home. Converging helicopters sighting Danny, trying to conceal himself in grass and brush, maintaining contact while a squad of twenty deputies with automatic weapons closed the ring on foot. Arraigned in San Jacinto on the second of July, for Reynold Johnson's murder, Figueroa would face other charges in the days to come. Convicted on three counts of murder in June 1987, he drew a prison term of 66 years to life.

Floyd, Charles

On July 10, 1942, the 20-year-old wife of William Brown, a Tulsa trucker, was strangled and raped in her Main Street apartment, on Tulsa's north side. Pregnant at the time of the attack, the victim had been six days from delivery of her child, who also died in what authorities would call a double homicide.

Six months went by before the next attack. Clara Stewart and her married daughter, Georgina Green, were sharing an apartment in the general neighborhood of the July attack, while Georgina's husband served in the army. Police suspected that the man who beat them both to death and raped their corpses one December night was drawn by the naturally red hair of his victims, a trait they shared in common with the wife of William Brown.

Another redhead, Panta Lou Niles, became the next victim on May 15, 1945. Bludgeoned in her sleep, by a man who entered through her open bedroom window, she was also raped after death. The killer was still in her room hours later, when a friend phoned to wake her for work. Alarmed at the sound of a man's voice on the line, the friend hung up and called police, but they arrived too late to bag their man.

A simple-minded drifter, Henry Owens, was arrested on suspicion of the latest homicide. Previously booked on charges of sexual assault, Owens agreed to a polygraph test but the results were inconclusive. He was still in custody when the killer struck again, on July 1, 1948.

Breaking into an apartment, the attacker clubbed the female tenant, her 12-year-old daughter, and a teenage girl who was sleeping over. Police reported that the girls were partially undressed and an "unnatural sex act" was performed on the woman before a neighbor arrived, drawn by their screaming, and put their assailant to flight. Two blocks away, he invaded the home of Ruth Norton—another redhead—fatally beating his last victim before raping her unconscious body.

This time, a witness came forward and offered police a description of Norton's attacker, including the piece of advice that he "looked like a truck driver." A survey of local trucking companies revealed that Charles Floyd, a driver known for his obsession with redheads, had quit his job on the morning of July 2. Police broadcast descriptions, leading to his ultimate arrest in Dallas, on November 22, 1949.

Despite assertions of "confusion," Floyd supplied detectives with substantial details of the crime known only to the killer and police. A lifelong "Peeping Tom," Floyd said that voyeurism sometimes failed to satisfy his cravings, and on those occasions he was moved to violence. Panta Niles had been a special target, fond of stripping down before an open window; Floyd had watched her for a period of weeks before lust exploded into rape and murder.

Psychiatric testing and the subject's low IQ saved Floyd from the electric chair in Oklahoma. On confession to the string of rapes and murders, he was packed off to a mental institution, where he subsequently died.

Fort Worth, TX— Unsolved Murders

Between September 1984 and January 1985, a string of brutal homicides and disappearances spread fear among the female residents of Tarrant County, Texas. Four young women and a teenage girl would lose their lives before the crime spree ended, as mysteriously as it had begun. Police have yet to name a suspect in the case, which still remains unsolved.

On the night of September 30, 1984, firefighers were called out to an apartment occupied by Cindy Davis, on the city's southwest side. They extinguished a small fire, traced to a cigarette dropped on the bed, but there was no sign of the 23-year-old aspiring model. Neighbors reported the sound of loud voices, raised in anger, and a car squealing away from the scene shortly before the blaze erupted.

Three weeks later, on October 22, 23-year-old Cindy Heller stopped to help stranded motorist Kazumi Gillespie on the southwestern side of Fort Worth. Though strangers, the women spent two hours together in a tavern, while Gillespie tried in vain to phone a friend. When they split up, Gillespie remaining at the bar, Heller agreed to drive by the friend's apartment and leave a note on his door. It was there when he came home at midnight, but Cindy Heller had vanished. Her car was found nearby, next morning, the interior gutted by fire, dry blood smeared on one door handle. No trace could be found of the two-time entrant in local beauty contests.

Police noted striking similarities in the apparent abductions—victims of identical age and given names, missing in circumstances that included suspicious fires—but they were not prepared to link the cases yet. Shortly before midnight on December 10, Angela Ewart left her fiancee's home in the Wedgewood section of southwest Fort Worth, stopping for gas at a station nearby. From there, the 21-year-old model and one-time beauty contestant vanished into limbo, her car discovered the next morning, doors locked, with a broken knife lying nearby. A flat tire, reported to police by passing motorists, had been switched with a spare by the time patrolmen arrived on the scene.

On December 30, 1984, 15-year-old Sarah Kashka left her home in Denton for a party in Fort Worth, arriving to find the festivities cancelled. Sarah's date dropped her off at a Wedgewood apartment, not far from the station where Angela Ewart was last seen alive, but her bad luck was holding. The friends she intended to visit were out for the evening, and Sarah had vanished before they came home. Two days later, her body was found in a marshy area near Mountain Creek, in southwest Dallas, torn by stab wounds that had caused her death. Police initially divorced her murder from the disappearances, citing "a difference we really can't talk about," but they later hedged their bets. As Detective Ben Dumas told newsmen, "We can't establish any thread, because we only have one girl found."

That changed on January 5, when children playing on the campus of Texas Christian University stumbled over Cindy Heller's decomposing corpse. She had been tortured, strangled, and beheaded, with her skull recovered from a nearby lake on January 9. That same day, 20-year-old Lisa Griffin was found, shot to death execution-style, in southwestern Fort Worth. Sheriff's deputies charged a former mental patient with that slaying, but he was released when his fingerprints failed to match others lifted from Griffin's abandoned car.

A final, grisly twist was added to the case on January 23, 1985, when construction workers uncovered human bones beside some railroad tracks, ten miles south of the Wedgewood "murder zone." Forensic tests identified the skeletal remains as those of Cindy Davis, missing since September, but the evidence would bring authorities no closer to a suspect in the case.

"Freeway Murders"— California

Between December 1972 and June 1980, authorities in seven Southern California counties recorded the violent deaths of at least 44 young men and boys, attributing their murders to an unknown "Freeway Killer." Of eleven victims slaughtered prior to 1976, most were known or suspected homosexuals, their deaths lending credence to the notion that the murderer himself was gay. While strangulation was the favored mode of death, some victims had been stabbed with knives or ice picks, and their bodies bore the earmarks of sadistic torture. Homicide investigators noted different hands at work in several of the murders, but they finally agreed that 21 were almost certainly connected. (Sixteen others would be solved in 1983, with the arrest of "Scorecard Killer" Randy Kraft.)

The first "definite" victim was 14-year-old Thomas Lundgren, abducted from Reseda on May 28, 1979, and discarded the same day, near Malibu. Mark Shelton, 17, was next, reported missing from Westminster on August 4, his body recovered a week later at Cajon Pass. The day after Shelton's disappearance, 17-year-old Marcus Grabs was kidnapped in Newport Beach, his violated corpse discovered at Agoura on August 6. Donald Hyden, 15, was also found in Agoura, on August 27—the same day he disappeared from Hollywood. On September 7, 17-year-old David Murillo vanished from La Mirada, his body found in Ventura five days later. The remains of Robert Wirostek were found off Interstate 10, between Banning and Palm Springs, on September 27, but eleven months would pass before he was identified. Another "John Doe" was discovered in Kern County, on November 30, with 18-year-old Frank Fox murdered at Long Beach two days later. The killer's last victim for 1979 was another unidentified male, aged 15 to 20, his violated body found on December 13.

The new year began badly in Southern California, with 16-year-old Michael McDonald abducted from Ontario on January 1, 1980, found dead two days later in San Bernardino County. Charles Miranda, 14, disappeared from Los Angeles on February 3, his body discarded in Hollywood later that day. On February 5, 12-year-old James McCabe was kidnapped in Huntington Beach, his body recovered three days later in Garden Grove. Ronald Gatlin, 18, disappeared from Van Nuys on March 14, found dead the next day in Duarte. Fifteen-year-old Russell Pugh was reported missing from Huntington Beach March 21, his body found next day at the Lower San Juan Campground, along with the corpse of 14-year-old victim Glen

Barker. Three days later, police found 15-year-old Harry Turner slain in Los Angeles proper.

The killer claimed two victims on April 10, 1980, abducting 16-year-old Steven Wood from Bellflower, rebounding to snatch 18-year-old Lawrence Sharp from Long Beach hours later. Wood's body was found April 11, at Long Beach, but Sharp remained missing until May 18, when his remains were discovered in Westminster. Meanwhile, on April 29, 19-year-old Daren Kendrick was reported missing in Stanton, his body recovered from Carson on May 10, with traces of chloral hydrate ("knockout drops") in his system. On May 19, 14-year-old Sean King vanished without a trace in South Gate; he remains among the missing. Eighteen-year-old Stephen Wells, the last to die, was kidnapped in Los Angeles June 2, his body discovered the next day at Huntington Beach.

Police got their break on June 10, when 18-year-old William Ray Pugh confessed "inside" knowledge of the murder series. Pugh identified the killer as William George Bonin, a 32-year-old Vietnam veteran and truck driver residing in Downey. A glance at the record revealed Bonin's 1969 conviction, in Torrance, on counts of kidnapping, sodomy, child molestation and forcible oral copulation. The charges stemmed from four separate attacks, between November 1968 and January 1969, with Bonin diagnosed as a mentally disordered sex offender, committed to Atascadero State Hospital. He was released in May 1974, on the recommendation of psychiatrists who found him "no longer dangerous." Two years later, he was back in prison, convicted of kidnapping and raping a 14-year-old boy. Bonin had been paroled in October 1978, seven months before the death of Thomas Lundgren.

Officers established round-the-clock surveillance on Bonin, striking paydirt after 24 hours. On the night of June 11, 1980, their suspect was arrested while sodomizing a young man in his van, booked on suspicion of murder and various sex charges. Held in lieu of $250,000 bond, Bonin was still in jail when police picked up 22-year-old Vernon Butts on July 25, charging him as an accomplice in six of the "freeway" murders. Between July 26 and 29, Bonin was formally charged with 14 counts of murder, eleven counts of robbery, plus one count each of sodomy and mayhem. Butts, facing six counts of murder and three counts of robbery, quickly began "singing" to police, naming more alleged accomplices in the murder ring. James Michael Munro, 19, was arrested in Michigan on July 31, returned to California for trial on charges of killing Stephen Wells. Three weeks later, on August 22, 19-year-old Gregory M. Miley was arrested in Texas, waiving extradition on charges of murdering Charles Miranda and James McCabe, plus two counts of robbery and one count of sodomy.

Orange County raised the ante on October 29, 1980, charging Vernon Butts with the murders of Mark Shelton, Robert Wirostek, and Darin Kendrick, plus 17 other felony counts including conspiracy, kidnapping, robbery, sodomy, oral copulation and sex perversion. Greg Miley was also charged with another Orange County murder, plus seven related felony counts. By December 8, suspect Eric Marten Wijnaendts—a 20-year-old Dutch immigrant—had been added to the roster, charged with complicity in the murder of Harry Turner.

Under California law, a murder committed under "special circumstances"—accompanied by robbery, torture, or rape—may be punished by death. In December, Bonin's playmates began cracking, pleading guilty on various felony charges and drawing life sentences in return for their promise of testimony against Bonin. They spelled out details of the torture suffered by assorted "freeway" victims, and the glee with which Bonin inflicted pain. As one remarked, "Bill said he loved those sounds of screams." On January 11, after telling police of Bonin's "hypnotic" control, Vernon Butts hanged himself in his cell, finally successful in the fifth suicide attempt since his arrest. With the new testimony in hand, Orange County indicted Bonin on eight more counts of murder, with 25 related counts of robbery and sexual assault.

William Bonin's trial on twelve counts of murder opened November 4, 1981, in Los Angeles. Greg Miley and James Munro testified for the prosecution, describing how Bonin—following his arrest—had urged them to "start going around grabbing anyone off the street and killing them," in a bid to convince authorities that the "Freeway Killer" was still at large. A television reporter divulged contents of a jailhouse interview, in which Bonin admitted participation in 21 murders. "I couldn't stop killing," the trucker had said. "It got easier with each one we did." On January 5, 1982, after eight days of deliberation, jurors convicted Bonin on ten counts of murder and ten of robbery. (He was acquitted in the deaths of Thomas Lundgren and Sean King.) Two weeks later, he was formally sentenced to death.

"Freeway Phantom, The"

A puzzling case recorded from the nation's capital, this murder series stands officially unsolved despite conviction of two defendants in one of seven similar homicides. Authorities have speculated on solutions in the case, asserting that "justice was served" by the round-up of suspects on unrelated charges, but their faith was shaken by an outbreak of look-alike murders in Maryland, during 1987. At this writing, some students of the case believe the "Phantom" has eluded homicide detectives altogether, shifting his field of operations to a more fertile hunting ground.

The stalker's first victim was 13-year-old Carole Denise Sparks, abducted on April 25, 1971, while en route to a neighborhood store in Southeast Washington. Her strangled, ravaged body was recovered six days later, a mile and a half from home, lying on the shoulder of Interstate Highway 295, one of several freeways passing through Washington east of the Anacostia River.

Ten weeks passed before 16-year-old Darlenia Denise Johnson disappeared, on July 8, from the same street where Carole Sparks was kidnapped. Strangled to death, she was found on July 19, within feet of the spot where Sparks was discovered on May 1. In the meantime, a third victim, 14-year-old Angela Denise Barnes, had been abducted from Southeast Washington on July 13, shot to death and dumped the same day at Waldorf, Maryland. Brenda Crockett, age ten, disappeared two weeks later, her strangled corpse recovered on July 28 near an underpass on U.S. Highway 50.

The killer took a two-month break in August and September, returning with a vengeance to abduct 12-year-old Nenomoshia Yates on October 1. Familiar marks of strangulation were apparent when her body was found six days later, discarded on Pennsylvania Avenue, near the Maryland state line. At eighteen, Brenda Denise Woodward was the oldest victim, kidnapped from a Washington bus stop November 15, stabbed to death and dumped the next day on an access road leading to Prince Georges County Hospital. A mocking note, its contents still unpublished, was discovered with the body, signed "The Freeway Phantom" in accordance with a nickname coined by journalists. In a macabre twist, FBI experts reported that Woodward had written the note herself, in a steady hand, betraying no hint of tension or fear.

For once, police had ample evidence of pattern, from the victims' race—all black—to the peculiar fact that four were named Denise. There seemed to be a geographical connection, both in the abductions and disposal of remains, but speculation brought authorities no closer to their goal of an arrest. Black Washington was up in arms, demanding a solution to the case, intent on proving that a white man was to blame, but angry rhetoric did nothing to advance the murder probe.

Ten months elapsed before the Phantom claimed his final victim, abducting 17-year-old Diane Williams on September 5, 1972. Her body was found the next day along I-295, five miles from the point where Carole Spinks was discovered in May 1971. Again, police noted striking similarities with the other crimes—and again, they found no evidence that would identify a suspect in the case.

In late March, Maryland state police arrested two black suspects—30-year-old Edward Leon Sellman and 26-year-old Tommie Bernard Simmons—on charges of murdering Angela Barnes. Both suspects were ex-policemen from Washington, and both had resigned in early 1971, before completion of their mandatory probation periods. Investigators now divorced the Barnes murder from other crimes in the Phantom series, filing additional charges against both suspects in the February 1971 abduction and rape of a Maryland waitress. Convicted of murder in 1974, both defendants were sentenced to life.

Meanwhile, a federal grand jury probing the Phantom murders focused its spotlight on a "loosely-knit group of persons" suspected of luring girls and young women into cars—sometimes rented for the hunt—then raping and/or murdering their victims for sport. Suspects John N. Davis, 28, and Morris Warren, 27, were already serving life on conviction for previous rapes when a series of new indictments were handed down in December 1974. Turning state's evidence, Warren received a grant of limited immunity in return for testimony against Davis and another defendant, 27-year-old Melvyn Sylvester Gray. As a government spokesman explained, "The ends of justice can be served just as well if a person is convicted and sentenced to life for kidnapping, than if he is jailed for the same term for murder."

Critics questioned the wisdom of that advice, thirteen years later, when a new series of unsolved murders was reported from neighboring Maryland. Again, the female victims were young and black, abducted and discarded in a manner reminiscent of the Freeway Phantom's style. Authorities refuse to speculate upon a link between the crimes, and so both cases are considered "open," with the killers still at large. (See also: Maryland—Unsolved Murders)

Gary, Carlton

A native of Columbus, Georgia, born December 15, 1952, Gary was blessed with a near-genius IQ, but that gift of nature was cruelly balanced by the rigors of childhood and adolescence. Rejected by his father at an early age, Gary was malnourished as a child, and he suffered at least one serious head trauma in elementary school, knocked cold in an accident that left him unconscious on the playground. A heavy drug abuser in his teens, he began logging arrests in 1966, his rap sheet listing charges of robbery, arson, and assault before he reached his eighteenth birthday.

Gary surfaced in Albany, New York, during the spring of 1970, in time for a series of rape-murders targeting elderly women. In May, Marion Brewer was strangled with a pillow case in her Albany hotel room, followed two months later by 85-year-old Nellie

Farmer, slain in a nearby apartment. Gary was arrested as a suspect in the latter case, and he admitted being on the scene, but he fingered an accomplice—John Lee Williams—as the killer. Williams was convicted and sentenced to prison on the basis of Gary's testimony, his verdict subsequently overturned after Gary recanted. Escaping prosecution for the murder, Gary was convicted of burglary, receiving stolen property, and possession of drugs, drawing a term in the Onondaga County Correctional Institution at Janesville, New York. He escaped from custody on August 22, 1977, and headed home to launch a one-man reign of terror.

On September 16, 60-year-old Ferne Jackson was raped, beaten and strangled to death at her home in the Wynnton district of Columbus, Georgia, found with a nylon stocking knotted tight around her neck. The same M.O. was demonstrated nine days later and a few blocks distant, in the slaying of 71-year-old Jean Dimenstein. Florence Scheible, age 89, was killed in identical fashion on October 21, and 69-year-old Martha Thurmond died the same way, two days later. On October 28, 74-year-old Kathleen Woodruff was raped, beaten, and manually strangled at her home, her slayer forgetting the traditional stocking in his haste to escape. Ruth Schwob survived the "Stocking Strangler's" attack on February 12, 1978, triggering a bedside alarm, but the killer was determined, traveling a mere two blocks before he raped and strangled 78-year-old Mildred Borom the same morning. By early March, police knew they were searching for a black man in the string of homicides, and since his victims had been white, a threat of mounting racial violence dogged investigators on the job. They were distracted, later in the month, by threatening communications from another killer—self-styled "Chairman of the Forces of Evil"—who threatened to murder selected black women if the stranger was not swiftly apprehended. Three deaths would be traced to the "chairman" before his arrest on April 4, but prosecution of the Stocking Strangler's competition brought police no closer to their man. On April 20, the killer claimed his final victim in Columbus, strangling 61-year-old Janet Cofer in her home, leaving the usual stocking knotted around her neck.

A week later, on April 27, 1978, Greenville, South Carolina experienced the first in a series of armed robberies by the "Steakhouse Bandit," a gunman who invaded restaurants near closing time. Eight months passed before Carlton Gary was arrested in nearby Gaffney, following a similar holdup, and he confessed to the entire series, drawing a sentence of 21 years in prison for armed robbery. Transferred to a minimum-security prison at Columbia, four years later, he escaped from custody on March 15, 1983.

Another fourteen months would pass before Gary's ultimate arrest, on May 3, 1984, at a motel in Albany, Georgia. Held as a fugitive from South Carolina, and linked with an October 1977 burglary in Columbus, Gary was charged with the Scheible, Thurmond, and Woodruff murders on May 4. A jury convicted him of all counts in August 1986, deliberating for three hours before his penalty was fixed at death. (See also: Hance, William)

Gaskins, Donald H.

Known as "Pee Wee" to his friends, South Carolina's premier serial killer liked to mix business with pleasure. Authorities believe that some of his nine victims were killed to cover the tracks of an auto theft ring, but others—including the girl whose disappearance led to Pee Wee's downfall—were slain for the pure thrill of it. Even behind prison walls, he could not be restrained.

Born in 1937, Gaskins earned his nickname from the

fact that he stood only five-feet-two in stocking feet. Ferocity cannot be judged by size, however, and where Pee Wee was concerned, sheer bloodlust made up for a lack of altitude. Convicted of ten murders so far, he has hinted at other victims, yet unnamed, their identities held in reserve against the day when he may need to bargain for a stay of execution.

Pee Wee's world began unraveling with the disappearance of 13-year-old Kim Ghelkins, in 1975. Investigation led authorities to property owned by Gaskins in a remote portion of northeastern South Carolina. By the time Ghelkins was unearthed, in January 1976, eight other victims had been discovered and Gaskins was facing trial on capital charges. The dead included Doreen Geddings and her two-year-old daughter, drowned together in 1973; Johnny Sellers, missing since June 1974; Kim Ghelkins and Dennis Bellamy, murdered in 1975; and Barnwell Yates, brutally knifed to death in an altercation with Gaskins.

Sentenced to die at his trial in May 1976, Gaskins later won commutation of his sentence, settling for ten life terms on nine counts of murder and one of burglary. Technically eligible for parole in 1985, Pee Wee never got the chance to bring his case before the board. On September 12, 1982, he booby-trapped a radio belonging to a death row inmate, Rudolph Tyner, killing his target with a homemade explosive charge. Gaskins denied the murder, but convict eyewitnesses testified against him, and authorities produced tapes of telephone conversations between Gaskins and relatives of a Tyner victim who commissioned the murder. Convicted of yet another slaying, Gaskins was once again sentenced to die.

Gay Murders—New York (1973)

In January 1973, a series of brutal stabbings cast a pall over New York City's free-wheeling homosexual community, sparking angry demands for police protection in quarters where officers are normally viewed as the enemy. Targeting denizens of the gay "leather" scene, a faceless butcher mutilated seven victims in a little over three weeks' time, ending the murder spree as suddenly and mysteriously as it began.

The first slaying was recorded on January 4, when neighbors found 29-year-old Ronald Cabo knifed to death in his apartment, laid out on a burning sofa. Four days later, on the Lower East Side, 40-year-old Donald MacNiven and his next-door neighbor, 53-year-old John Beardsley, were slaughtered in MacNiven's apartment, discovered by firemen called out to extinguish an arson fire at the scene. Police confirmed that all three victims were "leather boys," well-known in sado-masochistic circles, but rumors of other mutilation deaths were dismissed as "grossly exaggerated."

On January 18, victim Robben Borrero, 23, was pulled from the Hudson River off Greenwich Village, along with the body of a young "John Doe." Nine days later, the killer scored his last double-header in Brooklyn Heights invading the apartment that schoolteacher Nelson Roberts shared with his male lover. Neighbors used a pass key to investigate a blaring radio and stumbled on a scene of carnage. In the living room, hands bound behind his back, Roberts lay covered with a blanket, killed by multiple stab wounds in the back. His roommate was discovered in the bedroom, hog-tied, with a broken neck. The couple's pet, a miniature poodle, had been drowned in the sink.

The slayer's premature "retirement" after seven murders left police without a single piece of valid evidence. An undercover officer was fitted out with leather gear to infiltrate the seamy world of S & M, and while his exploits helped inspire the movie *Cruising,* they did not result in apprehension of the killer. (See also: Bateson, Paul)

Gay Murders—New York (1986)

On March 21, 1986, Pedro Gonzalez, a 43-year-old restaurant worker, was found tied up and strangled in his Corona, Queens, apartment. Six days later, homicide detectives told the press his death bore similarities to two other homicides in Queens, committed since July of 1985. All three victims were dark-skinned Hispanic homosexuals, known to frequent the same two bars in Queens and Manhattan. Each victim was beaten to death or asphyxiated in his own apartment, with the lights left on and a radio blaring loud music. Objects stolen by the killer included two videocassette recorders and a portable radio. At this writing, the case remains unsolved, the killer still at large.

Gay Murders—Washington, D.C.

On March 3, 1972, police in the District of Columbia announced that ten of 1971's thirty-eight unsolved murders were "homosexually motivated or related." Hesitant to speculate about connections in the crimes, investigators did report that they were searching for a single suspect, pictured in a photograph with victim James Williams, 55, found stabbed to death in his northwest apartment on April 13, 1971. The snapshot had been taken by a photographer known only as

"Bill," who ignored official pleas for help in solving the case. At this writing, the murders remain unsolved, the killer (or killers) still at large.

Gbrurek, Tillie

Born in 1865, in Chicago's "Little Poland," Tillie Gbrurek went to work in a sweatshop as a child. She grew up beefy, muscular, and unattractive, but she was a wizard in the kitchen, and her specialty was hearty stew. In 1885, a marriage broker paired her off with one John Mitkiewitz, a shiftless lay-about whom she supported, fed, and pampered for a quarter of a century before the tables finally turned.

One afternoon, in 1911, Tillie was working her usual job in the sweatshop when she observed her employer bullying a child. Fed up at last, she crossed the room and decked the foreman with a single punch. From there, with the applause still ringing in her ears, she turned for home and gave her worthless spouse a thrashing which induced him to evacuate the house and find a steady job.

Around the time of Tillie's sudden turn-around, she also started having "visions" which allowed her to "predict the future" with amazing accuracy. Staring at a mongrel dog one afternoon, she solemnly predicted it would die within a set amount of time. The mutt fell dead on cue, and others followed. Tillie Mitkiewitz was building up a reputation as a "seer."

In 1914, Tillie's "ancient powers" led her to announce that husband John had only three more weeks to live. Her prophecy was accurate, and with a thousand dollars from his life insurance in her purse, she paid another visit to the marriage broker. Soon, she was the blushing bride of John Ruskowski, but again the "powers" brought bad news. Three months after the wedding, Tillie began dropping hints that her husband would die in two weeks. Again, her reputation as a visionary was upheld—and more insurance money came her way.

Creeping up on fifty now, the portly widow had no time to spare for mourning. John was barely in the ground before she married Joe Guskowski, but her luck was running true to form. The "powers" spoke. Joe died. His life insurance paid. In 1916, Tillie married husband number four, Frank Kupczyk. She seemed happier with Frank—he managed to survive four anniversaries—but in the meantime, Tillie's extrasensory perception found another target. Neighbor Rose Chudzinsky made no secret of the fact that she regarded Tillie's miserable luck—and her predictions of disaster—with extreme suspicion. Tillie huddled with the spirits, and they told her that Chudzinsky's days were numbered. Neighbors waited patiently for yet another funeral, and no one seemed surprised when Rose collapsed on schedule.

Shortly after the removal of her neighbor, Tillie visited a fabric store and purchased black material to make a dress in preparation for her husband's funeral. The clerk was sympathetic. When had Mr. Kupczyk died? "Ten days from now," came the reply.

Frank kept his schedule, to the day, and Tillie married Anton Klimek, husband number five, in 1921. By now, Chicago's finest had become suspicious of the high mortality in Tillie's household. When detectives paid a visit on October 27, they discovered Anton Klimek sick in bed, his wife beside him, feeding him his stew. A stomach pump saved Anton's life, and lab analysis discovered arsenic in Tillie's winning recipe. She grappled with police, and sent a couple of patrolmen to emergency receiving as they dragged her to a cell, but Tillie's run was over. On conviction, she was sentenced to a term of life imprisonment, with the express condition that she never be allowed to cook for other inmates.

Goebbels, Peter

A weekend rapist who eliminated witnesses by strangling his victims, Peter Goebbels took to violent sex as a diversion from the daily grind of working in a factory. At twenty-three, he never let his pleasures interfere with earning money, but the ease with which he claimed his victims fostered over-confidence, and he grew careless in the end.

On Saturday, July 6, 1985, a teenage boy observed a man and woman grappling in an alley, in the Lichterfelde neighborhood of West Berlin. A lover's quarrel, perhaps. He thought no more about it at the time, until pedestrians discovered the body of Marion Bormann, 17, raped and strangled near the scene of the remembered altercation.

Frightened now, the boy approached police and offered them a fair description of the suspect. Meanwhile, homicide detectives had been paging through their files, compiling records of attacks that seemed to fit the killer's profile. Three more cases from the Lichterfelde district caught their eye.

On Sunday night, the twenty-sixth of August, 1984, Helga Kousdoerfer, age 22, had been strangled and raped in the area. Seven months later, on March 24—another Sunday—19-year-old Liselotte Mohn had suffered an identical fate. On Saturday, June 1, the victim was Karola Eisenstein, age 20, raped and strangled like the others.

In their search for likely suspects, the authorities examined one more case. A 20-year-old woman from the Lichterfelde neighborhood had been attacked in mid-July of 1984, her rapist startled into flight at the appearance of pedestrians. The suspect, Peter Goebbels, 23, had dropped his identification card at the scene, making conviction a virtual certainty, but there were problems with the case. The rape had taken place on Wednesday, and detectives in the string of homicides were searching for a killer who invariably struck on weekends.

Simple homework finally revealed the link. While suspect Goebbels worked a normal five-day week on the assembly line, his plant had been closed down for the retooling of machinery one Wednesday in July of 1984. Convicted of the rape, he drew a year's suspended sentence from the court, but homicide investigators kept the pressure on, including Goebbels in a lineup where the teenage witness in the Bormann case selected Peter as the girl's assailant. Goebbels broke down and confessed, denying all involvement in the other crimes while claiming he was "sick," in need of "help." A term of life in prison was prescribed as treatment for his "illness," while Berlin authorities continue seeking evidence to link him with three other identical homicides.

Gohl, Billy

Nothing of substance is known about Billy Gohl's first forty years, and the stories he told in response to occasional questions were riddled with holes, contradictions, and some outright lies. By his own reckoning, Gohl was born around 1860, spending most of the next four decades as a laborer, sailor, or both. In 1903, he surfaced in Aberdeen, Washington, as a delegate for the Sailors' Union of the Pacific. Gohl's stocky build and clean-shaven scalp made him memorable, but his tales about previous lives scarcely set him apart from the seamen he served.

The union office, in those days, functioned as a com-

bination mail drop, bank, and general employment office for its members. Sailors new in Port might check
for letters, scan the list of vessels needing crewmen, or
deposit valuables before they made the rounds of various saloons. In many cases, sailors back from months at
sea had large amounts of cash on hand. An honest union delegate would hold the money in a safe until it was
reclaimed. In Aberdeen, the spoils belonged to Billy
Gohl.

His method was simplicity itself. When sailors turned
up individually, Gohl checked the street for witnesses.
If it was clear, and something of substantial value was
entrusted to his care, he drew a pistol from his drawer
and shot his victim in the head. That done, he paused
to clean the weapon, stripped his prey of any extra cash
and all identifying documents. Gohl's building had a
trapdoor, with a chute extending to the Wishkah River,
just outside, with currents flowing toward Gray's Harbor and the sea beyond.

Within a few years after Billy Gohl's arrival, Aberdeen acquired a reputation as a "port of missing men."
No records exist for his first six years of operation, but
authorities pulled 41 "floaters" out of the water between 1909 and 1912, suggesting a prodigious body-
count. Most of the nameless dead were presumed to be
merchant seamen, and Billy Gohl was among the most
vocal critics of Aberdeen law enforcement, demanding
apprehension of the killers, more protection for his
men.

Gohl's downfall was precipitated by a timepiece and
his own attempt at cleverness. While rifling the pockets
of his latest victim, Billy came upon a watch bearing
the engraved name of August Schleuter, from Hamburg,
Germany. Alert to the potential for incrimination, he replaced the watch and dumped the corpse as always.
When the "floater" came ashore, Gohl was on hand to

identify Schleuter as one of his sailors, renewing demands for a thorough investigation of the murders.

This time, Billy got his wish. It took some time, but homicide investigators learned the victim was, in fact, a Danish sailor named Fred Nielssen. He had bought the watch in Hamburg, from a craftsman who identified each piece he made with an engraving of his name. Gohl's effort to identify the corpse as August Schleuter smacked of guilty knowledge, and detectives finally built a case that brought him into court, in 1913, on a double charge of murder.

Gohl was rescued from the gallows by Washington's repeal of the death penalty, in 1912. Convicted of two slayings, he rebuffed all efforts to compile a comprehensive list of victims. Even so, publicity surrounding Billy's case was adequate to win restoration of the death penalty in 1914. Safe in his prison cell, with no evidence to support further trials and possible execution, Gohl counted the years until his death, of natural causes, in 1928.

Gore, David Alan, and Waterfield, Fred

A Florida native, born in 1951, David Gore resembled the stereotypical Southern "redneck," tipping the scales at 275 pounds, so enamored of firearms that he studied gunsmithing in his free time. He studied women, too, but in a different fashion, losing one job as a gas station attendant after the owner found a peephole Gore had drilled between the men's and women's restrooms. A year younger, cousin Fred Waterfield was another product of Florida's Indian River County, a high school football star whose ugly temper and taste for violent sex perfectly meshed with Gore's. In 1976, they put their heads together and decided to combine their favorite sports by stalking human game.

Their early efforts were embarrassing. Trailing a female motorist outside Yeehaw Junction, Waterfield flattened her tires with rifle fire, but the intended victim escaped on foot. Later, they followed another woman from Vero Beach to Miami, giving up the pursuit when she parked on a busy street. Their first successful rape took place near Vero Beach, and while the victim notified police, she later dropped the charges to avoid embarrassment in court.

By early 1981, Gore was working days with his father, as caretaker of a citrus grove, patrolling the streets after dark as an auxiliary sheriff's deputy. Waterfield had moved north to Orlando, managing an automotive shop, but he made frequent visits home to Vero Beach. Together, they recognized the potential of Gore's situation—packing a badge by night, killing time in deserted orchards by day—and Fred offered to pay cousin Dave $1,000 for each pretty girl he could find. It was a proposition Gore could not refuse.

In February 1981, Gore spotted 17-year-old Ying Hua Ling disembarking from a school bus, tricking her into his car with a flash of his badge. Driving her home, Gore "arrested" her mother and handcuffed his captives together, phoning Waterfield in Orlando before he drove out to the orchard. Killing time while waiting for his cousin, Gore raped both victims, but Waterfield proved more selective. Rejecting Mrs. Ling as too old, Fred tied the woman up in such a fashion that she choked herself to death while struggling against her bonds. He then raped and murdered the teenager, slipping Gore $400 and leaving him to dispose of the corpses alone, in an orchard a mile from the Ling residence.

Five months later, on July 15, Gore made a tour of Round Island Park, seeking a blond to fill his cousin's latest order. Spotting a likely candidate in 35-year-old Judith Daley, Gore disabled her car, then played Good Samaritan, offering a lift to the nearest telephone. Once inside his pickup, Gore produced a pistol, cuffed his victim, and called cousin Fred on his way to the orchard. Waterfield was happier with this delivery, writing out a check for $1,500 after both men finished with their victim. Two years later, Gore would spell out Judith Daley's fate, describing how he "fed her to the alligators" in a swamp ten miles west of Interstate Highway 95.

A week later, Gore fell under suspicion when a local man reported that a deputy had stopped his teenage daughter on a rural highway, attempting to hold her "for questioning." Stripped of his badge, Gore was arrested days later, when officers found him crouched in the back seat of a woman's car outside a Vero Beach clinic, armed with a pistol, handcuffs, and a police radio scanner. A jury deliberated for thirty minutes before convicting him of armed trespass, and he was sentenced to five years in prison. Rejecting a psychiatric treatment recommended by the court, he was paroled in March of 1983.

A short time after Gore's release, his cousin moved back home to Vero Beach, and they resumed the hunt. On May 20, they tried to abduct an Orlando prostitute at gunpoint, but she slipped away and left them empty-handed. The next day, they picked up two 14-year-old hitchhikers—Angelica Lavallee and Barbara Byer—raping both before Gore shot the girls to death. Byer's body was dismembered, buried in a shallow grave, while Levallee's was dumped in a nearby canal.

On July 26, 1983, Vero Beach authorities received an emergency report of a nude man firing shots at a naked girl on a residential street. Converging on the suspect house—owned by relatives of Gore—officers found a car in the driveway with fresh blood dripping from its trunk. Inside, the body of 17-year-old Lynn Elliott lay curled in death, a bullet in her skull. Outgunned by the raiding party, Gore meekly surrendered, directing officers to the attic where a naked 14-year-old girl was tethered to the rafters.

As the surviving victim told police, she had been thumbing rides with Lynn Elliott when Gore and another man picked them up, flashing a pistol and driving them to the house, where they were stripped and raped repeatedly in separate rooms. Elliott had managed to free herself, escaping on foot with Gore in pursuit, but she had not been fast enough. Gore's companion had left in the meantime, and detectives turned to their suspect in quest of his identity.

Gore swiftly cracked in custody, enumerating crimes committed with his cousin, turning state's evidence to save himself from the electric chair. On January 21, 1985, Fred Waterfield was convicted in the Byer-Levallee murders, receiving two consecutive life terms with a specified minimum stint of 50 years before parole. Gore received an identical term, with, charges dismissed in four other cases to avoid redundant prosecution.

Graham, Harrison

A mentally-retarded drug abuser, Harrison Graham was well-known in his Philadelphia ghetto neighborhood. Sometimes, he would amuse the local children with his "Cookie Monster" puppet; other times they found him digging graves—for dogs, he said—in nearby vacant lots. Apparently, no one suspected that his simple mind might hide a darker urge, compelling him toward homicide.

In early August 1987, Graham quarreled with his landlord's nephew, afterward evacuating his apartment, nailing the door shut out of spite. Police were summoned on the afternoon of August 9, when neighbors filed complaints of a pervasive stench that emanated from the room. Inside, patrolmen found two strangled women's bodies, three more skeletons beneath a mound of garbage on the floor, another tied up in the closet. Graham had been living in the squalid hole since 1983, and he had not been idle.

Officers began to search the neighborhood for Graham, house by house, while newsmen noted that the suspect's dwelling stood a mere three miles from Gary Heidnik's "house of horrors," where another ghoulish scene had been discovered five months earlier. The roof of Graham's building yielded skeletal remains of victim number seven, but initial warrants simply charged the missing suspect with abuse of corpses. Murder was not proven until August 11, when a medical examiner reported that the freshest victims had been strangled some time in the past ten days.

On August 14, another skull and partial skeleton were excavated from the dirt floor of a row house three doors down from Graham's building. He surrendered two days later and confessed to seven murders since the winter months of 1986. According to his statement, Graham picked up female addicts on the street, enticing them with offers of a fix, and brought them home where they were murdered after sex. On August 26, psychiatrists declared that he was competent for trial.

In April 1988, dispensing with his right to trial by jury, Graham laid his case before a solitary judge. Convicted on seven counts of first-degree murder and seven counts of abusing a corpse, he was sentenced to life imprisonment, followed by six electrocutions. The unusual sentence—hailed by Graham's lawyer as "compassionate and brilliant"—theoretically assures that he will never be paroled.

Grant, Waldo

A Georgia native, Grant fled a failed marriage by migrating to New York City in 1971, settling in a bachelor apartment on Manhattan's Upper West Side. Neighbors knew him as a quiet loner, with detectives furnishing descriptions of "the kind of guy who lives in a tenement block for years, and nobody raises an eyebrow." More to the point, no one suspected that Grant's secret hobby was murder.

The first to die was 18-year-old Philip Mitchell, stabbed and bludgeoned with an iron bar on September 14, 1973, then hurled from the rooftop of Grant's apartment building in an effort to simulate suicide. Nearly two years elapsed before Grant struck again, stabbing 23-year-old George Muniz numerous times, dumping his corpse in a trash bin, a few doors down from Grant's residence. Number three was Harold Phillips, age 30, hammered to death in his own apartment on October 3, 1976. On December 29 of that year, police found 16-year-old Harry Carrillo in Central Park, his body sawed into three pieces, wrapped in plastic bags, and left in a shopping basket. All four victims were described as homosexuals by homicide investigators.

An acquaintance of Carrillo's, Grant was routinely questioned by police as part of their investigation, later singled out as a suspect on the basis of evidence found with the body. In custody, he confessed all four murders, citing an "uncontrollable urge" to kill in each case.

Gray, Ronald Adrian

A native of Miami, born in 1966, Gray joined the U.S. Army at age 18 and was trained as a cook. In

1986, he was posted to Fort Bragg, outside Fayetteville, North Carolina, and his arrival on the base unleashed a sudden reign of terror.

On April 29, 1986, 24-year-old Linda Coats was found dead in her trailer at Fayetteville, killed by a shot to the head after suffering sexual abuse. A university student enrolled in the army's ROTC program, Coats was scheduled to receive her commission the week she was murdered. A few days later, soldiers on the Ft. Bragg military reservation found the naked, battered corpse of Teresa Utley, a Fayetteville prostitute. Abducted from the streets where she plied her trade, Utley had been stripped and beaten, raped and knifed to death by her assailant.

On November 16, 1986, two Fayetteville women were abducted at gunpoint by a black man who raped them both, while threatening their lives. Neither victim reported the attack to police, but one staked out the neighborhood with her boyfriend, fingering Ronald Gray as her attacker on November 26. Still terrified, she kept the knowledge to herself.

By that time, Fayetteville's resident stalker had struck again, abducting a young woman on November 22, raping her and slashing her about the face and body, leaving her for dead in suburban Bonnie Doone. A female soldier was attacked the same night, at Fort Bragg, but both victims survived, and their assailant remained at large. He raped and stabbed another soldier on the base a few days later, but MPs had nothing that would bring them closer to a suspect.

On December 12, a soldier's wife, 18-year-old Tammy Wilson, was abducted from her home in Bonnie Doone. Her naked body was discovered hours later by her husband, in some nearby woods. She had been raped and shot at point-blank range. Three days later, Sgt. Michael Clay was called home from maneuvers to inspect the smoking ruins of his mobile home in

Fayetteville. His wife, Pvt. Laura Clay, was missing from the scene, and five more weeks would pass before her body was recovered from the nearby forest.

In the meantime, yet another female soldier was attacked on January 3, but she survived. Kimberly Ruggles, a 23-year-old Fayetteville cab driver, was less fortunate on January 7. Officers were still examining her taxi, found abandoned on a city street, when searchers on the Ft. Bragg reservation found her body. Raped and beaten, she had died when her assailant drew a knife across her throat.

The latest slaying prompted two surviving victims to report their own attacks, and one of them identified a suspect for police on January 8. After six months of investigation, Ronald Gray was formally indicted by civilian authorities on 23 felony charges, including two counts of first-degree murder (Coats and Wilson), five counts of first-degree rape and first-degree sex offense, four counts of first-degree kidnapping, two counts each of first-degree burglary and armed robbery, plus one count each of second-degree arson, attempted first-degree rape, and assault with a deadly weapon with intent to kill. Held in lieu of $420,000 bond, he was subsequently charged, on August 7, with two counts of murder (Clay and Ruggles) and two counts of attempted murder on a military reservation.

On November 5, 1987, Gray pled guilty to all charges in Fayetteville, receiving three consecutive terms of life imprisonment. Convicted on all remaining counts at his court-martial, on April 12, 1988, he was sentenced to death for the crimes committed at Ft. Bragg.

Greenawalt, Randy:
See Tison, Gary

Greenwood, Vaughn Orrin

The first of Southern California's several "Skid Row" slayers launched his one-man war in 1964, taking a decade off before he returned to terrorize Los Angeles with nine more murders, committed over the space of two months. Victims were ritually "posed" by the slasher in death, with salt sprinkled around their bodies and cups of blood standing nearby, their wounds surrounded by markings of unknown significance. Police recruited psychiatric "experts" to create a profile of the killer, publishing assorted sketches of their suspect, but the case was ultimately solved by accident, embarrassing authorities whose "profiles" of the murderer were sadly off the mark.

The "Skid Row Slasher's" first known victim was an aging transient, David Russell, found on the library steps with his throat cut and numerous stab wounds on November 13, 1964. The following day, 67-year-old Benjamin Hornberg was killed in the second-floor restroom of his seedy hotel, throat slashed from ear to ear, numerous stab wounds marking his head and upper torso.

Police saw a pattern of sorts, but it seemed to lead nowhere, and the early victims were forgotten by December 1974, when the killer returned with a vengeance. On December 1, he murdered 46-year-old Charles Jackson, an alcoholic drifter, on the spot where David Russell had been slain a decade earlier. Moses Yakanac, a 47-year-old Eskimo was knifed to death in a Skid Row alley on December 8, and 54-year-old Arthur Dahlstedt was slain outside an abandoned building three days later. On December 22, 42-year-old David Perez was found in some shrubbery adjacent to the Los Angeles public library. Casimir Strawinski, 58, was found in his hotel room January 9, and 46-year-old Robert Shannahan had been dead several days when another hotel maid discovered his body—a bayonet protruding from his chest—on January 17. The final Skid Row victim, 49-year-old Samuel Suarez, was also killed indoors, his body found in a sleazy fifth-floor hotel room.

Inexplicably, the killer switched his hunting ground to Hollywood on January 29, 1975, stabbing 45-year-old George Frias to death in his own apartment. Two days later, a cash register mechanic, 34-year-old Clyde Hay, was found in his Hollywood home, marked by the Slasher's characteristic mutilations.

By that time, L.A. detectives had formed a mental picture of their suspect, described as a white male in his late twenties or early thirties, six feet tall and 190 pounds, with shoulder-length stringy blond hair. A psychiatric profile, published on the morning of Clyde Hay's murder, described the killer as a "sexually impotent coward, venting his own feeling of worthlessness on hapless derelicts and down-and-outers ... He strongly identifies with the derelicts and drifters he kills, and we think he's trying to resolve his own inner conflicts by turning his wrath and hatred outward." The Slasher was further described as a friendless, poorly-educated loner, probably homosexual, with an unspecified physical deformity.

On February 2, a prowler invaded the Hollywood home of William Graham, assaulting him with a hatchet before houseguest Kenneth Richer intervened, and both men plunged through a plate-glass window. The attacker fled on foot, striking next at the home of actor Burt Reynolds, carelessly dropping a letter—addressed to himself—in the driveway. Police picked up Vaughn Greenwood, charging him with counts of burglary and assault, their search of his residence netting a pair of cufflinks stolen from victim George Frias. A year later, on January 23, 1976, Greenwood was indicted on eleven counts of murder in the Slasher crimes.

Unfortunately for police, the "suspect profile" was a stumbling block to their solution of the case. For openers, Vaughn Greenwood was a 32-year-old black man, lacking any obvious deformities, and from the testimony of acquaintances, he was not impotent. He *was* a loner and a homosexual, who finished seventh grade before he fled his Pennsylvania foster home and thumbed a ride to California. Most of his adult life was spent drifting from Chicago to the West Coast and back again, riding the rails and earning his keep as a migrant farm worker. In Chicago, during 1966, he had demanded cash from 70-year-old Mance Porter, following a sexual encounter in the latter's skid row apartment. When Porter refused, Greenwood slashed his throat and stabbed him repeatedly with two different knives, spending five and a half years in jail on conviction for aggravated battery.

While awaiting trial on murder charges, Greenwood was convicted of assaulting William Graham and Kenneth Richer, drawing a prison term of 32 years to life. On December 30, 1976, the defendant was convicted on nine counts of first-degree murder, jurors failing to reach a verdict in the case of victims David Russell and Charles Jackson. Greenwood was sentenced to life on January 19, 1977, the judge recommending that he never be released because "His presence in any community would constitute a menace."

Guatney, William

William "Freight Train" Guatney loved to ride the rails. For almost forty years he traveled the United States in box cars, living off the land and picking up odd jobs in towns where he was known as a "likeable hobo," described by his many friends as "the happy-go-lucky type." But Guatney also had a darker side. At fifty-seven, he had seen America the hard way, and he hated being called a bum. "I'm two people," he once told a female acquaintance. "I can also be mean." In retrospect, friends noted that "He was a strong man when he got mad."

The special target of his anger—and his lust— appeared to be young boys. In August 1979, Guatney was arrested in Illinois, charged with three counts of murder on warrants issued from Kansas and Nebraska. Homicide investigators viewed the charges merely as a starting point, suggesting Guatney might have murdered fifteen children in the past five years alone.

Nebraska charged him in the deaths of 13-year-old Jon Simpson and 12-year-old Jacob Surber, abducted from the state fair at Lincoln, in 1975. Both were discovered days later, and Guatney was arraigned on August 22, 1979, refusing to enter a plea.

The Kansas charge involved Jack Hanrahan, a 12-year-old who disappeared from his Topeka neighborhood on May 20, 1979. Molested and murdered, his corpse was found in a creek bed ten days later; on August 20, Guatney was charged with first-degree murder, kidnapping and sodomy.

At least two victims were suspected by police in Illinois, where 9-year-old Mark Helmig was murdered at Pekin, in 1976, and Marty Lancaster, 14, was killed at Normal two years later. The authorities considered Guatney a suspect in the deaths of at least ten other boys, scattered throughout the Southwest.

Hahn, Anna Marie

The first woman to die in Ohio's electric chair, Anna Hahn was a German native, born in 1906, who immigrated to Cincinnati at age 21. There, she married a young telephone operator, briefly managing a bakery in

Cincinnati's German district before she tired of the hours and set her sights on easy money. Life insurance seemed to be the answer, and she twice tried to insure her husband for $25,000, meeting resistance each time. Soon after rejecting her second demand, Philip Hahn fell suddenly ill, rushed to the hospital by his mother over Anna's objection. Physicians saved his life, but there was nothing they could do to save his marriage.

Despite a total lack of training or experience, Anna began to offer her services as a live-in "nurse" to elderly men in the German community. Her first client, septuagenarian Ernest Koch, seemed healthy in spite of his years, but that soon changed under Hahn's tender care. Koch died on May 6, 1932, leaving Anna a house in his will. Its ground floor was occupied by a doctor's office, and Hahn visited her new tenant frequently, stealing prescription blanks to keep herself supplied with "medicine" for her new "nursing" business.

Her next client, retired railroad man Albert Parker, died swiftly under Anna's ministrations. This time, she avoided the embarrassment of a convenient will by "borrowing" Parker's money before he died, signing an I.O.U. that predictably vanished as soon as he died. Jacob Wagner was next, willing a lump sum of $17,000 to his beloved "niece" Anna, and Hahn soon picked up another $15,000 for tending George Gsellman in the months before his death.

George Heiss was a rare survivor, growing suspicious one day after Anna served him a mug of beer. A couple of house flies had sampled the brew, dropping dead on the spot, and when Anna refused to share the drink herself, Heiss sent her packing. He did not inform police of his suspicions, though, and so the lethal nurse was free to go in search of other "patients."

George Obendoerfer was the last to die, in 1937, lured to Colorado on a supposed visit to Hahn's nonexistent ranch. Obendoerfer died in his hotel room, soon

after arriving in Denver, and Anna took the opportunity
to loot his bank account, pocketing $5,000 for her ef-
forts. Police became suspicious when she balked at
picking up the tab for George's funeral, demanding an
autopsy after they turned up evidence of the unorthodox
bank transfer. Arsenic was found in Obendoerfer's
body, and detectives were waiting for Hahn when she
reached Cincinnati, armed with arrest warrants and
court orders demanding exhumation of her previous clients. Each had been slain with a different potion, and a
search of Hahn's lodgings reportedly turned up "enough
poison to kill half of Cincinnati."

Convicted of multiple murder and sentenced to die,
Hahn kept her nerve, maintaining her pose as an "angel
of mercy." On June 20, 1938, she hosted a small party
for local newsmen in her cell, lapsing into hysterics as
she began her last walk to the death chamber. It took a
prison chaplain to restore her calm, holding her hand as
she was buckled into the chair. Facing the minister with
a level gaze, Hahn warned him, "You might be killed,
too, Father."

Haley, Kevin Bernard

The Haley brothers made a lethal team. Born in 1960
and 1964, respectively, Reginald and Kevin did everything together, sharing drugs and women, ultimately
joining forces in a two-man crime wave that would terrorize Los Angeles. Spurred on by what detectives
called "a burning cocaine habit," the brothers would
participate in an estimated 500 burglaries, 60 rapes, and
eight murders over a five-year period ending with their
arrest in 1984.

The first to die, in the official tally, was 90-year-old
Isabel Burton, beaten to death by the men who looted
and ransacked her home on April 20, 1983. Exactly

one year later, celebrating the event, 78-year-old D. Robinoff was beaten, raped and murdered in her small L.A. apartment. The brothers missed Willa Gerber, bungling a streetcorner abduction on May 12, but they rebounded five days later, gunning down 15-year-old Jodie Samuels as she ran to catch a school bus.

After their brief excursion into street violence, the brothers reverted to type, victimizing older women in their homes. Laverne Stolzy, 56, was raped and slain on June 26, followed by the beating death of 79-year-old Elizabeth Burns, and the strangulation of 89-year-old Elizibeth Karp. August's victim was T. Okauchi, 88, bludgeoned to death in her looted home, with 55-year-old Dolores Clement raped and murdered on September 27.

Arrested on October 11, 1984, the brothers cracked swiftly under interrogation, providing graphic details of previously unreported rapes. In addition to Kevin's various murder charges, the Haleys would rack up 42 felony charges involving 24 separate victims. Reginald led the field, with four counts of robbery, two burglaries, two rapes, two counts of sodomy, two of oral copulation, two sexual assaults, one kidnapping, and one auto theft. Kevin faced trial on thirteen burglaries, one robbery, one attempted rape, and one count of oral copulation. The brothers were jointly charged with six robberies, two kidnappings, one rape, and one count of sodomy. On August 8, 1987, Reginald Haley was convicted on 20 counts, drawing a sentence of 60 years plus one term of life imprisonment. While theoretically eligible for parole after 30 years, it seems unlikely he will ever walk the streets again. In June 1988, brother Kevin was convicted of murder, rape, sodomy, robbery and burglary in the Dolores Clement case, his jury fixing the penalty at death.

Hance, William Henry

On September 6, 1977, the nude and lifeless body of an army private, 24-year-old Karen Hickman, was discovered near the women's barracks at Fort Benning, near Columbus, Georgia. Beaten with a blunt instrument, then run over several times with a car, Hickman had been killed elsewhere, her corpse transported to the spot where it was found. Investigators learned that the victim—a white woman—had dated black soldiers exclusively, picking them up in bars near the post. An anonymous call led authorities to her missing clothes a month later, but no new evidence was found. The crime was treated as an isolated incident, almost forgotten in the manhunt for the "Stocking Strangler" who terrorized Columbus between September 1977 and April 1978.

By mid-February, the Strangler—described as a black man from evidence found at the crime scenes—had raped and murdered six elderly white women in Columbus. Georgia is Klan country, and racial tension was already mounting when, on March 3, 1978, the chief of police received a letter signed by the self-styled "Forces of Evil." "Since that coroner said the S-Strangler is black," the note read, "we decided to come here and try to catch him or put more pressure on you . . . From now on black women in Columbus, GA., will be disappearing if the Strangler is not caught." The first victim, a local black woman named Gail Jackson, had already been abducted by "an organization within an organization," and she was scheduled to die if the Stocking Strangler was not apprehended by June 1. Two more blacks would be killed, the author promised, if the murderer was still at large September 1.

Police could find no record of a Gail Jackson missing in Columbus, but they did discover that a black prostitute, Brenda Gail Faison, had disappeared from a local tavern on February 28. A second letter to the chief, arriving March 13, suggested that a ransom of $10,000 might secure the hostage's release, if homicide detectives could not find their man before the deadline. When police made no reply, a third note was delivered two weeks later, claiming that a second hostage named "Irene" had been abducted, scheduled to die on June 1. Detectives learned that 32-year-old Irene Thirkield was indeed missing, last seen on March 16 in the company of an unnamed black soldier.

In the predawn hours of March 30, 1978, an anonymous phone call led MPs to a shallow grave, just off the military reservation, where they uncovered the remains of Brenda Faison, her face and skull crushed into pulp by a savage beating. Four days later, another call directed CID agents to Maertens Range, on Fort Benning, and Irene Thirkield's headless body—plus scattered skull fragments—was found hidden behind a pile of logs.

On April 4, an officer reviewing tapes of the anonymous phone calls recognized the distinctive voice, fingering a 26-year-old private, William Hance, as the caller. An ammunition handler for the 10th Artillery, Hance was arrested that day, charged with murder and attempted extortion on April 5. A civilian jury convicted him of Brenda Faison's murder on December 16, 1978, voting the death penalty (plus five years on the extortion charge). Convicted of the Hickman and Thirkield murders at a subsequent court-martial, Hance drew a sentence of life imprisonment at hard labor.

Hansen, Robert

Born at Pocahontas, Idaho, in 1940, Hansen was the son of a Danish immigrant who followed in his father's footsteps as a baker. In his youth, Hansen was skinny and painfully shy, afflicted with a stammer and a severe case of acne that left him permanently scarred. (In later years, he would recall his face as "one big pimple.") Shunned by the attractive girls in school, he grew up hating them and nursing fantasies of cruel revenge.

Hansen was married in 1961 and divorced within the year, following his first arrest, on charges of arson. Six years later, he wed another Pocahontas native and she followed him to Anchorage, Alaska, where he opened his own bakery and prospered in a new land, safely removed from the painful memories of childhood and adolescence. Hansen took flying lessons and purchased his own private plane, earning a reputation as an outdoorsman and hunter who stalked Dahl sheep, wolves, and bear with a rifle or bow and arrow.

In 1972, Hansen was arrested twice more, charged with the abduction and attempted rape of a housewife (who escaped his clutches) and the rape of a prostitute (who did not). Serving less than six months on a reduced charge, he was picked up again, for shoplifting a chain saw, in 1976. Convicted of larceny, he was sentenced to five years in prison, but the verdict was overturned on appeal, the Alaska Supreme Court regarding his sentence as "too harsh."

Unknown to local authorities, Hansen's visible activities were only the tip of a very lethal iceberg. According to his subsequent confession, Hansen preyed consistently on women in the decade between 1973 and 1983, murdering 17 and raping another 30 who survived. As targets, he selected prostitutes, "exotic" dancers and the like, abducting them by airplane to the wilderness outside of Anchorage, where they were forced to act out Hansen's private fantasies. "If they came across with what I wanted," he explained, "we'd come back to town. I'd tell them if they made any trouble for me, I had connections and would have them put in jail for being prostitutes." Resistance—or demands for payment after sex—resulted in assorted victims being murdered, sometimes with the ghoulish touch of Hansen stripping them and stalking them like animals, making the kill with a hunting knife or his favorite big-game rifle.

The first indication of a killer at large came in 1980, when construction workers unearthed a woman's remains near Eklutna Road. Stabbed to death in 1979, she was never identified, dubbed "Eklutna Annie" by police assigned to work the case. Later that year, the corpse of Joanna Messina was found in a gravel pit near Seward, and a special task force was organized to probe the killings. Topless dancer Sherry Morrow had been dead ten months when hunters found her body in a shallow grave beside the Knik River, but the discovery brought authorities no closer to a solution in their case.

In 1983, Hansen decided to save time and energy by bringing his victims home. He called it his "summer project," laying the groundwork by packing his wife and two children off on a European vacation. Next, he began running ads in a local singles newspaper, seeking women to "join me in finding what's around the next bend, over the next hill."

On June 13, 1983, a 17-year-old captive escaped from Hansen en route to his airplane hangar, handcuffs still dangling from one wrist as she ran for help. Her charges brought Hansen to the attention of task force detectives, and he ultimately confessed to a series of 17 murders, including that of Paula Golding, found by hunters in September 1983. On a flying tour of the wilderness, Hansen began pointing out graves to state troopers, and they recovered eleven bodies over the next eight months. Several victims remained anonymous, their names unknown even to Hansen, but others were identified as Rox Easland, Lisa Futrell, Andrea Altiery, Angela Fetter, Tersa Watson, and Delynn

Frey—all reported missing from the Anchorage area during Hansen's reign of terror.

On February 18, 1984, Robert Hansen pled guilty on four counts of first-degree murder, in the cases of "Eklutna Annie," Joanna Messina, Sherry Morrow, and Paula Golding. Charges were dismissed in the other cases, but it scarcely mattered, as Hansen was sentenced to a term of life imprisonment plus 461 years.

Harrison, Lester

Logging his first arrest at age 22, in 1945, Harrison drew a term of five to ten years on conviction for a Chicago armed robbery. While locked up at Menard, he struck and killed another inmate—convicted murderer Norman Kimme—in November 1951, earning a stint in the state hospital after he was deemed incompetent for trial. Upon parole, there would be more convictions, eight in all, on various charges including larceny, attempted armed robbery, unlawful use of a weapon, battery, and indecent exposure. Harrison jumped bail twice, and twice more was sent back to state hospitals for diagnosis and treatment. Found competent for trial on robbery charges in March 1972, Harrison was convicted and sentenced to eighteen months, then released by a judge on the basis of time served during psychiatric evaluations. Through it all, no one suspected Harrison of possible involvement in a string of grisly homicides committed around Grant Park, in downtown Chicago.

Agnes Lehman was the first victim, beaten to death near the park's bandshell on July 10, 1970, her body found the next morning. A shoe recovered at the scene was linked to suspect Wilbur McDonald, arrested twelve days later as he lay unconscious by some railroad tracks, the victim of a mugging. McDonald admitted speaking with Lehman the night of her death, but insisted a black man had rushed from the darkness, assaulting them both and putting McDonald to flight. Skeptical jurors rejected the story, convicting McDonald of murder, and the court handed down a sentence of 100 to 150 years in prison.

Authorities saw no reason to reopen the case on September 5, 1972, when Judith Betteley was beaten to death a few yards from the old murder scene. Three weeks later, Lester Harrison was charged with assaulting 31-year-old Cozetta Gladys, knocking her down with a brick and dragging her through a Chicago alley. Released on $5,000 bond September 28, he was subsequently found competent for trial, and formally indicted on December 29. A judge allowed the meager bail to stand despite his violent record and long history of mental disorders.

Harrison's trial was still pending in July 1973, when Irene Koutros was stabbed to death in Grant Park's underground garage. Three weeks later, on August 3, Lee Wilson was fatally stabbed in the park proper, her assailant pausing to gnaw on the body before he escaped. On August 13, 28-year-old Judith Ott was knifed to death in a park restroom, a black man observed sprinting from the scene of the attack. The victim's husband, David Ott, gave chase and tackled Harrison, unaware that his wife had been murdered nearby.

In custody, Harrison confessed to four of the Grant Park murders, staunchly denying a role in the case of Irene Koutros. Aroused by the thought of female suffering, Harrison derived satisfaction from beating and stabbing his victims, once sampling cannibalism in the case of Lee Wilson. In addition to his confessed crimes, police sought links in the death of 28-year-old Elizabeth Dawson, recovered in August 1972 from a derelict building next door to Harrison's home.

Defense motions and psychiatric examinations delayed Harrison's murder trial until 1978, when he was acquitted on grounds of insanity. Unwilling to set the diagnosed schizophrenic "lust killer" free, prosecutors convened a special hearing to have Harrison declared "sexually dangerous," dusting off a little-used state law to have him confined while he remained a menace to society.

By May 1986, a 62-year-old quadriplegic, Harrison found attorneys to seek his release from state custody. Lawyers described Harrison as "harmless," asserting that he could "hardly" move in his present condition. The state countered with testimony from guards at Belleville State Hospital, suggesting that Harrison was capable of raising his arms, that he spoke incessantly of sexual activity, and that he was visibly aroused when certain nurses entered his room. As Terry Levin, spokesman for the state attorney's office, told the court, "If Lester Harrison were able to get his hands on any woman that woman would be in danger of being killed. If he could use one leg, he would try to use it to kick somebody to death. If he could use one arm, he would use it to try to beat somebody to death." The petition seeking Harrison's release was withdrawn on August 11, 1986.

Hatcher, Charles

Born in 1929, Hatcher spent half of his first 30 years in prison, convicted of numerous property crimes such as theft. He seemed to shift gears in 1959, with his arrest and conviction for the attempted abduction of a 16-year-old newsboy in St. Joseph, Missouri, moving on from that point to log convictions for sexual assaults and kidnapping of children in California, Nebraska, and Iowa. The latter charge, involving the March 1982 abduction of a boy at Bettendorf, sent Hatcher to a state mental institution, where psychiatrists pondered his case for two months before setting him free.

On July 29, hikers found the nude, ravaged body of 11-year-old Michelle Steele, beaten and strangled to death on a bank of the Missouri River near St. Louis. Hatcher was arrested next day, as he tried to check in at the St. Joseph State Hospital. While awaiting trial, he confessed to fifteen other child-murders dating from 1969. The first victim, 12-year-old William Freeman, had disappeared from Antioch, California, in August of that year, one day before Hatcher was charged with child molestation in nearby San Francisco. In another case, Hatcher penned a crude map that led searchers to the remains of James Churchill, buried on the grounds of the Rock Island Army Arsenal, near Davenport, Iowa. Innocent suspect Melvin Reynolds was already serving life for another of Hatcher's crimes—the sex-murder of four-year-old Eric Christgen, but Hatcher's confession released him from custody.

Convicted of the Christgen homicide in October 1983, Hatcher drew a term of life imprisonment with no parole for at least 50 years. Facing his second Missouri conviction a year later, in the Steele case, Hatcher requested a death sentence but the jury refused, recommending life on December 3, 1984. Four days later, the child-killer hanged himself in his cell, at the state prison in Jefferson City.

Herrington, Michael Lee

The son of a Kansas City policeman, born in 1943, Herrington was regularly beaten by his mother, with a belt, until age 12 when he "got tired and took it away from her." By age 23, he was working in Milwaukee as a shipping clerk, married, with his wife expecting their first child. A jet-black 1957 Chevy was his pride and joy, but it would also prove to be his downfall, as internal pressures mounted toward the point of "an explosion of all this anger that I built up over the years."

On September 1, 1966, Mrs. Duane Troyer, a 34-year-old Oak Creek resident, was driving to work when another motorist pulled her over by means of a ruse. Emerging from his car—described by Troyer as a "gray 1956 Chevrolet"—the stranger slashed her with a knife, then fled when she began to scream. She would survive her wounds, but other victims proved less fortunate.

On September 3, 10-year-old Julia Beckwith was raped, beaten and stabbed to death on a vacant lot in Milwaukee. Herrington was questioned as a suspect in the case, and then released. Six weeks later, 18-year-old Sherryl Thompson was found by her brother behind a Catholic church, partially nude, her body torn by 22 stab wounds resulting in death. The scene was even more horrific on November 4, when 19-year-old Diane Olkwitz was slain, stabbed more than 100 times, at the factory where she worked in Menomonee Falls.

A week later, 11-year-old Kathleen Dreyer was accosted by a man who slashed her with a knife and left her bleeding on the street, escaping in a 1957 Chevrolet. A neighborhood boy spotted the car at a nearby gas station and summoned police from the crime scene. Herrington was arrested on the spot, a search of his vehicle turning up drugs and a stockpile of surgical instruments.

In custody, Herrington confessed to the Beckwith and Thompson murders, along with the stabbing of Kathleen Dreyer. Found competent for trial, he was convicted by a jury on July 7, 1967, after 35 minutes of terse deliberation. Herrington was sentenced to consecutive life terms for the two murders, with an additional 30 years tacked on for attempted murder.

"Highway Murders"—Canada

For the best part of a decade, between 1973 and '81, Canadian authorities were baffled by a series of unsolved sex-murders along the Trans-Canada Highway, spanning the provinces of Alberta and British Columbia. Victims ranged in age from 12 years old to 35, and while published sources could never agree on a body-count—citing various totals from 11 to 33 victims—the most frequent tally lists 28 slayings spread over eight years. Many of the victims were apparently hitchhikers, sexually assaulted before they were beaten, strangled, or stabbed to death, with some of the bodies revealing post-mortem mutilations.

Generally acknowledged as the first "Highway" victim, 19-year-old Gale Weys was thumbing her way home to Kamloops, from a job in Clearwater, when she met her killer on October 19, 1973. Her naked, decomposing corpse was found a few miles south of Clearwater, on April 6, 1974.

By that time, the killer had claimed another victim, picking off 19-year-old Pamela Darlington, at Kamloops, on November 6. Her ravaged body was fished out of the Thompson River next day, and a train crew reported sighting a man with "messy blond hair" near the scene of the crime, but the vague description led detectives nowhere.

Colleen McMillan, 16, was last seen alive on August 9, 1974, thumbing rides near Lac La Hache. A month later, on September 4, her nude, decomposing remains were found some 35 miles away. Police suspected a drug addict, who confessed the murder and then recanted before committing suicide. The case remains officially unsolved.

On January 9, 1976, 16-year-old Pauline Brazeau was found stabbed to death, outside Calgary. Six months later, on July 1, 19-year-old Tera White disappeared from Banff, her skeletal remains discovered near Calgary in March 1981. Marie Goudreau, 17, was murdered near Devon on August 2, 1976, and 20-year-old Melissa Rehorek was murdered near Calgary on September 15, her body discarded 12 miles from the spot where Pauline Brazeau was discovered.

Barbara McLean, age 26, traveled all the way from Nova Scotia to meet her death near Calgary, by strangulation, on February 26, 1977. Monica Jack, 14, disappeared while bicycling near Merritt, on May 6, 1978, and she has not been seen since, though her bike was recovered at the bottom of a highway embankment. On September 26, 1979, 12-year-old Susan Duff went biking near Penticton, her body recovered from the outskirts of town on October 21. Mary Jamieson, 17, disappeared while hitchhiking near Davis Bay, on August 7, 1980; nine days later, when her body was discovered in the nearby woods, the cause of death was listed as asphyxiation.

On February 28, 1981, victim Oanh Ha—a 19-year-old Vietnamese refugee—was raped and strangled near Golden, her body mutilated after death. Two months later, on April 22, 15-year-old Kelly Cook was reported missing, her body recovered near Taber, Alberta, on June 29. The only male victim in the series, transvestite Frederick Savoy, was parading in drag when the killer mistook him for a woman, knifing him to death in a Vancouver parking lot. Maureen Mosie, generally described as the last "Highway" victim, was beaten to death at Kamloops on May 8, 1981.

Six months later, Canadian authorities convened a special summit meeting to discuss 33 of western Canada's 200 unsolved murders, and while they generally agreed that they were seeking several killers—possibly as many as 18—in the "Highway" series, no solid suspects were identified. A ray of hope broke through in 1983, with the marathon confessions of serial slayers

Henry Lucas and Ottis Toole including references to "several" Canadian victims, but no charges have been filed to date, and the slayings remain unsolved. (See also: Lucas, Henry, Vol. 1; Toole, Ottis, Vol. 1)

Hill, Clarence

In serial murder, as in American society at large, blacks have always constituted a statistical minority. Only in the 1980s have their numbers been significant, but every generation has produced some interesting cases, bold exceptions that defy the rule. In the 1940s, Jake Bird and Jarvis Catoe did their part to raise white hackles, but they were assisted by the efforts of a grim soul brother in New Jersey.

Duck Island, in the years surrounding World War II, consisted of a dreary landfill on the Delaware River, in Hamilton Township, near Trenton, New Jersey. Devoid of any residential or commercial value, it became a "lover's lane," where trysting couples came by night to grapple in the dark, professing love—or its facsimile—in breathless whispers. In the period from 1938 to 1942, the lovers did not have Duck Island to themselves.

The first attack took place on November 8, 1938, when 20-year-old Vincent Tonzello pulled his car off the Duck Island road, to spend a few pleasant hours with Mary Mytovich, 16. Next morning, when patrolmen reached the scene, Tonzello lay dead in the car, riddled with buckshot; his date was found nearby, gravely wounded. Before she died in a Trenton hospital, Mary described the attack. A black man had approached the car, she said, shooting Tonzello when Vincent rejected a demand for money. The assailant then dragged Mary from the car, raped her, shot her, and left her for dead.

Eleven months later, on October 3, 1939, Frank Casper and Katherine Werner were killed near the same spot, in almost identical fashion. A junk dealer, prowling Duck Island for saleable refuse, found Casper dead in his car; Werner's body lay nearby, partially buried in garbage, one arm severed by a shotgun blast that had cut her down as she ran from the car.

The scene changed slightly for the third attack, in 1940. Ludovicum Kovacs, 25, and Carolina Maroconi, 24, were parked off Cypress Lane, several miles from Duck Island, when close-range shotgun blasts snuffed out their lives. Again, no clues were left behind that might identify the stalker.

Police would document three more attacks in 1941 and '42, but the killer had lost his touch and all six victims survived. A piece of the murder weapon, carelessly dropped at the scene of a shooting in 1942, eventually led detectives to question Clarence Hill in January 1944. A father of two, Hill had been drafted into the army eighteen months before, and was stationed at Fort Dix, in New Jersey. Detained there for questioning by military authorities, Hill confessed to the series of murders and assaults on January 28, 1944.

Considering the link between his own confessions and the deathbed testimony of his victim, Hill was brought to trial for killing Mary Mytovich. Convicted on December 29, 1944, he was sentenced to a term of life imprisonment.

Hilley, Audrey Marie

A native of Anniston, Alabama, Hilley was born in 1933 and seemed to enjoy a normal childhood. Married at 18, she was having marital problems nine years later when her second daughter—Carol—was born. Psychiatrists, applying hindsight, feel the birth may have somehow triggered a radical shift in Hilley's personality, resentment of the new child simmering over time, finally surfacing in a series of lethal attacks upon family members.

When Audrey's husband, Frank, passed on in 1975, cancer was blamed for his death. The same diagnosis was made two years later, in the death of Hilley's mother, Lucille Frazier. By 1979, victims had begun to pile up, with daughter Carol lingering on the brink of death for several weeks before doctors managed to pull her back. They were too late for mother-in-law Carrie Hilley, who died in November after a prolonged illness.

By that time, authorities were already closing the ring around Audrey. Doctors had discovered abnormal levels of arsenic in Carol's blood, and on a hunch, they started checking other family members recently deceased. On October 25, 1979, Hilley was indicted for attempted murder of her daughter, plus an unrelated charge of check fraud. Three weeks later, free on $14,000 bond, she vanished from a Birmingham motel where she had been awaiting trial. Indictments were handed down in the murder of her husband on January 11, 1980, but they meant little without a suspect in custody.

In flight, Hilley adopted the identity of "Robbi Hannon," attaching herself to bachelor John Homan in Marlow, New Hampshire. They lived together for several months before they were married, in May 1981, and "Robbi" was talking divorce a month later, lighting out for Texas in a search for "space." She spent that summer in the Lone Star State, occasionally telephoning Homan as herself, and in the guise of her own alleged twin, "Teri Martin." A brief reconciliation with Homan was followed by yet another separation, in September 1982, and "Robbi" moved on to Florida, where she contrived to fake her own death. Incredibly, she then returned to New Hampshire—as "Teri Martin"—

and spent time consoling her "brother-in-law" before moving on to Vermont. There, her suspicious behavior finally alerted authorities, and Hilley was arrested in January 1983.

Her trial opened in Anniston four months later, and Hilley was convicted on two counts, receiving a life term for the murder of husband Frank Hilley, plus twenty years for the attempted murder of her daughter. On February 9, 1987, Hilley was granted a three-day furlough from the women's prison at Wetumpka, Alabama, and she never returned. Discovered on the porch of an Anniston home February 26, in the midst of a winter rainstorm, Hilley was soaked to the skin and spattered with mud, suffering from severe hypothermia. Fading in and out of consciousness, she gave her name as "Sellers," but authorities identified her from the wanted posters issued after her escape. Stricken by a heart attack en route to the local hospital, Hilley was beyond the help of medical science, and doctors pronounced her dead that afternoon.

In retrospect, there seems to be no rational motive for Hilley's various crimes. She maintained her innocence to the end, while complaining of various "blackouts" and memory lapses, but she remains a suspect in several other cases. In the late 1970s, Hilley repeatedly complained to police about prowlers and threatening phone calls, always greeting patrolmen with fresh pots of coffee when they arrived at her home. At least two of those officers later complained of severe stomach cramps and nausea after drinking the coffee, and Hilley was also linked with the chronic, unexplained illness of various neighborhood children who played with her daughter around Hilley's home. One such playmate, eleven-year-old Sonya Gibson, died of unknown causes in 1975, but a 1983 autopsy revealed only "normal" levels of arsenic in her remains. The final count of Marie Hilley's victims—like her motive itself—remains unknown.

Hoch, Johann Otto

Born John Schmidt in 1855, at Horweiler, Germany, Hoch immigrated to the United States as a young man and dropped his given name in favor of assorted pseudonyms, frequently taking the name of his most recent victim. At age 51, Chicago police would dub him "America's greatest mass murderer," but statistics remain vague in this puzzling case. We know that Hoch bigamously married at least 55 women between 1890 and 1905, bilking all of them for cash and slaying many, but the final number of his victims is a matter of conjecture. Sensational reports credit Hoch with 25 to 50 murders, but police were only certain of 15, and in the end he went to trial (and to the gallows) for a single homicide.

Hoch's first—and only legal—wife was Christine Ramb, who bore him three children before he deserted her in 1887. By February 1895, as "Jacob Huff," he had surfaced in Wheeling, West Virginia, where he won the heart and hand of a middle-aged widow, Caroline Hoch. They were married in April, and Caroline fell gravely ill three months later. Called to her bedside, Rev. Hermann Haas watched "Huff" administer a potion that Haas believed to be poison, but the minister took no action and Caroline died days later, in agony. "Huff" cleaned out her $900 bank account, sold their house, collected $2,500 in life insurance benefits—and vanished. Suicide was suspected, with his clothing, his watch, and a note discovered on the bank of the Ohio River, but no body was found.

Hoch kept his latest victim's surname—described by prosecutors as "a warped keepsake stored in an evil mind"—and moved on to Chicago, finding work in the meat packing plants when he was not engaged with the business of swindling women. Selecting his victims from newspaper "lonely-hearts" columns, Hoch went merrily about his business until 1898, when he was sentenced to a year in jail for swindling a used-furniture dealer. Police Inspector George Shippy also suspected Hoch of bigamy, and murder was added to the list on receipt of a letter from Rev. Haas in West Virginia. Shippy started digging into Hoch's background, turning up dozens of missing or deserted women from San Francisco to New York City, but solid evidence remained elusive. In Wheeling, Caroline Hoch was exhumed in a search for arsenic traces, but surgeons found the body gutted, all her vital organs missing.

Hoch was released at the end of his jail term, chalking up another fifteen wives before his ultimate arrest in 1905. Aware that Shippy and others were charting his movements, Hoch killed more often and more swiftly now, relying on primitive embalming fluids—with their high arsenic content—to cover any traces of poison in his victims. On December 5, 1904, he married Marie Walcker in Chicago, killing her almost at once. Wasting no time, Hoch proposed to his new sister-in-law on the night of Marie's death, and they were married six days after the hasty funeral. Amelia Hoch bestowed a gift of $750 on her husband, prompting him to vanish with the cash, and she immediately summoned police.

Modern science was Hoch's downfall, his late wife's mortician employing a new embalming fluid with no taint of arsenic. Medical examiners found poison in Marie Walcker's system and Hoch was charged with her murder, his photograph mailed off to every major American newspaper. In New York City, a middle-aged landlady recognized "Henry Bartels," a new tenant who had proposed marriage twenty minutes after renting a room. At his arrest, police recovered a revolver, several wedding rings with the inscriptions filed off, and a fountain pen filled with arsenic. (Hoch claimed the arsenic was purchased as a step toward suicide!)

Chicago journalists dubbed Hoch the "Stockyard Bluebeard," trumpeting the speculative details of his criminal career. At trial, he whistled, hummed, and twirled his thumbs throughout the prosecution's case, apparently well pleased by his position in the limelight. On conviction of Marie Walcker's murder, he was sentenced to hang, telling the court, "It's all over with Johann. It serves me right." Mounting the gallows on February 23, 1906, Hoch maintained his innocence, declaring, "I am done with this world. I have done with everybody." As the trap was sprung, a local newsman quipped, "Yes, Mr. Hoch, but the question remains: *What* have you done with everybody?"

Part of the solution was unearthed in 1955, when human bones were found inside the wall of a Chicago cottage occupied by Hoch. It was a meager bit of evidence, the victim unidentified, and Johann's final body count, the names and number of his murdered wives, will probably remain a mystery forever.

Hoffman, Ronald

The month preceding Christmas 1978 brought sudden terror to Chicago's quiet northwest side, a neighborhood traditionally occupied by law-abiding citizens of old Germanic stock. Beginning in November, residents were haunted by the shadow of a gunman—dubbed the "Sunshine Sniper" for his daring daylight raids—who claimed his victims seemingly at random, showing no respect for sex or age.

The first to die was 90-year-old Emmanuel Dahl, gunned down without motive in his vitamin shop, on

William G. Bonin

(Courtesy of The Los Angeles County Sheriff's Department)

Joseph Francis Bryan, Jr.

(Courtesy of The Federal Bureau of Investigation)

Vernon Butts

(Courtesy of The Los Angeles County Sheriff's Department)

Robert C. Hansen

October 1983
(Courtesy of The
Anchorage, Alaska,
Police Department)

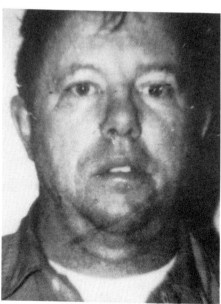

Robert C. Hansen

May 1988
(Courtesy of The
Anchorage, Alaska,
Police Department)

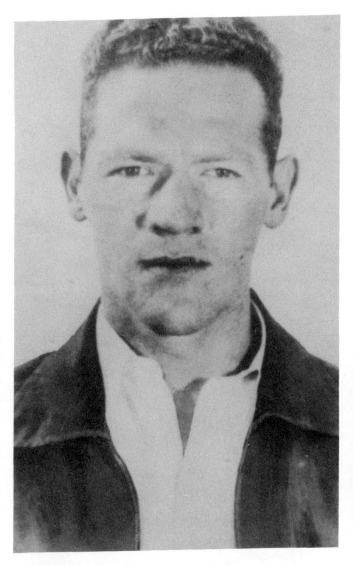

Richard Laurence Marquette

(Courtesy of The Federal Bureau of Investigation)

Gregory
M. Miley

(Courtesy of The
Los Angeles County
Sheriff's Department)

Darren
D. O'Neal

(Courtesy of The
Federal Bureau of
Investigation)

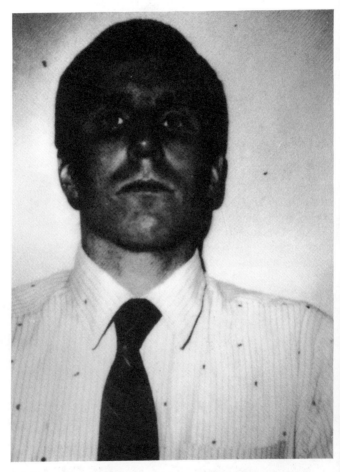

Dr. Michael Swango

(Courtesy of The Federal Bureau of Investigation)

William Albert Autur Tahl

(Courtesy of The Federal Bureau of Investigation)

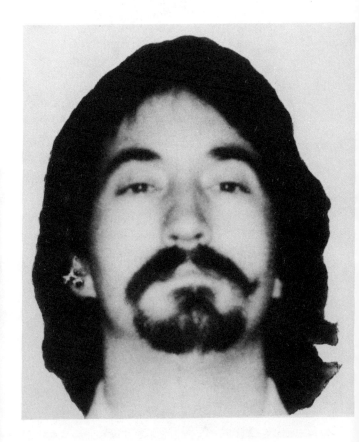

Billy Ray Waldon

(Courtesy of The Federal Bureau of Investigation)

November 11. Detectives found no evidence of robbery, and friends recalled no prior threats of any kind against the murdered man. Four weeks later, 65-year-old Sophie Schwartz was crossing Sunnyside Street, at Wells Park, when she collapsed on the pavement, crying out in pain. She died an hour later at emergency receiving, with doctors locating a bullet wound in her back moments after her death. Again, there was no evidence of robbery, no history of harassment or threats.

On December 18, 35-year-old Diamond Menodinez was approaching his office, on foot, when a bullet slammed into his arm. A survivor, he could offer no description of the gunman who had fired from ambush, but police got lucky five days later, on their own. Arrested on December 23, 35-year-old Ronald Hoffman was carrying a .357 magnum revolver and 40 spare rounds of ammunition when two patrolmen slapped the cuffs on (earning themselves immediate promotion to the rank of inspector). Ballistics tests connected Hoffman's weapon with the random shootings and he was detained for trial, unable—or unwilling—to provide a motive for the crimes.

Hohenberger, Robert Carl

An ex-convict and one-time California sheriff's deputy, Hohenberger was linked with the abduction, rape and murder of five Morgan City, Louisiana teenagers over a three-month period of 1978. Two of the victims were discovered on May 25, their bodies secured to weights and dumped in a septic tank; a third was found two days later, with all three reportedly strangled after sex. Still missing at the time of Hohenberger's identification were 14-year-old Bertha Gould, vanished from a high school fair on May 11, and 16-year-old Leah Rodermund, lost on a trip to the neighborhood drugstore. FBI agents described sex as the motive for slayings committed by Hohenberger, a drifter since his release from prison who found temporary employment around Morgan City. As an afterthought to the case, city councilmen passed an ordinance requiring all transients to register and have their fingerprints taken by police, in an effort to "discourage the criminal element from coming down here and looking for a job."

Holmes, Edward J.

On November 27, 1973, 11-year-old Penny Schroeder vanished from her school in Clinton, Maryland. As the daughter of a police lieutenant, her disappearance prompted a swift law enforcement response, and her body was found hours later, in some woods five blocks from school. The child had been molested, strangled, stabbed repeatedly, her skull fractured by crushing blows in a grisly example of overkill.

Penny's murder came nine weeks after the slaying of 21-year-old Susan Fallin, whose charred body was recovered from a burned-out car near Brandywine, October 5. Police had no evidence to link the crimes, but this time there were witnesses who told of seeing Penny with a teenage boy before she disappeared. Descriptions led authorities to janitor Edward Holmes, 19, and he was taken into custody November 28, charged the same day with the murders of two children in Washington, D.C.

The capital victims were listed as nine-year-old Stanford Kendrick, abducted from school on September 20, and 12-year-old Joanie Bradley, kidnapped in similar fashion October 16. Like Penny Schroeder, both of the earlier victims had been molested, their bodies discarded in woods near their respective schools. Again, like Penny, Joanie Bradley was a campus monitor, apparently snatched while "on duty," patrolling the playground. In custody, Holmes freely confessed to the three murders charged against him.

Horton, Wayne Donald

A native of Las Vegas, born in 1956, Horton was possessed of an explosive temper and "a bad habit of pulling the trigger" when quarrels erupted into violence. Between the ages of 16 and 20, he dispatched at least one victim per year, regaling the judge at his murder trial with a promise to take more lives in the future, if the opportunity arose.

Horton's first victim was a "Jane Doe," picked up at a liquor store in the latter half of 1972, beaten to death with a jack handle and dumped in the desert when she objected to Wayne's smoking marijuana while driving. Her skeletal remains, complete with shattered skull, were found on February 4, 1973, but the woman remains unidentified today.

On May 12, 1975, Horton tried to rob Edward Buccieri, a 52-year-old shift boss at Caesar's Palace, shooting his victim five times in the head after Buccieri "called him dirty names." Three months later, Horton repeated the performance—down to the number of gunshots—with Las Vegas cab driver William Tinnell. Far from insulting Horton, the cabbie was on his knees, pleading for mercy when he died, but Wayne felt no sympathy. As he explained in court, "I don't think he deserved to live."

On April 21, 1976, Horton was jailed in Las Vegas, awaiting trial on charges of rape, robbery, and kidnapping, when he led two cellmates in fatally stabbing 19-year-old Calvin Brinson. All three prisoners were charged with murder, but Horton freely confessed his role in the unprovoked attack, blaming Brinson's death on his own "frustration" at confinement.

On June 5, 1976, Horton pled guilty to the Buccieri and Tinnell murders, giggling as he described the crimes in court. In return for his guilty plea, various other felony charges were dismissed, including the August 1975 strangulation murder of Delmar Bright, later charged to serial slayer Billy Chadd. Three weeks later, Horton received two consecutive terms of life imprisonment without parole, publicly lamenting the fact that he would not be executed. Voicing his intention to claim future victims, Horton said, "There are several people I'm going to kill if I can." When a black prisoner began chuckling nervously, Horton swung around to face him. "Go ahead and laugh, nigger," he snarled. "You might just be the first one."

The killer was more subdued on August 3, when he filed guilty pleas in the deaths of Calvin Brinson and the "Jane Doe" victim, drawing two more terms of life without parole. Nevada authorities announced their intention of seeking Horton's transfer to a California prison, where he would be permanently out of touch with other inmates he has vowed to murder.

Hospital Murders—Georgia

In November 1985, administrators at Phoebe Putney Hospital, in Albany, Georgia, were alarmed by a sudden rash of cardiac arrests in the intensive care unit. A review of hospital records showed six suspicious deaths, with an equal number of near-misses, since late October, and police were quietly notified. Post-mortem examinations blamed the six deaths on injections of potassium chloride, and homicide investigators went to work on the case full-time.

The first apparent victim had been 68-year-old

Milton Lucas, pronounced dead on October 19, 1985. Next up was Minnie Houck, age 58, lost on November 7. Three days later, 36-year-old Joe Irwin joined the list, and Roger Parker, also 36, died on November 15. Andrew Daniels, age 73, lost his struggle for life on November 24, and he was followed two days later by three-year-old Norris Morgan. Survivors included patients Sam Bentley, George Whiting, Frances Freeman, and Jack Stephens, all of whom had suffered one or more unexplained cardiac arrests in ICU.

By New Year's, authorities were confident of six victims, but there may have been more. Lee Creech, a 26-year-old jail inmate, had died under treatment on December 21, and detectives were suspicious of three or four other deaths, dating back to mid-August. By March, their investigation had focused on a 24-year-old nurse, Terri Eden Maples Rachals, and on March 13 she reportedly confessed to injecting five patients with lethal doses of potassium chloride.

On March 25, 1986, Rachals was indicted on six counts of murder and 20 counts of aggravated assault against nine patients. Some of them had received multiple injections, with Creech and Parker holding the record at six and four jolts, respectively.

At trial, in September, the prosecution contended that Rachals "felt like a second-class citizen all her life," desirous of "power and control" that she ultimately sought "on the dark side of the street," by murdering her patients. Reference was made to her confessions, but Terri took the stand on September 23, recanting her statements, denying any memory of the attacks. On September 26, jurors returned a verdict of guilty but mentally ill on one count of aggravated assault, acquitting Rachals on all other charges. Members of the panel said that, while she may indeed have been responsible for several deaths, the prosecution simply had not proved its case. On October 1, Rachals was sentenced to a 17-year prison term, with three years of probation on release.

Hospital Murders— Maryland (1984–85)

Jane Bolding was employed as a nurse at Prince George's Hospital, in a Maryland suburb of Washington, D.C., for nine years before authorities became suspicious of her conduct on the job. For much of that time, she worked the intensive care unit, tending patients in the direst extreme. Death is a daily fact of life in ICU, but during 1984 and early 1985, Jane Bolding's patients died like flies, a startling number suffering from cardiac arrest. On March 9, 1985, she was relieved of duty pending an internal probe of what administrators called "a pattern of unsubstantiated but suspicious information relating to incidents in the intensive care unit."

The investigation yielded grim results. According to statistical analysis, performed by the Federal Center for Disease Control in Atlanta, Georgia, Bolding had been the attending nurse in 40 percent of all ICU deaths between January 1984 and March 1985. In concrete terms, she had witnessed the deaths of 57 patients; her closest competitor on staff had lost only five patients in the same period, and none of the hospital's remaining 93 nurses had lost more than four. Additionally, Bolding was the Prince George's nurse attending 65 percent of all the patients who experienced a cardiac arrest in ICU during the night shift.

On March 20, 1985, Bolding was charged with first-degree murder in the death of Elinor Dickerson, age 70, who died in ICU at 12:05 a.m., September 29, 1984. According to police, their suspect confessed to injecting the patient with potassium, inducing cardiac arrest in the name of "mercy." While Bolding was released on bond to stay with relatives, authorities announced that they were checking into other recent deaths. It was suggested that the final body-count might run as high as seventeen.

Dismissed from her job on March 26, Bolding was encouraged when the prosecution's case appeared to crumble two days later. The state's attorney for Prince George's County scolded police for arresting the nurse against his wishes, branding her confession insufficient to support a case in court. Bolding's charges were dropped in mid-May, but detectives returned to the search with a vengeance, seizing 200 boxes of hospital records on May 31, scouring the files for information on twenty-two "suspicious" deaths.

On December 16, 1986, a Maryland grand jury indicted Jane Bolding on three counts of murder and seven counts of assault with intent to kill. Elinor Dickerson was back on the list as a victim, joined by patients Isadore Scheiber and Martha Moore. Scheiber allegedly survived two potassium injections, on October 2 and 11, 1984, before a third injection killed him on October 12. Martha Moore was less hardy, surviving only one attack—on October 27—before a second injection finished her off the next day. Patient Mary Morbeto survived a single injection, in March 1984, while Gary Dodson weathered three consecutive attacks a year later, in the week before Bolding's suspension from duty.

After various delays, Jane Bolding's murder trial began in May of 1988, with prosecutors dubbing her a "killing angel." Bolding waived her right to trial by jury, placing her fate in the hands of a judge who promptly declared her confession—obtained after 33 hours of grilling without an attorney—inadmissible as evidence. Deprived of the confession, lacking any witnesses, the prosecution had no case. On June 20, 1988, Bolding was acquitted on all counts. At this writing, the Maryland hospital murders remain unsolved.

Hospital Murders—
New Jersey

In 1966, authorities in Bergen County launched a probe of nine suspicious deaths at Riverdell Hospital, a small osteopathic facility located in Oradell, New Jersey. In each case, patients were admitted to the hospital for surgery and died of unrelated causes, before or after routine surgical procedures. Despite the identification and trial of a suspect on murder charges, this intriguing case is still unsolved.

Carl Rohrbeck, age 73, was the first to die, admitted for hernia surgery on December 12, 1965, and lost to a diagnosed "coronary occlusion" the next day. Four-year-old Nancy Savino was signed in for an appendectomy on March 19, 1966, her death on March 21 attributed to some "undetermined physiological reaction." Margaret Henderson, 26, was admitted to Riverdell on April 22; she died the following day, after successful exploratory surgery. On May 15, 62-year-old Edith Post was booked in for surgery, lost two days later to undetermined causes. Ira Holster, 64, entered Riverdell for gall bladder surgery on July 12, dying without apparent cause on the twenty-ninth. Frank Biggs was complaining of an ulcer when he checked in on August 20; a week later, the 59-year-old patient was dead. Eighty-year-old Mary Muentener died on September 1, seven days after she was admitted for gall bladder surgery. Emma Arzt, age 70, was another gall bladder patient, admitted on September 18, dead by September 23. Eileen Shaw, 36, also lasted five days at

Riverdell, dying on October 23, after a successful Caesarian section.

Hospital administrators launched their investigation on November 1, 1966, after a Riverdell surgeon found eighteen vials of curare—most nearly empty—in the locker assigned to Dr. Mario Jascalevich. An Argentine immigrant, Jascalevich—dubbed "Dr. X" by the press—moved to the United States in 1955, setting up his practice in New Jersey. Confronted with the vials of poison, he explained that he had been involved in personal experiments with dogs. No motive could be ascertained for homicide, and ten years passed before the state charged Jascalevich with five counts of murder, in May 1976. Formally accused of slaying patients Savino, Henderson, Rohrbeck, Biggs and Arzt, the 39-year-old physician surrendered his medical license pending resolution of the case.

At trial, in 1978, two of the murder counts were dismissed for lack of evidence. After 34 weeks of testimony, Jascalevich was acquitted by jurors on October 24, returning to his native Argentina a short time later. He died there, of a cerebral hemorrhage, in September 1984. The case of the curare deaths at Riverdell remains officially unsolved today.

"I-35 Murders"—Texas

Interstate Highway 35 covers some 740 miles from Salina, Kansas, in the north, to Laredo, Texas, on the Mexican border. More than half the highway's length—in excess of 420 miles—runs north-to-south across the Lone Star State, past Gainesville, Denton, splitting to accommodate the twin giants of Dallas-Ft. Worth, reuniting above Hillsboro for the long run south, through Waco, Temple, Austin, San Antonio. Between 1976 and 1981 the Texas stretch of I-35 was the hunting ground for a killer (or killers) who preyed on hitchhikers and motorists in trouble, claiming at least 22 victims in five years time. Some officers believe the stalker is at large today.

The first "official" victim was 21-year-old Lesa Haley, found two miles north of Waxahachie, Texas, on August 23, 1976. Bound for Oklahoma City, traveling by thumb, she was last seen climbing into a van at Waco. Haley was stabbed in the neck with an awl before she was dumped on the shoulder of I-35.

On the night of November 5, 1978, 19-year-old Frank Key and 18-year-old Rita Salazar ran out of gas on a date in Austin. Next morning, Key was found north of Georgetown, shot nine times with a .22-caliber pistol, including four post-mortem shots in the back of the head. Salazar's body, shot six times with the same gun, was found on a frontage road near Waco.

Sharon Schilling, age 27, was found on a street in San Marcos, Texas, on Labor Day 1979, a few blocks from I-35. Shot once in the abdomen with a .410-gauge shotgun, she died on September 13, without regaining consciousness. Less than a month later, on October 8, Sandra Dubbs was kidnapped after her car broke down on the drive from St. Louis to San Antonio. Her body, stabbed 35 times, was discovered in Travis County, Texas. On Halloween, the strangled body of a "Jane Doe" victim, nude except for a pair of orange socks, was found in a highway culvert near Georgetown.

On June 23, 1980, victim Rodney Massey, shot four times, was found in a field near Temple, Texas, 70 miles north of the state capital at Austin. "On July 9 of that year, a Hispanic "Jane Doe" was discovered near Pflugerville, stabbed 27 times with a screwdriver; her pants had been pulled down, although there was no evidence of sexual assault. In May 1981, yet another "Jane Doe" was found near New Braunfels, shot six times in the head with a .25-caliber pistol.

Authorities convened in Austin to discuss the murders on October 30, 1981, but their review of the case produced no solid suspects. Two years later, serial slayers Henry Lucas and Ottis Toole confessed to most of the I-35 murders—and Lucas was sentenced to die on conviction in the "orange socks" case—but subsequent renunciation of the Lucas confessions, in 1985, has returned several cases to the "unsolved" column. Texas authorities remain divided on the question of Lucas's guilt, or the involvement of multiple killers in the I-35 murder series. (See also: Lucas, Henry, Vol. 1; Toole, Ottis, Vol. 1)

Infant Murders— New Hampshire

The town of Somersworth, New Hampshire, is a peaceful place, immune to the endemic violence that has blighted larger cities in the years since World War II. It is a place of simple pleasures, a traditional respect for God and country, unaccustomed to the limelight of publicity. That changed in April 1982, when residents Earl and Ruth Davis opened an old steamer trunk in their basement, releasing the contents of a grim Pandora's box.

The trunk had lain unopened in the dust and damp for 20 years, ever since Shirley Thomas—a friend from nearby Rochester—had asked the Davises to store it for her, pleading lack of space. Curiosity finally got the better of Ruth Davis, and she recruited her husband's help to spring the rusty locks on April 6, 1982. Inside, they found four tiny suitcases, each containing the mummified remains of a newborn infant, wrapped in local newspapers spanning the years between 1949 and 1952.

Authorities speculated that the infants may have been

slain in a cold-blooded "baby-snuffing" scheme, with unwed mothers giving up babies for adoption to someone who killed them instead. New Hampshire State Attorney General Gregory Smith declined to prosecute Shirley Thomas, believing the trunk was entrusted to her by a deceased third party. Somersworth Police Chief Ronald Perron summed up the local feelings of shock in a comment to *Newsweek* reporters. "It's almost too bizarre to be true," he remarked. "You don't think these things happen in our part of the country—maybe down South."

On November 27, 1988, the New Hampshire state attorney general's office released an investigative report on the case, hoping that new leads might develop through publicity. In that report, pathologists describe the four infants as newborn or premature babies, suggesting that an unidentified "piece of metal" found in the trunk may have been an abortion tool. According to former co-workers, the trunk's original owner often looked pregnant but never had children. To date, no arrests have been made in the case, and none are anticipated.

Ionosyan, Vladimir M.

In early January 1964, residents of Moscow whispered warnings to their neighbors of a mysterious, long-nosed killer prowling the city, knocking on doors at random, gaining entry to the homes of his victims by posing as a meter-reader for Moscow Gas. It seemed a nearly fool-proof gimmick, since the men from Mosgas made their rounds each month and were unlikely to arouse suspicion.

In the absence of reliable reports, with widespread tales of women slain and children mutilated, paranoia took control. By mid-month, the authorities reported that at least two Mosgas workers had been violently assaulted on their rounds, roughed up by tenants who were not inclined to scrutinize credentials. It became a standing joke for friends to telephone each other, hanging on the line in silence for a while before they whispered, "Mosgas calling."

On January 16, Moscow police announced the arrest of a suspect in the case. Vladimir Ionosyan, 26, was an unemployed actor fallen on hard times. He had turned to burglary as a source of revenue, reportedly killing in the process. Charged with the ax murders of two boys and a woman in downtown Moscow, Ionosyan was also linked with two similar killings in a suburban district.

Vladimir's arrest resulted from a general police alert to taxi drivers, circulating suspect sketches with instructions to beware of anyone who looked suspicious. Officers were summoned after Ionosyan stopped a trucker on the street and tried to sell a television set—a luxury in Soviet society—at bargain prices.

A three-day trial resulted in Ionosyan's conviction on five counts of murder. Sentenced to death on January 31, 1964, he was shot by a firing squad the next day. Vladimir's female accomplice, former ballerina Alevtina Dmitrieva, received a sentence of fifteen years in prison.

"Ivan the Ripper"

A decade after Vladimir Ionosyan sparked a local panic with the "Mosgas" murders, residents of Moscow circulated rumors of another homicidal maniac at large. According to reports, the slayer was a fair-haired, handsome young man, armed with a cobbler's bodkin or similar instrument, who trailed his female victims from the ornate subway stations, stabbing them to death in nearby streets and alleys.

Manhunting is doubly difficult in a society that admits to no crime problem, but Moscow police indirectly confirmed at least some of the rumors. By October 19, extra police and militia patrols were at large, their activity officially explained as preparation for the upcoming celebration of the Bolshevik revolution, on November 7. At the same time, posters bearing sketches of a suspect surfaced in the city's seventeen taxi garages, enlisting cab drivers as lookouts in the search.

By October 21, police confirmed that they were searching for the killer of "a woman." Inside sources put the body-count at seven, with the latest murder five days earlier. An eighth intended victim had survived her wounds, providing homicide investigators with the likeness reproduced in suspect sketches.

Five days later, on October 26, authorities reported they were holding a suspect in a series of stabbings that had killed at least eleven Moscow women. The prisoner, unnamed, had been arrested on the evening of October 24, after three victims were slain in a period of twenty-four hours.

Police maintained their news blackout as the suspect was shuffled off for psychiatric evaluation, and the disposition of his case remains unknown, but this time silence backfired. On the streets, a population starved for solid news fell back on rumor, doubting that the killer had been captured. "They caught one, but there is a second killer," one woman confided to a Western journalist. "They still have not caught the main one."

"Jack the Ripper"— Atlanta, GA

In the twelve months between May 1911 and May 1912, black residents of Georgia's capital were terrorized by the activities of a knife-wielding maniac who preyed exclusively on women of color, leaving them with throats slashed and bodies mutilated after death. Inevitably, he was christened "Jack the Ripper" by the local press, and like his namesake, he was never captured or identified. Unlike his predecessor, though, Atlanta's ripper claimed an even twenty victims, while the 19th-century practitioner had satisfied himself with five.

The early murders in Atlanta were committed with a shocking regularity, the slayer claiming victims on seven successive Saturday nights, between May 20 and July 1, 1911. White newsmen were quick to report that the victims were all attractive, well-dressed mulattoes, with no "out-and-out black women" slain by the stalker. In each case, there was evidence of the woman being choked unconscious, after which her throat was slit from ear to ear and "the carving of the victim—always in the same area of the body—begins." None of the women had been raped, but from the nature of the mutilations—tactfully unspecified in media reports—it was apparent that the crimes were sexual in nature. As in the case of London's Jack (and nearly all his imitators), newsmen noted that the killer "seems to possess some knowledge of anatomy."

Number seven on the Ripper's hit list was 40-year-old Lena Sharp, slain in the late hours of July 1, her head nearly severed, her body "horribly mutilated" after death. Concerned when Sharp was late arriving home, her daughter started searching in the streets. She was accosted by a well-dressed black man, but his mannerisms frightened her, and as she turned to flee he stabbed her in the back. Escaping with her life, she offered homicide investigators a description of the man, but no arrests resulted from the lead.

The Ripper's first near-miss resulted in a change of schedule, slowing down his pace. He would require ten months to claim another thirteen victims in Atlanta, mutilating his last target—a "comely yellow girl" of 19 years—on Friday, May 10, 1912. A large reward collected by the black community produced no takers, and the case remains unsolved today. It is, perhaps, coincidental that the years 1911 and 1912 also witnessed the unsolved ax murders of more than 40 mulatto victims in Texas and Louisiana.

"Jack the Ripper"— New York City

At five years old, Lenora Cohn was used to running errands for her mother. She was not required to leave the tenement that housed her family, except on rare occasions, and her chores were never rigorous, but she was learning to rely upon herself. The lesson would have served her well, had she survived.

At 7:30 on the evening of March 19, 1915, Lenora's mother sent her for a pail of milk. It was a simple task—she merely had to run downstairs—and neighbors saw her toiling homeward with a brimming pail ten minutes later. She was nearly home, already climbing toward the third-floor landing and her own apartment, when she passed out of their sight. At 7:45, Augusta Johnson heard an infant's cry outside her door, directly opposite the stairwell. Peering out, she saw a small child lying on her face, apparently the victim of a fall. Concerned, Miss Johnson rushed to help. The child was cradled in her arms before she saw the dark blood welling out of ragged knife wounds, soaking through the tiny dress.

Police were summoned to the tenement, along Third Avenue, but they found little in the way of clues. Lenora's pail of milk was sitting at the bottom of the stairs, where she was found, and not a drop had spilled. Detectives scouring the tenement found drops of blood on two steps of another staircase, on the far side of the house, but their significance remains obscure. Lenora's left hand clenched a tuft of short, gray hair, and bruises on her throat reflected violent contact with a larger-than-average hand. She had apparently been choked unconscious, stabbed and mutilated afterward with something like a leather worker's knife.

As if the nightmare of a murdered child were not enough, Lenora's mother soon became the target of sadistic letters, written by an individual who claimed to be the killer. Picking up on garish headlines in the press, the author signed his letters "Jack the Ripper," after London's gaslight ghoul of 1888. The notes were handed over to police, who passed them on to United States postal inspectors. On April 29, a 27-year-old Austrian named Edward Richman was arrested in connection with the mailings, quickly cleared of actual involvement in the homicide.

But the arrest of Richman did not stop the letters. One day after he was jailed, another note was posted to Lenora's mother. It read:

Dear Mrs. Cohn: Just a line to let you know that the person that is accused of writing letters to you is innocent. I am the fellow that wrote you the letters, and as I said before a man that keeps his ears open and mouth shut will always get along and never get caught. Some day thats if I get the chair I may confess. But as long as I am out they can never get me. Kindly give the enclosed letter to the police and tell them I wrote it. From

H.B. RICHMOND, Jack-the-Ripper

Enclosed with the letter was a second envelope, marked "Give this to the police." Inside was a letter that read:

Why don't you drop this case? You know that man can't get me in 100 years from now so its no youse in sirchen for me. I am a wise guy you know but wise guys never get caught. You may think that I am a fool to write you. But I am writing just to show that I aint afraid. Mr. Richmond is innocent of the letter which you accuse him of writing to Mrs. Cohn. I am the one that wrote all of them. As I told you in one of my letters that is going to be the biggest murders to be committed in N.Y. that was ever known. Now do you see I am true.

H.B. RICHMOND
JACK-THE-RIPPER

Police initially suspected Edward Richman of attempting to divert suspicion from himself, and visitors who called on him in jail were shadowed as potential cohorts, but no link between the suspect and the final "Ripper" letters was established. Officers intent on tracing "H.B. Richmond" came up empty-handed, still concerned about the recent note's allusion to the possibility of further slayings.

On May 3, the threat was realized. Charles Murray, four years old, did not respond when members of his family called him in from play at 7:30 in the evening. A hasty search was organized, uncovering his mutilated body tucked beneath a staircase in the family's First

Avenue tenement. Police responding to the call announced that Murray's killer "very likely" was the same man who had slashed Lenora Cohn on March 19. The victim's sister, Mamie, offered a description of the killer, but police eventually dismissed it as the product of a child's imagination.

Meanwhile, homicide detectives and patrolmen fanned out through the neighborhood in search of clues. Five doors up the street, they met the frantic parents of Louisa Niedig, six, who had apparently escaped the killer's clutches moments earlier. While playing on the street outside a bakery, waiting for her aunt to get off work, Louisa was approached by a neatly-dressed man, wearing a black derby hat and sporting a dark mustache. When she refused to speak with him, he grabbed her arm and dragged Louisa through an open doorway, but her screams brought neighbors on the run and her attacker fled before she suffered any harm.

At 47th Street and Third, Patrolman Curry was approached by several girls, aged eight to twelve, who said two men were chasing them with knives. Just then, the suspects came around a corner, stopping short at sight of Curry's badge. When Curry ordered them to halt, they rushed him, drawing blades and slashing him across the hand before he battered one assailant to the ground. The other fled, abandoning a stunned James Daly to his fate, but no connection was established with the Ripper crimes.

Reports kept pouring in, but all of them were vague, and none contained the crucial information that would crack the case. At Stuyvesant Park, twelve- and thirteen-year-old girls informed detectives that a stranger with a dark mustache and Van Dyke beard had been "annoying" them for several months. Inspector Joseph Faurot informed reporters that "the ripper type ... is one of the shrewdest and most elusive of criminals," an opinion seconded by Coroner Israel Feinberg. More murders were expected, Feinberg said, unless the killer could be found "within ten days."

The panic spread. On May 8, fifty men and boys attacked a Ripper suspect after two small boys accused him of "suspicious" actions. Rescued by police, the bloodied victim proved to be a Polish shoemaker, visiting friends on the street where he once had his shop.

On Sunday, May 9, two neighborhood housewives found crude, pencilled notes on their doormats, signed "The Ripper Jack." In each, the author threatened death to children of the target families; they would be killed on Monday afternoon, the letters said, or kidnapped from their homes that night if all else failed. There were no incidents on Monday, and on May 12 officers secured confessions from two girls who wrote the notes "for fun." That afternoon, another "Ripper" note was traced to its author, an eighteen-year-old, who had threatened her employer's children out of spite.

Exposure of such childish hoaxes did not ease the local atmosphere of tension. On the evening of May 15, six-year-old Anna Lombardi was lured into a basement by a man who raped her there. A mob went looking for the suspect, but police—who claimed to know his name—denied a link between the rape and murders. Two days later, when patrolmen arrested Stephen Lukovich for beating his wife and child, rumors spread that "a ripper" was in custody, drawing 1,000 outraged vigilantes to the street outside the precinct house.

Nor was the Ripper scare confined to New York City. On June 22, Inspector Faurot visited Philadelphia, where a man in custody had recently confessed to murdering a child "on 15th Street." Detectives had no knowledge of the crime, but young Charles Murray had been slain near 16th Street, and so the suspect warranted an interview. Faurot found his man confined in the mental ward of a local hospital, coming away from the interrogation convinced of his innocence in the Ripper crimes. In August, Lieutenant Patrick Gildea was dispatched to Baltimore, where Ripper suspect Edward Jones was being held on charges of defrauding his landlady. Informant Grace Elliott had denounced her common-law husband as the slayer, and while the woman's own behavior seemed erratic, irresponsible, New York authorities were notified. It was revealed that Jones and Elliott had lived in New York City when the homicides occurred, but there was nothing to connect them with the crimes. Interrogated by Gildea, Grace Elliott withdrew her charges, denying earlier statements that Jones had "confessed" the murders in her presence. Rather, she decided, he was simply interested in reading articles about the crimes.

The trail grew cold, and local panic faded over time. Despite assignment of 100 homicide detectives to the case, interrogation of innumerable "witnesses" and suspects, no solution was forthcoming in the case. As with Atlanta's Ripper—and his several predecessors of the 19th century—the New York crimes remain unsolved.

"Jack the Stripper"

Seventy years after Jack the Ripper murdered and disemboweled prostitutes in London's East End, a new generation of hookers learned to live with the ever-present fear of a lurking killer. This "Jack" carried no knife and penned no jaunty letters to the press, but he was every bit as lethal (claiming eight victims to the Ripper's five) and possessed of far greater longevity (operating over nearly six years, instead of the Ripper's ten weeks). At the "conclusion" of the case, both slayers shared a common attribute: despite a wealth of theories and assertions, neither "Jack" was ever publicly identified.

On June 17, 1959, prostitute Elizabeth Figg, 21, was

found floating in the Thames, clad only in a slip, her death attributed to strangulation. Four and a half years passed before discovery of the next murder, with the skeleton of 22-year-old Gwynneth Rees unearthed during clearance of a Thames-side rubbish dump, on November 8, 1963. The cause of death was difficult to ascertain, and homicide investigators later tried to disconnect both murders from the "Stripper" series, but today the better evidence suggests that these were practice runs, the early crimes committed by a killer who had yet to hit his stride.

Thirty-year-old Hannah Tailford was the next to die, her naked corpse discovered in the Thames by boatmen on February 2, 1964. Her stockings were pulled down around her ankles, panties stuffed inside her mouth, but she had drowned, and the inquest produced an "open" verdict, refusing to rule out suicide, however improbable it seemed.

On April 9, 1964, 20-year-old Irene Lockwood was found naked and dead in the Thames, floating 300 yards from the spot where Tailford was found. Another drowning victim, she was four months pregnant when she died. Suspect Kenneth Archibald confessed to the murder later that month, then recanted his statement, blaming depression. He was subsequently cleared at trial.

Helen Barthelemy, age 20, was the first victim found away from the river. On April 24, her naked body was discovered near a sports field in Brentwood, four front teeth missing, with part of one lodged in her throat. Traces of multi-colored spray paint on the body suggested that she had been kept for a while after death in a paint shop, before she was dumped in the field.

On July 14, 21-year-old Mary Fleming was discarded, nude and lifeless, on a dead-end London street. Witnesses glimpsed a van driver near the scene, but none could finally describe the man or vehicle with any certainty. Missing since July 11, Fleming had apparently been suffocated or choked to death—as opposed to strangled—and her dentures were missing from the scene.

Margaret McGowan, 21, had been missing a month when her nude corpse was found in Kensington, on November 25, 1964. Police noted the familiar traces of paint on her skin, and one of her teeth had been forced from its socket in front. The last to die was 27-year-old Bridget O'Hara, last seen alive on January 11, 1965, her body found on February 16, hidden in some shrubbery on the Heron Trading Estate, in Acton. Her front teeth were missing, and pathologists determined she had died on her knees. The corpse was partially mummified, as if from prolonged storage in a cool, dry place.

Despite appeals to prostitutes for information on their "kinky" customers, police were groping in the dark. Inspector John Du Rose suggested that the last six victims had been literally choked to death by oral sex, removal of the teeth in four cases offering vague support for the hypothesis. A list of suspects had supposedly been narrowed down from 20 men to three when one of those committed suicide, gassing himself in the kitchen and leaving a cryptic note: "I cannot go on." It might mean anything—or nothing—but the murders ended with the nameless suspect's death, and so police seem satisfied, although the case remains officially unsolved.

Who *was* the Stripper? Suspects range from a deceased prize fighter to an unnamed ex-policeman, but police favored a private security guard who worked the night shift on the Heron Trading Estate, his rounds including the paint shop where at least some of the victims were apparently stashed after death. The only "evidence" of guilt is the cessation of similar crimes after the suspect's suicide, but numerous serial killers—from the Ripper to the modern Zodiac and Babysitter—have "retired" once they achieved a certain body-count. The best that we can say for Scotland Yard's solution is that it is plausible, but unconfirmed.

Jackson, Anthony J.

Eight years after the solution of the "Boston Strangler" case, Massachusetts co-eds were terrorized by a new series of brutal rape-murders. Unlike one strangler's crimes, all victims in the latest series were young, between 18 and 22 years of age, and none were killed in their homes. As bodies were retrieved and evidence compiled, it soon became apparent that Boston's new slayer was preying on attractive hitchhikers, selecting his victims as random "targets of opportunity."

The killer claimed his first two victims in late September 1972, picking off 18-year-old Kathleen Randall a week after she enrolled at Boston University. Last seen thumbing rides near the campus, she was found two weeks later, raped and strangled in rural New Hampshire. Two days after Randall's disappearance, 19-year-old Debra Stevens was raped and strangled to death at Lynn, Massachusetts, her body discarded within 50 yards of home.

Victim Ellen Reich was another habitual hitchhiker. A 19-year-old sophomore at Emerson College, she lived off campus in the Back Bay area, traveling by thumb in preference to laying out the money for a car. The practice cost her life on November 9. Strangled and stabbed several times, she had been dead at least four days when searchers found her body on November 14, nailed inside the closet of an abandoned house in Boston's Roxbury district.

Sandra Ehramjian, age 21, also liked to hitchhike

when she wasn't earning money as a Boston taxi driver. A resident of Cambridge, she vanished November 27, en route to a dentist's appointment, her strangled corpse found the next day in a culvert near Waldo Lake, in suburban Brockton. Two days later, honor student Synge Gillespie vanished while thumbing rides in Boston. A telephone ransom demand for $25,000 brought relatives no closer to recovery of their loved one, and the Boston slayer had claimed three more victims by Christmas, all strangled or suffocated, with some stabbed for good measure.

Police got their break on December 26, when 33-year-old Anthony Jackson was arrested following a high-speed chase and shootout with Cambridge patrolmen. Booked on charges of assault with a deadly weapon, operating an automobile to endanger, and illegal possession of firearms, he was indicted for the Gillespie murder on February 3, 1973. A blood-soaked Cadillac, discovered in a Brockton junkyard, was believed to be the murder scene, and while evidence would remain elusive in several cases, investigators noted that the co-ed killings stopped abruptly with Jackson's arrest.

Jackson, Calvin

A small-time thief who sold his loot to buy narcotics, Calvin Jackson might have been ignored in New York City, ranked with thousands like himself and hastily forgotten, if his petty crimes had not accelerated into rape and brutal murder. As it was, complacent homicide investigators failed to recognize a pattern in his crimes for better than a year. Before they ran their man to earth, he claimed nine lives.

West 77th may fairly be classified as one of New

York's mean streets. It is better than some, worse than many, and no prize by any standards. In spite of its pretentious name, the Park Plaza Hotel, on West 77th, was a flea-bag catering to middle-aged and older women, scaling its facilities and rates to accommodate fixed incomes. Death was not the most unusual means of checking out, considering the average age of tenants, but in 1973 and '74 a lethal specter stalked the Park Plaza's corridors, driving the mortality rate sky-high.

Theresa Jordan was the first to die, on April 10, 1973. The youngest of the killer's victims at age thirty-nine, she was discovered, raped and suffocated, in her tiny room. From all appearances, a thief had torn the place apart.

Kate Lewisohn, age 65, was murdered on July 19. A caller found her trussed up on the bed, her small apartment looted. After being raped, she had been strangled, with her skull bashed in.

Police examining the crimes in search of a pattern soon lost interest, when the killer took a nine-month leave of absence. His return, on April 24, 1974, was nearly overlooked, authorities ascribing 60-year-old Mable Hartmeyer's death to arteriosclerosis. A second, closer look revealed the victim had been raped and strangled, with assorted items missing from her room.

On April 28, Yetta Vishnefsky, age 79, was found dead in her room at the Park Plaza. She had been raped, bound with her own nylon stockings, a butcher knife plunged to the hilt in her back. Items of clothing and jewelry were missing, along with a portable television set.

As spring gave way to summer, terror descended on the lonely tenants of the Park Plaza Hotel. Winifred Miller, 47, was strangled, raped, and robbed on June 8. Eleven days later, Blanche Vincent, 71, was suffocated and raped in her room, with death initially blamed on "alcoholism." Martha Carpenter, age 69, was suffocated and raped July 1. The death of Eleanor Platt, 64, on August 30, was initially dubbed "suspicious," without known cause; autopsy results confirmed she had been suffocated and raped after death. In each case, the murderer stole radios, televisions, or similar items worth a few hundred dollars.

On September 12, 1974, the slayer left his chosen hunting ground for the first time, striking one block away, on West 77th. That morning, Pauline Spanierman, 59, was found dead in her apartment, raped and strangled, with her television missing. A neighbor recalled seeing a man on the fire escape, lugging a TV set, around three o'clock in the morning, and detectives started searching door-to-door. They soon turned up the missing television, in a nearby flat, and were informed that it belonged to Calvin Jackson, who was staying with the tenants temporarily.

Police knew Jackson as a junkie-mugger, with a record of arrests for robbery and assault. His latest bust had occurred in November 1973; charged with burglary and felonious robbery, Jackson had bargained down to a misdemeanor, serving only thirty days. In retrospect, detectives wondered if they might be looking at a partial explanation for the killer's "vacation" during the winter of 1973–74. The clincher came when officers discovered that their suspect, 26 years old, was employed as a janitor at the Park Plaza Hotel.

In custody, Jackson readily confessed to all nine murders, stating that he often lingered with his victims for an hour or more, eating food from their refrigerators, watching carefully to make sure they were dead. When victims were molested, Jackson said, he always raped them after death. In testimony at his six-week trial, Calvin testified that his crimes were all committed to support his habit, leading prosecutors to inquire why it was necessary for his victims to be killed, their corpses violated. "Well," he told the court, "I guess I kind of broke wild there, you know?"

Convicted on an epic list of charges, Jackson was sentenced to eighteen consecutive terms of life imprisonment. With time for good behavior, he will theoretically be eligible for parole in the year 2030 A.D.

Japanese Sex Murders

Racism has played a role in various serial murders, but none more pathetic than the case of a 16-year-old auto mechanic arrested at Kashiwa, near Tokyo, in January 1967. Unidentified in the press because of his age, the prisoner's mother was Japanese, his father a black American soldier killed in the Korean war. The boy's mother subsequently married another American and moved to the United States, leaving her son behind in the care of relatives.

Shunned by other children as a half-breed, ridiculed for his appearance, the boy grew up wild and undisciplined, with a record of thievery beginning in junior high school. One of his teachers recalled that the youth "had a complex about his color," and he quickly learned to despise females since, in the words of the Japanese press, "every young woman laughed at him with scorn."

His answer to that scorn, between December 1966 and January 1967, was a spree of rape and murder, claiming three victims in different towns over a six-week period. Arrested January 27, he confessed his crimes and offered detectives the only available motive. "I hate my hair and skin," he said.

Johnson, Milton

An Illinois native, born in 1951, Johnson was convicted at age 19 of raping a Joliet woman, torturing his victim with a cigarette lighter in the process. The charge carried a sentence of 25 to 35 years in prison, with a consecutive term of five to ten years added on conviction for burglary. Even with "good time," Johnson should have been confined until April 1986, but authorities saw fit to release him more than three years prematurely, on March 10, 1983. Their generosity would cost at least ten lives.

For two long months, between June 25 and August 25, 1983, Joliet and surrounding communities were terrorized by a series of random "weekend murders," marked by savage violence. Law enforcement officers were mobilized to sweep Will County in a search for suspects, but the killer managed to elude them, slaughtering his victims with impunity, while residents stocked up on guns and ammunition in their own defense.

The crime spree started with the death of two Will County sisters on Saturday, June 25. A week later, on July 2, Kenneth and Terri Johnson were shot to death without apparent motive, the woman's body discarded in southwestern Cook County. Five persons—including two deputy sheriffs—were killed on Saturday, July 16, in what authorities termed a "random wholesale slaughter." The next evening, 18-year-old Anthony Wackett was shot to death, his fiancee raped and stabbed by a black assailant who left her for dead.

The violence escalated a month later. On Saturday, August 20, four women were shot and stabbed to death in a Joliet pottery shop, their handbags dumped nearby with money still inside. Once more, police were left without a solid clue in the slayings of proprietor Marilyn Baers, 46, and her three customers: 75-year-old

Anna Ryan; 29-year-old Pamela Ryan; and 39-year-old Barbara Dunbar. On August 21, the killer(s) shifted to Park Forest, in Cook County, binding 40-year-old Ralph Dixon and 25-year-old Crystal Knight before slashing their throats in Dixon's apartment, stabbing the woman 20 times. The murder of 82-year-old Anna Johnson broke the pattern, falling on Thursday, August 25, and a suspect was swiftly apprehended in that case, leaving seventeen murders unsolved.

On March 9, 1984, Milton Johnson was arrested while visiting his parole officer, charged with aggravated battery and deviate sexual assault in the rape of Anthony Hackett's fiancee. Officers focused on Johnson after repeated complaints of a black pickup driver harassing Joliet women over the past two weeks, ending when one of the victims memorized Johnson's license. Evidence collected at various murder scenes—including fibers, fingerprints, and a sales receipt bearing the name of Johnson's step-father—linked Johnson to ten of the Will County murders, including Hackett's, the pottery shop massacre, and the carnage of July 16. (The receipt had been found beneath one of the murdered officers.) In addition to those cases, police saw a "strong possibility" of Milton's participation in the July 2 murders of Kenneth and Terri Johnson.

Granted a change of venue on grounds of pretrial publicity, the defendant waived his right to trial by jury in the Hackett case. Convicted on all counts in September 1984, he was sentenced to death. Four months later, on January 23, 1986, Johnson was convicted of quadruple murder in the ceramic shop massacre, a second death sentence pronounced five days later. Prosecution in five other slayings was indefinitely deferred.

Jones, Genene

In February 1983, a special grand jury convened in San Antonio, Texas, investigating the "suspicious" deaths of 47 children at Bexar County's Medical Center Hospital over the past four years. A similar probe in neighboring Kerr County was focused upon the hospitalization of eight infants who developed respiratory problems during treatment at a local clinic. One of those children had also died, and authorities were concerned over allegations that deaths in both counties were caused by deliberate injections of muscle-relaxing drugs.

Genene Jones, a 32-year-old licensed vocational nurse, was one of three former hospital employees subpoenaed by both grand juries. With nurse Deborah Saltenfuss, Jones had resigned from Medical Center Hospital in March 1982, moving on to a job at the Kerr County clinic run by another subpoenaed witness, Dr. Kathleen Holland. By the time the grand juries convened, Jones and Holland had both been named as defendants in a lawsuit filed by the parents of 15-month-old Chelsea McClellan, lost en route to the hospital after treatment at Holland's clinic, in September 1982.

On May 26, 1983, Jones was indicted on two counts of murder in Kerr County, charged with injecting lethal doses of a muscle-relaxant and another unknown drug to deliberately cause Chelsea McClellan's death. Additional charges of injury were filed in the cases of six other children, reportedly injected with drugs including succinylincholine during their visits to the Holland clinic. Facing a maximum sentence of 99 years in prison, Jones was held in lieu of $225,000 bond.

An ex-beautician, Jones had entered nursing in 1977, working at several hospitals around San Antonio over the next five years. In early 1982, she followed Dr.

Holland in the move to private practice, but her performance at the clinic left much to be desired. In August and September 1982, seven children suffered mysterious seizures while visiting Dr. Holland's office, their cases arousing suspicion at Kerr County's Sid Peterson Hospital, where they were transferred for treatment. Jones was fired from her job on September 26, after "finding" a bottle of succinylincholine reported "lost" three weeks earlier, its plastic cap missing, the rubber top pocked with needle marks.

(In retrospect, Dr. Holland's choice of nurses seemed peculiar, at the very least. Her depositions, filed with the authorities, maintain that hospital administrators had "indirectly cautioned" her against hiring Jones, describing Genene as a possible suspect in hospital deaths dating back to October 1981. Three separate investigations were conducted at Bexar County's hospital between November 1981 and February 1983, all without cracking the string of mysterious deaths.)

On November 21, Jones was indicted in San Antonio, on charges of injuring four-week-old Rolando Santos by deliberately injecting him with heparin, an anticoagulant, in January 1982. Santos had been undergoing treatment for pneumonia when he suffered "spontaneous" hemorrhaging, but physicians managed to save his life. Their probe continuing, authorities branded Jones as a suspect in at least ten infant deaths at Bexar County's pediatric ward.

Genene's murder trial opened at Georgetown, Texas, on January 15, 1984, with prosecutors introducing an ego motive. Like New York's Richard Angelo, Jones allegedly sought to become a hero or "miracle worker" by "saving" children in life-and-death situations. Nurses from Bexar County also recalled Genene's plan to promote a pediatric intensive care unit in San Antonio, ostensibly by raising the number of seriously-ill children. "They're out there," she once told a colleague. "All you have to do is find them."

Jurors deliberated for three hours before convicting Jones of murder on February 15, fixing her penalty at 99 years in prison. Eight months later, on October 24, she was convicted of injuring Rolando Santos in San Antonio, sentenced to a concurrent term of 60 years. Suspected in at least ten other homicides, Jones was spared further prosecution when Bexar County hospital administrators shredded 9,000 pounds of pharmaceutical records in March 1984, destroying numerous pieces of evidence then under subpoena by the local grand jury.

Jones, Harold

In February 1921, eight-year-old Freda Burnell was abducted from her home at Abertillery, Wales, found raped and strangled next morning, in the outhouse behind a local shop. Suspicion focused on 15-year-old Harold Jones, an employee at the shop, and he was finally charged with the murder, acquitted by jurors on June 23 after a long and controversial trial.

Many locals still believed Jones was guilty, and their suspicions were born out in early July. On July 8, 11-year-old Florence Little disappeared from her home, and searchers launched a house-to-house sweep through Abertillery two days later, when no trace of the girl could be found in the surrounding mountains. At the Jones residence, officers found a trapdoor leading from Harold's bedroom into the attic, and there they discovered his latest victim, her throat slashed from ear to ear.

A measure of confusion was added to the case on July 14, with the arrival of a semi-literate note, allegedly penned by the killer. Signing himself "Duffy," the author described himself as a 46-year-old Irishman active in the militant Sinn Fein movement. "I think it very right," he wrote, "to kill all I can of England lad and girls."

Dismissing the letter as a hoax, authorities indicted Harold Jones for murder on July 22. In November, based upon Jones's confession to both murders, a magistrate imposed the maximum possible sentence for killers under sixteen, ordering that Jones be "detained during his Majesty's pleasure."

Jones, Jeffrey Gerard

A Sacramento native, born in 1960, Jones attended college in Arizona, and was sent home at age 22, after he "began to exhibit abnormal behavior." Psychiatrists diagnosed him as a chronic paranoid schizophrenic, prescribing anti-psychotic medication, but nothing seemed to help his condition. In early 1984, John Jones awoke one night to find his son beside the bed, a knife in hand, and by May Jeffrey was charged with robbing a disabled Davis resident, filing a plea of not guilty by reason of insanity. That November a probation report filed with the Yolo County court noted that therapy and medication had "stabilized" Jones, so that "the probability of threat to others is not significant at this time."

The full enormity of the mistake was driven home in early 1985. On January 21, Jones waylaid Harry Dong at Sutter's Fort, near Sacramento, using a claw hammer to slaughter his victim in a public restroom. Hours later, he struck at the University of California in Davis, battering John Rowland and leaving him for dead in a men's room at the campus medical center. On January 22, he staked out another restroom in the same building, hammering Dr. Michael Corbett to death. On February 18, Fred Morris was killed in identical fashion, at the UC Davis physics-geology building. In the wake of Jones's arrest and indictment, it was revealed that he had threatened "to do something bad" in a bid for commitment and psychiatric care.

Kelly, Horace Edward

On November 16, 1984, police officers in San Bernardino, California, were alerted to the discovery of a woman's body at a local cemetery. Nude from the waist down, with her bra unfastened, the victim had been raped before she was shot in the chest and neck with a .357 magnum revolver. She was identified as 25-year-old Sonia Reed, last seen at a drug party the night of November 15.

The following day, 42-year-old Ursula Houser was found dead in a San Bernardino alley, two miles from the Reed murder scene. Shot twice from behind with a .357, the victim had then been dragged 35 feet to concealment, where the gunman finished his assault by raping her corpse. Ballistics tests matched bullets from the two shootings, and investigators knew they had a serial killer on their hands.

Eight days elapsed before the next attack, in Riverside. Daniel Osentkowski, age 11, was walking his 13-year-old cousin home from a neighborhood store when they were accosted by a black man in uniform. The stranger drew a pistol and grabbed Osentkowski's cousin, dragging the girl toward a van parked nearby. Daniel waded in on the attacker, kicking the man's shins, freeing his cousin before the gunman opened fire. Osentkowski was fatally wounded, but the gunman fled empty-handed, his would-be victim providing police with descriptions of both man and vehicle.

That evening, 25-year-old Horace Kelly was stopped in a light green van, arrested when officers found a recently-fired .357 magnum in his vehicle. A native of

New Jersey, employed for the past two years as a security guard, Kelly first denied everything, then confessed when his surviving victim made a positive I.D. Convicted of murder and attempted murder in the Osentkowski incident, Kelly was sentenced to death on May 21, 1986. Eight months later, he was convicted on two counts of murder in San Bernardino, receiving another death sentence.

Khan, Sohrab Aslam

A Pakistani-born physician, Sohrab Khan obtained his medical training in the United States, specializing in cardiology. In the 1970s, he served as a fellow at Baylor University Medical Center Hospital in Dallas, Texas, returning to his native city of Lahore in 1981. Whatever homicidal fantasies were cultivated in his mind, Khan managed to conceal them through the fall of 1986, until, at forty-two, he lapsed into a month-long homicidal binge and slaughtered thirteen victims.

Four of those were gunned down on the evening of November 13, as Khan cruised Mall Road on a motorcycle, randomly blasting a dogcatcher, a night watchman, a laborer, and an unidentified transient. A week later, he shot two more night watchmen and a rickshaw driver, dumping their bodies in a canal. Another of his victims was a waiter, shot—Khan said—because he moved too slowly with the doctor's order.

Arrested on December 11, 1986, Khan was charged with thirteen murders and quickly obliged police with confessions in nine of the cases. A search of his home turned up a cache of unlicensed weapons, along with several false passports and sketches of various murder scenes, drawn from memory. Dubbing Khan "a maniac or saboteur who killed for the fun of it," Punjab Province Police Chief Sabahuddin Jami declared, "He is a beast, not a human being."

Kinne, Sharon

When James and Sharon Kinne were married in October 1956, it was a matter of necessity. At sixteen, she was pregnant, and while neither loved the other, marriage was "the thing to do" for teenage parents-to-be in Independence, Missouri. A miscarriage later removed the necessity of their union, but by then it was too late. By March of 1960, the Kinnes had a mortgage and two other children, but Sharon was restless, yearning for a life with someone other than a hometown boy who still included "shucks" in his vocabulary.

On March 19, police were summoned to the Kinne residence, where they found James lying on the bed, a bullet in his brain. Sharon told detectives that, apparently, their two-year-old daughter had been playing with a pistol when the weapon discharged, striking James. Police remarked upon the youngster's seeming familiarity with the weapon, including manipulation of its safety lever, and the death was ultimately ruled an accident.

Suddenly flush with insurance money, Sharon bought herself a new car, becoming "friendly" with the salesman, Walter Jones. On May 27, 1960, she placed a second call to the police, reporting her discovery of a woman's lifeless body on a lonely, wooded lane in rural Jackson County. Shot four times, the victim proved to be Patricia Jones, Walter's wife. Sharon explained that she was helping Walter look for his missing wife, whom he suspected of meeting another man in the secluded lover's lane. Instead of catching Patricia in *flagrante delicto*, they found her dead and called for the authorities.

Patricia Jones had been shot with a .22-caliber pistol, and investigators learned that Sharon had recently acquired such a weapon. She had asked a male co-worker to buy the gun for her, specifically requesting that it not be registered in her name. Indicted for murder in September 1960, Sharon was subsequently acquitted when ballistics tests indicated that the gun in her possession was not the murder weapon.

Upon release, Sharon was immediately re-arrested for the murder of her husband, homicide detectives having chucked the "accident" theory in favor of darker suspicions. A two-year-old child, experts testified at Sharon's trial in January 1962, could not have pulled the trigger on the gun that killed James Kinne. Convicted of murder and sentenced to life, Sharon fought the verdict through a series of appeals. The jury deadlocked in her third trial, unable to reach a decision; a fourth trial was scheduled for October 1964, but Sharon Kinne had other plans.

On September 14, Sharon and her new boyfriend, Frank Puglise, checked into the Hotel Gin, in Mexico City. Quarreling with her lover four days later, she went out alone and picked up a local radio announcer, Francisco Ordonez, returning with him to his motel room. A short time later, the proprietor heard shots and rushed to Ordonez's room, surprised to find Ordonez sprawled on the floor, two bullets in his heart. Sharon stood over the corpse, gun in hand, and as the manager retreated, she shot him in the shoulder. They were grappling for the gun when officers arrived, responding to reports of gunfire.

A Mexican court was unimpressed with Sharon's tale of self-defense, and she was sentenced to ten years in prison; an unsuccessful appeal resulted in three more years being added to her term. In the meantime, Kansas authorities had a chance to examine the gun that had killed Ordonez, discovering that it had also killed Patricia

Jones. New charges would be waiting if and when the prisoner discharged her sentence in a foreign jail.

Kipp, Martin

A full-blooded Blackfoot Indian, Kipp was the son of a prostitute who abandoned him at the age of twenty-two months. Adopted by relatives, he was raised by an alcoholic "father" who frequently beat Martin in public. Liberated by his guardian's death, Kipp left the reservation for a stint in the Marine Corps and was briefly stationed in Japan, where he won divisional honors in boxing.

Reassigned to the base at El Toro, California, Kipp began playing with a rock band in his leisure time. In June of 1981 he was accused of abducting and raping a woman he met at a tavern in Long Beach. Martin went AWOL in lieu of facing the charges, but was captured in Idaho and returned to California for trial. Convicted of rape, he was sentenced to three years in prison, serving an actual nineteen months before his release in 1983. (Early release was granted, in part, because Kipp had himself become a rape victim in prison.) He was already registered with Southern California authorities as a convicted sex offender when his violent urges surfaced once again.

On the evening of September 16, 1983, 19-year-old Tiffany Frizzell checked into the Ramada Inn on Pacific Highway, in Long Beach, California. A native of Washington state, she was hoping for a good night's rest before she had to register at Brooks College the next morning, signing up for classes and attempting to secure a dormitory room.

She never made it to the campus.

On September 17, a maid at the Ramada found the co-ed's body stretched out on her bed, stripped naked from the waist. She had been beaten, raped, and strangled in a cruel assault that the medical examiner called "animalistic," so swift and violent that self-defense was probably impossible.

Fifteen months elapsed before the killer struck again, just after Christmas 1984. Antaya Howard, 19, left her Orange County home to buy a pack of cigarettes on December 29 and never returned. On January 3, 1985, her car was found in Huntington Beach; inside, beneath a blanket, lay Antaya's body, fully-dressed, but with her clothing disarranged. Like Tiffany Frizzell, she had been strangled.

In the minds of homicide investigators, there was nothing to initially connect the crimes. Los Angeles and Orange Counties chalk up several hundred murder victims every year, and strangulation is a common mode of death. Moreover, there were obvious dissimilarities: Tiffany Frizzell, was white, Antaya Howard black; the former had been killed in her motel room, while the latter was abducted from the street, abandoned in her car. In short, aside from cause of death, there was no pattern visible to overworked investigators.

Working from a matchbook found beside Antaya Howard's body, officers checked out an all-night restaurant in Newport Beach, where witnesses recalled the victim talking to a man identified as Martin Kipp. A quick scan of Kipp's record put detectives on alert; they visited his Long Beach address and discovered he had lately been evicted by the paying tenants, who returned the evening of December 30 to find Kipp sleeping in a closet, clothing torn, deep scratches on his face. While they initially accepted Kipp's explanation that he had suffered a "hard night," his continual mooching of food and liquor led his long-suffering roommates to show him the gate in early January.

The coincidence of dates was damning, and a check of fingerprints on file matched Kipp's with latent prints recovered from Antaya Howard's car. Coincidentally arrested in Laguna Beach, on outstanding traffic warrants, Kipp was remanded to Orange County authorities for booking on a charge of rape and murder. Once in custody, Kipp faced a second murder charge filed in the case of Tiffany Frizzell, with police keeping mum on the nature of their evidence.

Delays kept Martin out of court until the latter part of 1987. In the meantime, still incarcerated, he was married to a paralegal aide assigned to help with details of his case. In April 1987, Kipp's bride was arrested on conspiracy charges, after she approached an undercover officer with plans to break Martin out of the Orange County jail. Pleading guilty, she escaped with probation, on the condition that she refrain from visiting her husband.

Kipp's trial, for murdering Antaya Howard, covered two full weeks in August 1987. Convicted on August 15, he was sentenced to die in the gas chamber at San Quentin. At this writing, he has not been tried for the murder of Tiffany Frizzell.

Klenner, Frederick Robert

Police knew Fred Klenner was dangerous when they spotted his van on the outskirts of Greensboro, North Carolina, on June 3, 1985. A month earlier, he had slaughtered a family of three at Winston-Salem, and he was also sought in connection with the 1984 murders of a mother and daughter in Prospect, Kentucky. Authorities were ready to subdue him in the case of physical resistance, but they never got the chance. When Klenner's van was stopped, he opened fire with a machine gun, wounding three officers in the initial burst of fire. Before they could respond in kind, he threw a switch and detonated an explosive charge inside the van, killing himself and his three passengers. Identified as 39-year-old Susie Lynch and her two sons, the latest dead were related by blood or marriage to all of Klenner's previous victims.

Klosovski, Severin Antoniovitch

Born in Poland on December 14, 1865, Klosovski was apprenticed to a surgeon at age fifteen. He studied for six years without obtaining a degree, later traveling the country as a barber-surgeon. Married in Prague, he was briefly employed at a hospital there, before spending a year and a half in the Russian army. Klosovski left his wife behind and moved to London in the early part of 1888, settling in the East End's dismal Whitechapel district.

Setting up shop as a hairdresser, Klosovski became a suspect in Scotland Yard's search for "Jack the Ripper" after police informants reported his attempts to purchase poison. Based upon that testimony, and the evidence presented at his murder trial fourteen years later, it seems improbable that Klosovski, a consistent poisoner, would change his modus operandi by slashing streetwalkers to death.

In London, Klosovski "married" a Polish immigrant, but their honeymoon was disrupted by his lawful wife's arrival on the scene. The women shared Klosovski for a time, living under the same roof, but his first wife soon grew tired of the threesome and vanished. Klosovski and his second "wife" moved to the United States in 1890; she returned to London without him in 1891, and Klosovski followed a year later, calling himself "George Chapman." Thereafter, "Chapman's" true name would remain a closely guarded secret, the diversion helping to obscure his past.

Klosovski/Chapman met his first known murder victim during 1895. An alcoholic matron of independent means, Mary Spinks lived with her new paramour for two years before moving to Hastings, where Klosovski used her money to open a hairdresser's shop in 1897. He sold out after only six months, returning to London and there leasing a tavern. Mary was taken ill a short time later, racked with convulsions and vomiting. When she died, on Christmas Day, the death certificate attributed her passage to "consumption."

In need of help, Klosovski advertised for a barmaid, selecting Bessie Taylor from the crop of applicants. They later "married," and Klosovski grew increasingly abusive over time, his violence making matters worse as Bessie's health began to fail. She died on February 13, 1901, of what physicians called "exhaustion from vomiting and diarrhea."

Maud Marsh was Bessie's new replacement in the bar and in Klosovski's bed. She became his "wife" in 1902, and soon displayed the familiar symptoms of her predecessors. The attending physician suspected poison, his questions prompting Klosovski to finish the job with a hefty dose on October 22, 1902. An unauthorized autopsy turned up lethal traces of antimony, and Klosovski was charged with murder on October 25.

Receiving word that "Chapman" was in custody, retired Inspector Frederick Abberline declared, "You've caught Jack the Ripper at last!" In fact, Klosovski never went to trial for any of the Ripper slayings, and the final number of his victims is unknown. Charged only in the murder of Maud Marsh, he was convicted on March 16, 1903, and sentenced to hang. He stepped through the trap three weeks later, on April 7.

Knoppa, Anthony Michael:
See Lanham, Harry

Knowles, Paul John

A Florida native, born in 1946, Knowles logged his first arrest at age 19, spending roughly six months of each year thereafter in jail, on various convictions for burglary and auto theft. He was serving time in Raiford when he began corresponding with California divorcee Angela Covic, and she visited the prison long enough to accept his proposal of marriage, shelling out money for lawyers to win his release. Parole came through in May 1974, and Knowles flew directly to San Francisco for the nuptials, but Covic had changed her mind, warned off by a psychic who foresaw the entry of a new, dangerous man in her life. The night she dumped him, Knowles allegedly went out and killed three people on the streets of San Francisco, but his claim has not been verified.

Back home in Jacksonville, Knowles was jailed after a bar fight, but he picked a lock and escaped on July 26, 1974. That night, he invaded the home of 65-year-old Alice Curtis, leaving her bound and gagged as he ransacked her house for money, finally taking off in her car. She choked to death on the gag, but Knowles hung around town for a few days, using her vehicle, until police connected him with the crime and his picture began turning up on TV. Preparing to drop the hot car on a quiet residential street, he spied 11-year-old Lillian Anderson and her seven-year-old sister Mylette, recognizing them as friends of his mother. Convinced the girls had seen him and would notify police, he kidnapped both of them and dumped their strangled bodies in a swamp outside of town.

The next day, in Atlantic Beach, Florida, Knowles broke into the home of Marjorie Howe, strangling her with a nylon stocking and stealing her television set. His next victim was a teenage "Jane Doe" hitchhiker, raped and strangled for sport as he drifted aimlessly, working his way north. On August 23, he invaded the home of Kathie Pierce, at Musella, strangling her with a telephone cord while her three-year-old son looked on, leaving the child unharmed.

On September 3, Knowles met businessman William Bates at a tavern in Lima, Ohio, sharing a few drinks before he strangled Bates and dumped his body in some nearby woods, where it would be discovered in October. Stealing money, credit cards, and Bates's car, Knowles made his way to Sacramento, back through Utah, pausing at Ely, Nevada, long enough to murder campers Emmett and Lois Johnson on September 18.

Three days later, passing through Sequin, Texas, he spotted a female motorist stranded at roadside and stopped "to help," raping her before he strangled her to death and dragged her body through a tangled barbed-wire fence. On September 23, he met beautician Ann Dawson in Birmingham and instantly caught her fancy; they traveled together, at her expense, until Knowles tired of the game and killed her September 29. Her body has never been found.

Knowles drifted on through Oklahoma, Missouri, Iowa and Minnesota, apparently keeping his nose clean, leaving no bodies behind. By October 19, he needed a "fix," and he found it in Woodford, Virginia, barging into the home of 53-year-old Doris Hovey, shooting her dead with her own husband's rifle, then wiping his prints from the gun and placing it beside her body. Afterward, police would find no signs of sex or robbery to offer them a motive in the case.

Still driving Bates's stolen car, Knowles picked up two hitchers in Key West, planning to kill them both, but his scheme went awry when a policeman stopped him for traffic violations. The careless officer let Knowles go with a warning, but the experience had shaken him. Dropping his passengers off in Miami, Knowles phoned his lawyer for advice. Rejecting a suggestion of surrender, he met the attorney long enough to hand over a taped confession, then slipped out of town before police were informed of his presence.

On November 6, in Macon, Georgia, Knowles befriended Carswell Carr and was invited home to spend the night. Over drinks, he stabbed Carr to death and then strangled Carr's 15-year-old daughter, failing in his attempt to have sex with her corpse. In the wake of his flight from Macon, Knowles was also suspected in the November 2 murder of hitchhiker Edward Hilliard, found in some nearby woods, and his companion Debbie Griffin (still, among the missing).

Bar-hopping in Atlanta on November 8, Knowles met British journalist Sandy Fawkes, impressing her with his "gaunt good looks." They spent the night together, Knowles unable to perform in bed, and he failed repeatedly at sex over the next two days, suggesting possible impotence with a willing companion. They separated on November 10, but Knowles picked up one of Sandy's friends, Susan MacKenzie, the next day, demanding sex at gunpoint. She escaped and notified police, but when patrolmen tried to stop him, Knowles brandished a sawed-off shotgun and made his escape.

In West Palm Beach, he invaded the home of invalid Beverly Mabee, abducting her sister and stealing their car, dropping his hostage off in Fort Pierce, Florida, the following night. A police officer recognized the stolen car next morning and pulled Knowles over, but Knowles was faster on the draw. Taking the officer hostage, he drove away in the patrol car, using its siren to stop motorist James Meyer, switching cars a second time. Burdened with two prisoners now, Knowles handcuffed both men to a tree in Pulaski County, Georgia, and shot each one in the head at close range.

A short time later, Knowles tried to crash through a police roadblock, losing control of his car and smashing into a tree. A chaotic foot chase ensued, with Knowles pursued by dogs and helicopters, finally cornered by an armed civilian on November 17. In custody, he claimed 35 murders, but only 18 could be verified. On November 18, while being transferred to maximum security, Knowles made a grab for the sheriff's revolver, and FBI agent Ron Angel shot him dead in his tracks.

Koedatich, James J.

Born in 1948, Koedatich committed his first known murder in Dade County, Florida, on June 13, 1971. The victim was his roommate, 40-year-old Robert Anderson, and Koedatich served eleven years on conviction of murder and robbery, winning parole from Raiford prison in August 1982. He moved north with the state's permission, settling in Morristown, New Jersey, and he lasted all of two months before his bloodlust surfaced again.

On November 23, 1982, Amy Hoffman, a high school cheerleader, was kidnapped from a Morristown shopping mall, fatally stabbed in the chest and back with a long-bladed knife, her body recovered from a rural water tank on Thanksgiving Day. Witnesses described her abductor, but police had no suspects in sight twelve days later, when 29-year-old Deirdre O'Brian was snatched from her car on a dark country road, raped and stabbed, then left for dead near Allamuchy, 20 miles from Morristown. She lived long enough to describe her attacker as "resembling a truck driver."

On the night of January 16, James Koedatich phoned police in Morristown, complaining that he had been stopped by an unknown assailant and stabbed in the back while driving through Morris Township, a quarter-mile from the scene of Deirdre O'Brian's murder. Authorities routinely checked his car as part of their investigation, noting that his tires matched tracks dis-

covered at the latest murder site. A further search
turned up sufficient evidence to warrant his arrest, and
Koedatich was held in lieu of $250,000 bail, formally
charged with Deirdre O'Brian's murder on May 12.
Seven months later, on December 15, he was also indicted for murdering Amy Hoffman.

Tried on the latter charge first, in October 1984,
Koedatich was convicted of murder, kidnapping, aggravated sexual assault, and unlawful possession of a
weapon with intent to kill. On October 29, he became
the first man sentenced to die under New Jersey's revised capital punishment statute. (Serial slayer Richard
Biegenwald was the second, in 1985.) Convicted of
Deirdre O'Brian's murder in May 1985, Koedatich received a sentence of life imprisonment when three jurors balked at voting the death penalty.

Komaroff, Vasili

Vasili Komaroff was known among his neighbors as
a friendly, smiling family man. He dealt in horses, and
maintained a stable at his home, in Moscow's
Shabolovki district. None who knew him well suspected that he might have been the "Wolf of Moscow,"
an elusive killer who had terrorized the neighborhood
and foiled police investigators in a two-year manhunt.

Times were hard and life was cheap in Russia, in the
early 1920s. Revolution and a grueling civil war had
trained the populace to live with danger, but the recent
spate of murders in the nation's capital were something
else, entirely. From the latter part of 1921, through
early 1923, police pursued the brutal executioner of
twenty-one male victims, each of whom had been discovered tightly bound in sacks, their bodies dumped on
waste ground in the Shabolovki neighborhood. The
corpses had been "trussed like chickens for roasting,"

and detectives noted they were nearly always found on Thursday or on Saturday.

The timing seemed to be no mere coincidence, considering the fact that horses went to market in the neighborhood on Wednesday afternoons and Fridays. It seemed probable that victims were selected from the market crowds, but probability and proof were two entirely different things.

At length, investigators heard about Vasili Komaroff from other traders in the district. It was curious, they said, that while Vasili seldom brought a horse to market, he was often seen to leave with customers. It might have been coincidence, and then again . . .

Detectives questioned neighbors of the Komaroffs, and learned that family man Vasili had a nasty, violent streak behind the ever-present smile. On one occasion, they were told, he tried to hang his eldest son—an eight-year-old—but was prevented by his wife, who cut the struggling victim down. A raiding party visited Vasili's stable, on the pretext of a search for bootleg liquor, and they found his latest victim, trussed and bagged, beneath a pile of hay.

In custody, the Wolf of Moscow readily confessed his crimes. In all, he reckoned he had murdered thirty-three prospective buyers, luring each in turn with promises of bargain prices, killing them in the seclusion of his stable. Robbery was cited as the motive, though he averaged barely eighty cents per man—a miserable $26.40 for the entire series of crimes. Vasili led his captors to the dumping grounds where five more corpses lay in burlap bags. He had disposed of half a dozen others in the Moskva River; their remains were never found.

The prisoner tried suicide three times, without success, thereafter trusting in the court to grant him speedy trial and execution. "I am fifty-two," he told reporters from his cell. "I have had a good time and don't want to live any longer." Questioned on the nature of his crimes, he spoke of murder as "an awfully easy job." Vasili told the press, "I killed a man who tried to beat me in a horse trade. He was the only one who ever resisted. It was very easy. I just knocked them on their heads with a hammer or strangled them."

His murder trial convened on June 7, 1923. Vasili's wife was also charged with murder, on the theory that she scarcely could have overlooked her husband's grisly homework. The proceedings were conducted in Moscow's huge Polytechnic Museum to accommodate gawkers, and Vasili seemed to take it well when, in the predawn hours of June 8, the court condemned him to be shot within the next three days. Departing for his cell, the Wolf of Moscow quipped, "Well, it's my turn to be put in the sack now."

An eleventh-hour change of heart resulted in appeals, delaying the inevitable, but the fate of the defendants had been sealed. On June 18, the Komaroffs were executed by a Moscow firing squad.

Landru, Henri Desiré

Born in Paris during 1869, the future "Bluebeard" was a bright student who studied mechanical engineering at age sixteen. He served four years in the army, rising to the rank of sergeant before his discharge in 1894. During the same period, Landru seduced his cousin and she bore him a daughter in 1891, becoming his wife two years later. On discharge from the service, he enlisted with a Paris firm requiring cash deposits from its new employees, but the owner soon absconded with his money, leaving Landru bitter at society in general.

He logged the first of seven felony arrests in 1900, sentenced to a two-year term for fraud. He drew another two years in 1904, thirteen months in 1906, and three years in 1908. While still imprisoned on the latter term, he was returned to Lille for trial on charges of swindling 15,000 francs from a middle-aged widow he met through a lonely-hearts ad in the newspaper. That conviction earned him another three years, but Landru accepted his punishment philosophically, fathering three more children during his brief vacations from prison.

Free on parole in 1914, Landru was suspected by police of various offenses and convicted in absentia, sentenced to a four-year prison term and lifelong deportation to New Caledonia, to be imposed upon his apprehension. He had nothing left to lose except his life, and by the outbreak of the war in Europe, he was risking that, as well.

In 1914, posing as "Monsieur Diard," he struck up an acquaintance with a widow, Madame Cuchet, and her 16-year-old son. Despite warnings from her family, the lady furnished a villa at Vernouillet and the three of them set up housekeeping. The Cuchets disappeared in January 1915, with Landru pocketing 5,000 francs on the deal and presenting his wife with the woman's gold watch, as a gift.

In early June 1915, Landru began courting another widow, Madame Laborde-Line. She sold off her furniture on June 21, telling friends she was going to live with her future husband at Vernouillet. Madame Laborde-Line was last seen alive on June 26, after which Landru sold her securities and other belongings for cash.

Meeting his victims through lonely-hearts ads had become a routine, and by the time he disposed of his second mark, Landru had two more waiting in the wings. A Madame Guillin, 51, joined him at Vernouillet on August 2, and Landru sold off her securities a few days later. By December, a series of forged documents had siphoned 12,000 francs from the missing woman's account.

Calling himself "Dupont," Landru rented a villa at Gambais, south of Paris, in December 1915. His latest paramour, Madame Heon, joined him there on December 8, and was never seen again. Her friends were briefly pacified by notes from Landru, each explaining that the woman could no longer write herself, because of failing health.

Victim number six, Madame Collomb, had maintained correspondence with Landru since May 1915, accepting his pledges of true-blue affection. She moved into his Gambais villa in November 1916, but their romance was short lived, the lady vanishing on Christmas day.

In January 1917, Landru met a young servant girl, Andree Babelay, at the railway station, offering her a place to stay while she looked for work. On March 11, Andree told her mother she was engaged, and she moved in with Landru full-time on March 29. Penniless, she had nothing to offer in terms of financial rewards, but her days were still numbered. By April 12, she had vanished without a trace.

In July, after more than two years of running correspondence, Landru began courting Madame Buisson. They boarded the train for Gambais on August 19, and she was seen no more. Suspicious relatives launched their own investigation in the face of police indifference, and began comparing notes with the family of Madame Collomb.

Landru, meanwhile, continued his courting apace. Madame Jaune met her husband-to-be through a matrimonial agent, moving to Gambais on November 25, 1917; five days later, Landru cleaned out her bank account. Madame Pascal joined the list on April 5, 1918, her furniture sold as an afterthought. Madame Marchadier accepted Landru's proposal on New Year's Day, 1919; she moved to Gambais two weeks later ... and vanished.

Pressure from the Buisson and Collomb families eventually forced police to arrest Landru on April 12, 1919. A notebook was found, bearing cryptic notations of each of his victims, but excavations around his villa unearthed only the remains of three dogs. No trace of his human prey was ever found, and Landru remained uncooperative, certain that he must go free in the absence of bodies.

Prosecutors disagreed, and his trial at Versailles, in November, became a sensation. Neighbors from Gambais recalled the rancid smoke sporadically produced by Landru's chimney, and the court was satisfied. Convicted of murder, he was sentenced to die in spite of the jury's recommendation for clemency. Taking his secrets to the grave, Landru was guillotined on February 23, 1922.

Lanham, Harry, and Knoppa, Antony Michael

On November 3, 1971, the body of 16-year-old Adele Crabtree was found outside Conroe, Texas. Last seen alive at a "hippy" commune in Houston, she was fully clothed when found, her death attributed to close-range shotgun blasts. The same day, Linda Sutherlin was reported missing in Houston, when she failed to come home after work. Police retrieved her blood-stained car, but five more days would pass before her corpse was found near Pearland, in Brazoria County. A pair of nylon pantyhose was tied around her neck, but death was the result of shotgun blasts.

Investigators learned that Sutherlin had stopped in a neighborhood bar after work, on the night she disappeared. Witnesses recalled her talking to one Harry Lanham, a tow-truck driver once convicted of rape, more recently charged with beating his girlfriend and her five-year-old daughter. Picked up for questioning on December 8, Lanham refused to cooperate with police, but he was careless with his cellmate, making reference to "his own private graveyard."

The pressure of surveillance and interrogation finally got to Lanham, during April 1972, and he fingered an acquaintance, 24-year-old Tony Knoppa, in the Sutherlin murder. Previously charged with rape, Knoppa had been sentenced to seven months even after the victim changed her story. Back in jail on suspicion of murder, he was outraged by Lanham's fancy footwork, informing detectives that Harry was the triggerman in both the Sutherlin and Crabtree slayings.

In the wake of his prior rape conviction, Knoppa said, Lanham had vowed to silence his future victims, insuring against further jail time. "He said I should stick with him," Knoppa testified, "then I'd see a lot of women killed." Their typical M.O. involved picking up hitchhikers, women in bars, or stranded motorists, transporting them to a vacant house for multiple rapes, after which they were driven into the countryside and shot. In custody, Lanham was also linked with the murder of 13-year-old Collette Wilson, from Alvin, Texas, whose bones were found with those of Houston victim Gloria Gonzales, missing since October 1971. Convicted on all counts, Lanham and Knoppa were sentenced to life imprisonment.

Laskey, Posteal

Between October 1965 and December 1966, female Cincinnati residents were terrorized by a series of stranglings and sexual assaults, recalling memories of recent turmoil generated by the "Boston Strangler." Seven women died and one was injured in the space of fourteen months, the ultimate conviction of a suspect in a single case relaxing tension only when the murders ceased, thereby supporting homicide detectives in their claim that all eight crimes had been committed by a single man.

The killer blew his first attempt, on October 12, 1965, when he beat and raped a 65-year-old woman, failing in his effort to strangle her with a length of plastic clothesline. Two months later, on December 2, his weapon was the same, employed to strangle Emogene Harrington in the basement of her own apartment building. Police linked the two crimes in theory, but the panic was yet to come.

On April 4, 1966, 58-year-old Lois Dant was raped and strangled in her first-floor Cincinnati apartment. Two months later, on June 10, 56-year-old Jeannette Messer was found in a city park, raped and strangled with a necktie. On October 12, Mrs. Carl Hochhausler, 51, was found by her daughter in the family garage, beaten, raped and strangled to death by an unknown assailant. Eight days later, in a crime that police called "an exact copy" of the previous murders, 81-year-old Rose Winstsel was savagely beaten in her home, strangled with the electric cord of a heating pad. Authorities were less certain in the death of octogenarian Lula Kerrick, found in the elevator of her apartment building on December 9. The strangulation looked familiar, granted, but she had not suffered sexual assault.

A few days later, suspect Posteal Laskey was arrested and charged with the "similar" slaying of a seventh victim, Barbara Bowman. Convicted and sentenced to life for that crime, Laskey was never charged in the other stranglings, but police remain confident of his guilt, an assumption seemingly supported by the abrupt cessation of murders after his arrest.

Lee, Bruce

Born Peter George Dinsdale in 1960, Lee was the son of a British prostitute, afflicted from birth with epilepsy, partial paralysis, and a deformed right arm. Until the age of three, he lived with his maternal grandmother, afterward joining his mother and her common-law husband until the relationship disintegrated. Until the age of sixteen, he attended a school for the physically handicapped, and was there introduced to homosexual practices that, in the words of his prosecutors, "eventually led to his downfall and discovery." At age nineteen, Lee changed his name to emulate the famous kung-fu film star whom he idolized.

A classic pyromaniac, Lee would explain in his confessions that a tingling in his fingers signalled him that it was time to light a fire. His first act of arson, at age nine, caused more than $30,000 damage to a shopping center. Lee's normal technique involved dumping paraffin through a mail slot, followed by a match to light the fuel.

Lee scored his first fatality in June of 1973. On January 5, 1977, eleven elderly men were killed and six rescuers injured when he torched a local rest home. Slapped by an old man in an altercation over Lee's disturbing some pigeons, Bruce threatened to kill his assailant. Later, the birds were all found with their necks wrung, and the man was burned to death in his armchair. The death was ruled an accident until, years later, Lee confessed that he had found the man asleep and set his clothes on fire with paraffin.

In 1980, a house fire on Selby Street, in Hull, killed Edith Hastie and her three sons. Police found paper, soaked in paraffin, near the front door, but the Hasties were so unpopular with their neighbors that everyone in the vicinity was suspect. Some 18,000 persons were questioned before police discovered that Charles Hastie, one of the victims, was acquainted with various homosexuals who patronized public restrooms near his home. A group of suspects were rounded up, including Lee, who confessed to a series of fires spanning the past eleven years. In all, 26 persons had died by his hand, and multiple charges of manslaughter were filed.

Pleading guilty on all counts, Lee was sentenced to an indefinite term in a mental hospital. As his prosecutor remarked, "The sad fact is that this is his only real accomplishment in life, and something he had expressed himself as being proud of." Lee described his motive more compellingly. "I am devoted to fire," he said. "Fire is my master, and that is why I cause these fires."

Lehman, Christa

Born in 1922 at Worms, Germany, young Christa Ambros lost her mother to an asylum while still in her teens. Neglected by her father, she grew up wild and undisciplined, serving a term of probation on conviction for petty theft. In 1944, she married an alcoholic named Karl Lehman, responding to his inattention with several affairs that became open secrets in her hometown.

On September 17, 1952, Karl Lehman died at his home, in convulsions, a doctor listing the cause of death as a ruptured stomach ulcer. Thirteen months later, on October 14, 1953, Christa's father-in-law collapsed on the street and died in convulsions, twenty minutes after leaving her house. Ignoring the strange coincidence, authorities accepted another verdict of death by natural causes, and the case was closed.

On February 15, 1954, Christa handed out chocolate truffles to some of her neighbors, with startling results. One recipient, Annie Hamann, bit into a piece and pronounced it bitter, lapsing into convulsions and death a short time later. A dog that ate the truffles also died, and tests revealed traces of a new phosphorous-based pesticide, known as E-605.

Arrested on February 23, Lehman confessed to spiking the truffles with poison in an effort to kill elderly Eva Ruh, a neighbor who lived with Annie Hamann. Ruh had earned Christa's animosity by criticizing her friendship with Hamann, but the murder scheme backfired, landing her in court on multiple homicide charges. Lehman was convicted on September 20 and sentenced to life, reports of her trial ironically prompting dozens of Germans to purchase E-605 and commit suicide.

Lewingdon, Gary James and Lewingdon, Thaddeus Charles

Between February and December 1978, residents of Columbus, Ohio, were panicked by a string of random, senseless murders, characterized by nocturnal ambush and home invasions, with victims shot numerous times in the head at close range. Police were stymied in their search for the ".22-caliber Killer," and only a clumsy mistake by one gunman prevented the crimes from continuing indefinitely.

On February 12, 1978, a prowler invaded the home of nightclub owner Robert McCann, executing McCann, his mother Dorothy, and live-in girlfriend Christine Herdman with multiple shots to the head. Robbery appeared to be the motive, but police were less certain on April 8, when 77-year-old Jenkin Jones was gunned down in his home, shot six times in the head, with four dogs killed nearby.

The same gun was used in both crimes, and ballistics tests matched again, on April 30, when Rev. Gerald

Fields was killed in Columbus, while working part-time as a security guard. Three weeks later, on May 21, the gunman cornered 47-year-old Jerry Martin and his wife, 51-year-old Martha, in their home, snuffing both victims with close-range shots to the head.

Police played a hunch, dusting off their files on an unsolved shooting from December 1977. Joyce Vermillion and Karen Dodrill had been ambushed on December 10, gunned down after work at a Newark, Ohio, restaurant, and detectives examined the nine rounds retrieved from their bodies. Again, the bullets matched, and that made nine dead, in a little over five months time.

The final victim, 56-year-old Joseph Annick, was robbed of his wallet and shot nine times in his own garage, on December 4, 1978. A different .22 was used, but homicide investigators recognized the classic style of over-kill, and none of them had any doubts when Annick joined the victims list as number ten.

The case broke on December 9, when 38-year-old Gary Lewingdon presented Annick's stolen credit card to a clerk in a local department store. Arrested on the spot, he was detained on suspicion of murder while detectives examined his rap sheet. Discharged from the air force in 1962, Lewingdon had lived with his mother until 1977, when he married one of victim Robert McCann's nightclub waitresses. Along the way, he had logged arrests for petty larceny, possession of criminal tools, indecent exposure, and carrying a concealed weapon. None of the charges had led to conviction, but this time detectives were sure that they had their man cold.

In custody, Lewingdon swiftly confessed his role in the ".22-caliber murders," fingering his brother, Thaddeus, as the other trigger man. Search parties recovered the murder weapons, stolen from a gunshop in November 1977, and the brothers were indicted on December 14, with Gary facing 20 felony counts, while Thaddeus was hit with 17.

On February 19, 1979, Thaddeus Lewingdon was convicted of the Vermillion, Dodrill, and Jones homicides. A month later, on March 26, he was convicted of the McCann-Martin murders and sentenced to six terms of life imprisonment. Brother Gary went to trial, for all ten homicides, on May 14; twelve days later, the jury convicted him of eight counts, failing to reach a verdict on two others. His sentence was fixed at eight consecutive life terms, plus a $45,000 fine.

Liberty, Robert Willard

Robert Liberty first met Marcela Landis in an Orange County, California, mental institution, where both were confined after failed suicide attempts. He was attracted to the woman, eight years older than himself, and their relationship appeared to blossom on release, but Liberty was closer to the edge than anyone had realized. In 1966, he strangled Landis in her Westminster apartment, laying her body out on the couch with a Bible on her chest and candles burning at her feet. When the police arrived, he sat nearby, strumming a guitar by candlelight and humming to himself.

The courts found Liberty insane and packed him off to a state hospital for treatment. He was released September 15, 1969, after a panel of six psychiatrists voted him sane, no further menace to society. As we have seen too often in the past, their vote of confidence was rather premature.

On March 12, 1970, in Huntington Beach, California, Liberty shot and killed his former roommate, Thomas Astorina, in an argument about a television set. Police were still without a suspect three months later, on June 7, when authorities in San Diego found the battered corpse of Robert Irion, age 53, in his apartment. There were candles burning near his body, and a note was mounted on the closet door. It read: "The candle-light killer strikes again."

Investigators learned that Irion and Liberty had logged some time together, in the state hospital, and the killer's MO made a positive match. Liberty and a female companion had fled San Diego in Irion's car, but they were captured three days later, by police in Colorado Springs. Returned for trial, the slayer with a taste for candlelight would find the courts less sympathetic on the second time around.

Lockhart, Michael Lee

A drifter who has left his tracks from coast to coast, Mike Lockhart was paroled from a Wyoming prison in December 1986. Authorities suggest that over fifteen months, from Christmas 1986 through March of 1988, he was responsible for crimes including grand theft, robbery and rape, selecting victims from Wyoming to the Florida panhandle, with intermediate stops in Missouri, Illinois, Indiana, Ohio, Texas, and Louisiana. If detectives are correct, he also claimed at least four lives along the way.

By June 1988, Lockhart was back in jail, charged with raping his wife in Toledo, Ohio, and stealing a salesman's new car. Police "know for a fact" that Lockhart assaulted a Chicago woman on October 12, 1987, forcing her into an alley where he stole her purse and slashed her skirt with a knife. The killings charged against him started one day later, fifty miles away.

On October 13, Wendy Gallagher was murdered in Griffith, Indiana, southeast of Chicago, stabbed 21 times by her killer. Three months later, on January 20, 1988, a 14-year-old girl was knifed to death in Land

O'Lakes, Florida. Both victims were attacked in their homes, choked unconscious and raped before their assailant wielded his knife in a maniacal frenzy.

On March 22, Lockhart surfaced in Beaumont, Texas, where he killed a police officer and was subsequently arrested, held in lieu of $1 million bond. He was connected with the Indiana case when homicide detectives started sharing information, and his fingerprints were matched to suspect prints from Wendy Gallagher's apartment. Charged with Wendy's homicide June 17, the drifter faces further accusations in the murder of a co-ed at Vincennes University, in Indiana. At this writing, police in several other states are scrutinizing unsolved murders and assaults, in search of Lockhart's grisly "signature."

Long, Neal Bradley

A native of Dayton, Ohio, born in 1927, Long was a violent racist who could not abide the specter of black progress in his home community. In 1966, he approached local police and confessed to stabbing a black man in 1944, but he was released when detectives could find no record of the crime in their files. They had forgotten about Long by the early 1970s, when a three-year series of shootings left six blacks dead and fourteen others wounded, pushing Dayton toward the brink of racial war.

The catalyst for Long's final rampage was a school desegregation program that included busing students— Neal's 12-year-old son among them—from one school to another in the interest of "racial balance." On September 19, 1975, Long picked his boy up from school at the end of the day and promised, "You won't be bused any more, son."

An hour later, Dayton's white desegregation

planner—Dr. Charles Glatt—was shot four times and fatally wounded in his office at the federal building. Long was arrested near the scene, and FBI agents noted his resemblance to descriptions of an unknown gunman in a score of shootings logged since 1972. Indicted on seven counts of murder, Long was found competent for trial in November 1975 and was eventually convicted of two counts, drawing consecutive terms of life imprisonment. To protect him from black inmates—and vice versa—Long was confined at the U.S. Medical Center for federal prisoners in Springfield, Missouri, under conditions of maximum security.

Los Angeles—
Unsolved Murders (1982)

Between the months of August and October 1982, Los Angeles police were mobilized to track a prowling gunman who selected random motorists as targets, imitating New York's "Son of Sam." Before the rampage ended—with the gunman still at large—two victims had been killed and three more wounded in a spate of sudden, unprovoked attacks.

The first two victims, killed in August, were a local oceanographer and a vacationing student from Princeton University. On September 4, 51-year-old Jack Listman was wounded by shots fired through a window of his car, while he was waiting for the lights to change at a Los Angeles intersection. In the week of October 11 to 15, two Beverly Hills women were wounded in separate shooting incidents, apparently by the same gunman.

Detective Sherman Oakes could offer little hope for a solution in the case when he addressed the media in mid-October. Describing the gunman's technique,

Oakes said, "He just walks up, never says a word, and starts shooting. Once the victim is dead, he then goes through the victim's pockets." Moving on or tiring of his game with the October shootings, L.A.'s phantom gunman faded from the scene, still unidentified, to be replaced by other random killers in the coming months.

Lover's Lane Gunman— Atlanta, GA

While homicide detectives in New York were stalking the elusive "Son of Sam," their counterparts in Georgia were attempting to identify a killer with a similar M.O., who preyed on couples parked on darkened lanes, attacking from the shadows, interrupting passion with the searing blasts of point-blank gunfire. In Manhattan, officers eventually bagged a suspect; in Atlanta, there was no such luck. As this is written, Georgia's phantom gunman still remains at large.

The stalker's one-man war began on January 16, 1977, when police were summoned to the scene of a peculiar auto accident. A single vehicle had veered across an intersection, terminating its erratic course when it collided with a traffic sign. Inside, a naked man lay slumped behind the steering wheel, his face and body streaked with blood. A woman—also nude and bloody—lay behind him, in the back seat, covered by a coat.

The victims were identified as LaBrian Lovett, 26, and Veronica Hill, age 20. Lovett had been shot four times—in the head, stomach, right leg, and left arm; his companion had suffered two wounds, in the left leg and abdomen. Both died at the hospital, but investigators determined they were shot while making love in nearby Adams Park.

Police were playing the percentages, investigating jealous friends and lovers, when the killer struck a second time, attacking in the pre-dawn hours of February 12. This time, his targets were a teenage couple necking in West Manor Park, three miles northwest of Adams Park. Approaching their car at 2:45 a.m., the assailant—described as a large black man—fired six shots into the car before trying to open the locked doors. Frustrated, he fled on foot, leaving both victims with non-fatal chest wounds.

Jealousy went out the window as a motive when ballistics tests revealed that the same .38-caliber weapon had been used in both recent shootings. Likewise, the gunman seemed to have no interest in robbing his victims, nor in raping the women. Detectives were still puzzling over the motiveless crimes when their adversary made his third appearance in Atlanta.

On the night of March 12, Diane Collins, 20, was cuddling with her fiancee in Adams Park. They had announced their engagement a few days earlier, taking in a movie that evening before stopping in the park. Distracted, neither saw the gunman as he approached their vehicle, pumping six rounds through the window on the passenger's side. Diane was killed instantly, her fiancee wounded in the head. Despite the spurting blood that nearly blinded him, he put the car in motion, driving home on instinct, there to telephone an ambulance.

Police were baffled, but at least they had the bare suggestion of a pattern now. Twenty-seven days had elapsed between the first two attacks. Twenty-eight between their second and third shootings. If their man was hunting on a four-week cycle, homicide investigators theorized, they stood a decent chance of catching him by staking out the local parks on April 6–8.

The plan was logical enough, but it was wasted as the gunman vanished, calling off his lethal feud as suddenly and inexplicably as it began. Weeks lengthened into months without a new attack, and by the time a local newsman wrote a two-year retrospective article about the shootings, in March 1979, police were frank in their admission that they had no leads, no suspects in the case. Atlanta's phantom gunman—like the ripper who preceded him in 1912—is one of those who got away.

Ludke, Bruno

German born in 1909, Ludke was a petty thief and mental defective who derived sadistic pleasure from torturing animals. At age eighteen, he made the shift to human victims, stalking girls and women who aroused his hyperactive sexual desires. On one occasion, working as a roundsman for a laundry, he allegedly ran down a woman with his horse-drawn wagon, leaving her for dead. The atmosphere of violence in Nazi Germany facilitated Ludke's crimes, and if his own confessions are accepted, he was highly active in the early years of World War II. Arrested on a charge of sexual assault, he was sterilized on order of Himmler's SS, but the operation seemingly had no effect on his libido.

On January 29, 1943, Frieda Rosner, age 51, was found strangled in the woods outside Berlin, where she had been collecting firewood. Kriminal Kommissar Franz headed the investigation, beginning with a canvas of known criminals in the nearby village of Kopenick. One of them was Bruno Ludke, who admitted an acquaintance with the victim. When police asked Ludke if he was responsible for Rosner's death, he ran amok, assaulting his interrogators, and was physically subdued.

Upon reflection, Ludke made a full confession to the homicide, informing officers that under Paragraph 51—a law dealing with mental defectives—he was immune from indictment. Once he started talking, Ludke could not seem to stop, and his confessions ultimately listed eighty-five murders, committed since 1928. Although his victims were occasionally robbed, Ludke claimed rape as his primary motive. Kommissar Franz spent a year checking Ludke's confessions, emerging convinced that his suspect was guilty of numerous murders; conversely, some critics maintain that police saw the chance to unload open cases on Ludke and thereby save face.

Embarrassed by a case that now included the arrest of several blameless men for crimes confessed by Ludke, Nazi prosecutors opted for a cover-up. Immune to prosecution under law, Ludke was dispatched to Vienna as a subject for medical experimentation. He died there, from a chemical injection, on April 8, 1944.

Lyles, Anjette Donovan

A self-styled practitioner of black magic and voodoo, Anjette Lyles was born in Georgia during 1917. In 1958, authorities in Macon received an anonymous letter, charging that Lyles' daughter Marcia was being poisoned at home, and they felt obliged to investigate. The girl died before police intervened, but an autopsy revealed lethal traces of arsenic. The grieving mother spun a tale of accidental death, with Marcia eating poison during a game of "doctor and nurse," but homicide investigators weren't convinced. Their background search had turned up other family skeletons, including Anjette's last two husbands and one of her mothers-in-law. On exhumation, all three victims tested positive for arsenic, and Lyles was shown to have received insurance benefits upon the death of each. Convicted and sentenced to death at her trial, the defendant was later ruled insane by court psychiatrists, packed off to the state hospital at Milledgeville for life.

Macek, Richard O.

A native of McHenry, Illinois, Macek was 26 years old when he launched a two-state murder spree in 1974. On August 15 of that year, in Fontana, Wisconsin, he cornered Paula Cupit, a 24-year-old hotel maid, in one of the rooms she was assigned to clean, beating her and stabbing her in the heart before he began to gnaw and mutilate her body. Two months later, in Wauwatosa, the "Mad Biter" struck again, raping another maid, but his second victim survived to offer police a description of her assailant.

Macek shifted back to Illinois, murdering 26-year-old Nancy Lossman and her three-year-old daughter, Lisa, at Crystal Lake, before the end of the year. In July 1975, he invaded a Woodstock laundromat, battering a 20-year-old woman and leaving her for dead. Traced to San Bernardino, California, Macek was arrested on December 5, charged with the Wauwatosa rape and held in lieu of $175,000 bond. In custody, he signed confessions to the Fontana and Wauwatosa attacks.

In April 1976, Macek was committed to Wisconsin's Central State Hospital for an indefinite term, under provisions of the state's sex deviate statutes. Six months later, in Illinois, he drew a term of 50 to 70 years for attempted murder at Woodstock. On February 22, 1977, Macek pled guilty to Paula Cupit's murder in Wisconsin, receiving a life term from Judge Robert Gollmar (who also handled the case of Ed Gein). In September 1980, Macek was sentenced to 30 years for the Wauwatosa rape, and conviction of double homicide in Illinois earned him another sentence of 200 to 400 years in prison.

Depressed by the prospect of perpetual confinement, Macek opted for a shortcut. On March 2, 1987, he was found dead in his prison cell, hanging from an air vent with a pair of shoestrings looped around his neck. The death was ruled a suicide.

Mansfield, William, Jr.

The oldest son of a Florida child molester, Mansfield was born in 1956. In line with family tradition, he boasted a police record that included a one-year sentence for sex crimes in Michigan. Paroled in March 1980, he returned to the family home—a six-acre junk yard at Weeki Wachee Acres, near Tampa—and managed to last for three months before clashing with the law. A June 19 incident saw him charged with battery and false imprisonment of a young woman, and Mansfield departed for California in early September. Arrested in Santa Cruz on November 23, he was released on $1,500 bond. Two weeks later, when officers tried to correct the mistake, it was already too late for one of his victims.

Rene Sailing, age 30, was last seen alive when she left a California tavern with Mansfield, on December 6, 1980. Next morning her bullet-punctured body was recovered from a drainage ditch, and warrants were issued for Mansfield's arrest. He was captured days later, with 23-year-old brother Gary Mansfield, in Winnemucca, Nevada. William was held on charges of first-degree murder, his brother accused as an accessory after the fact.

On March 16, 1981, Hernando County deputies descended on the Mansfield home at Weeki Wachee Acres, bearing warrants for a search of the premises. Tipsters had informed them that a missing woman, 21-year-old Sandra Graham, of Tampa, might be buried on the property, and officers came prepared for full-scale excavation.

The first female skeleton, unearthed on March 17,

was identified only as a white woman in her twenties. Number two, discovered a week later, was that of 15-year-old Elaine Zeigler, a tourist from Ohio who disappeared from a nearby campground on July 1, 1976. Another "Jane Doe" surfaced on April 3, but authorities got lucky with the next skeleton, four days later, finally identifying the remains of Sandra Graham.

Two of the junkyard victims remain unidentified today, but Mansfield is also a suspect in other Florida homicides. Melinda Harder, 21, was a neighbor of Mansfield's, in St. Petersburg, when she disappeared on July 27, 1980. Another Ohio native, Carrol Barret, was abducted from her Daytona Beach motel room in 1980, shot to death and dumped beside a highway near Jacksonville. Mansfield fit the description of her killer, but eyewitnesses could make no positive I.D.

Ironically, police maintain that William Mansfield, Sr.—serving 30 years on a plea bargain to charges of child molestation—is not implicated in the series of murders. Neither, apparently, is Mansfield's mother, who claims total ignorance of the corpses planted within 40 feet of her home. No further skeletons were found at Weeki Wachee, and the excavations were abandoned by police in mid-April 1980.

Manuel, Peter

Born in New York City during 1927, Manuel was the son of British parents who returned to England five years later. He logged his first arrest, for burglary, at Coventry in October 1939, drawing a term of probation. Five weeks later, he was packed off to reform school on a charge of housebreaking. Manuel escaped to commit more thefts, and by 1942 he had been returned to the school eleven times. He committed his first sexual offense—an indecent assault on the wife of a school employee—shortly before Christmas 1942. Jailed for that offense in March 1943, he was released two years later. In March 1946, he was convicted on 15 counts of housebreaking and sentenced to prison; while serving his time, Manuel was also convicted of rape, with eight more years appended to his sentence. Released in 1953, he was briefly engaged, the relationship broken off after he mailed his fiancee an anonymous letter, detailing his criminal record.

On January 4, 1956, 17-year-old Anne Kneilands was found on a golf course at East Kilbride, south of Glasgow, her skull crushed by heavy blows. Although her clothing had been disarranged, there was no evidence of rape. Manuel was questioned in the case, as an habitual criminal, but he was released with no charges filed.

On September 17, 1956, Lanarkshire resident William Watt returned from a fishing trip to find his wife, their 16-year-old daughter, and a visiting sister-in-law murdered at his home, each shot through the head as they slept. Held for two months as a suspect in the massacre, Watt was finally released for lack of evidence. Ironically, he had been jailed with Peter Manuel, then serving time on an October burglary conviction that kept him behind bars until December 1957.

On December 20, 1957, 17-year-old Isabelle Cooke disappeared from her home in Mount Vernon. Nine days later, Peter Smart, his wife and 11-year-old son were found dead in their home at Uddingston, each shot through the head as they slept. Reckless spending led to Manuel's arrest on burglary charges, and he was charged with the Smart murders on January 14, 1958. Two days later, he signed confessions to eight homicides spanning the past two years, leading police to the buried remains of Isabelle Cooke, near her home.

Despite the confessions, Manuel mounted a spirited defense at his murder trial, in May 1958. Convicted on all counts, he was sentenced to die for his crimes, and he mounted the gallows on July 11.

Marquette, Richard Lawrence

A native Oregonian, from Portland, Marquette logged his first arrest in June 1956, on a charge of attempted rape. His victim failed to press the charge, and so her 21-year-old assailant was released. A few months later, he was held a second time, for disorderly conduct. In August 1957, Marquette tried to rob a Portland service station, clubbing the attendant with a sack full of wrenches. His guilty plea earned Richard eighteen months in jail, but he was turned out after twelve—for good behavior—and returned at once to Portland.

On June 5, 1961, a Portland housewife, Joan Rae Caudle, was reported missing by her husband when she failed to come home after shopping. Three days later, parts of a dismembered woman's body were discovered, scattered over several vacant lots around the southeast side of Portland.

Fingerprints identified Joan Caudle as the victim on June 14. Eyewitnesses had seen the murdered woman in a tavern on the night she disappeared; she had been killing time with Dick Marquette, a regular, and they had left the bar together.

A murder charge was filed against Marquette on June 19, and one day later he was named a federal fugitive, on charges of unlawful flight. His name was added to the FBI's "Ten Most Wanted" list June 29—the first time that the list had been expanded to include eleven names. The extraordinary step was warranted, the FBI decided, based on Marquette's demonstrated tendency toward violence and the threat he posed to women.

On June 30, one day after the release of Marquette's WANTED flyers, the manager of an employment agency in Santa Maria, California, recognized his newest client in the mug shots. Agents of the FBI were notified, and they surprised Marquette at work, repairing furniture for resale in a thrift shop. Seemingly relieved, the killer offered no resistance. "I knew the FBI would get me sooner or later," he told his captors.

According to Marquette, his victim had been picked up in a bar, and they had argued after having sex. He strangled her and then, impulsively, cut up her body to facilitate disposal. On July 2, Marquette led authorities to the missing remains. Convicted of first-degree murder in December, sentenced to a term of life imprisonment, his parting words to the court were a heartfelt "Thank God."

Paroled after only twelve years, Marquette slaughtered another female victim soon after his release, but escaped detection in that case. In April 1975, he dissected Betty Wilson in Salem, Oregon, and was arrested once again. In the absence of capital punishment, Marquette's second murder conviction earned him another sentence of life imprisonment, with theoretical eligibility for parole.

Maryland—Unsolved Murders

Between December 1986 and January 1987, five black women from the District of Columbia were murdered and their bodies dumped near Suitland, in Prince Georges County, Maryland. By September 1987, at least four more women were murdered in Washington, but the conviction of a suspect in one case has brought authorities no closer to solution of the rest.

The first victim, 20-year-old Dorothy Miller, was found in the woods near Suitland's Bradbury Recreation Center, on December 13, 1986. Killed by an apparent drug overdose, Miller had also been violently sodomized, a fact that linked her death with those of four other victims discovered a month later.

On January 11, 1987, young patrons of the recreation center noticed women's clothing hanging in a tree, nearby. Investigating, they discovered the body of 25-year-old Pamela Malcolm, missing from her Suitland home since October 22. An autopsy revealed she had been sodomized and stabbed to death.

On January 12, a team of 50 police recruits swept through the forest north of the U.S. Census Bureau's headquarters, seeking more clues in the two homicides. Instead of evidence, they found two more corpses, identified as 22-year-old Cynthia Westbury and 26-year-old Juanita Walls. Both had been reported missing from the District of Columbia—Westbury in mid-November— and both were sodomized, before or after they were stabbed to death.

Number five, 22-year-old Angela Wilkerson, was found near Suitland on January 13, and authorities reported that four of the victims had lived within a one-mile radius of each other, in Southeast Washington. All four of the D.C. victims were unemployed, and at least two had frequented the same restaurant, on Good Hope Road.

On January 15, another "profile" victim, 20-year-old Janice Morton, was found naked and beaten and strangled to death in a Northeast Washington alley. That investigation was still underway on April 5, when a nude "Jane Doe" was discovered near Euclid and 13th Street, Northwest, her body dumped in a secluded driveway. A 31-year-old suspect, Alton Alonzo Best, was indicted for Norton's slaying on April 7, and he confessed to the crime on June 9. Authorities say Best knew two of the Maryland victims, but the fact remains that his conviction did not stop the killing.

On April 10, with Best in jail, an unknown suspect in a van attempted to abduct a 25-year-old woman one block from the home of Suitland victim Pamela Malcolm. Police were still checking the facts five days later, when another black victim, Donna Nichols, was beaten to death in a Washington alley. On June 24, 21-year-old Cheryl Henderson was found in a wooded area of Southeast Washington, less than two miles from Suitland, with her throat slashed from ear to ear. Another female victim was discovered on September 21, at a Southeast Washington apartment complex, authorities refusing to discuss the cause of death or possible connections to their other "open" cases.

At this writing, the Maryland-Washington series of murders remains unsolved, the killer(s) still at large. His preference for blacks has led to speculation that the "Freeway Phantom" may have surfaced, after fifteen years of inactivity, but homicide detectives have revealed no evidence of a connection to the early unsolved crimes.

Matajke, Dorothy Jean

A resident of Nevada, Iowa, Dorothy Matajke began working as a nurse's aide and professional companion for the elderly and ailing in the 1970s. It came as no surprise to anyone when several of her patients died, and there were no suggestions of foul play except where money was concerned. In 1973, Matajke was convicted of fraud and sentenced to five years in prison. She escaped in February 1974 and remained at large until 1980, when she was recaptured and returned to finish out her sentence. Despite the prison break, she won parole in 1983, serving less than the original five years.

Upon release, Matajke moved to Little Rock and picked up with her old profession as a live-in nurse. On March 24, 1985, she moved in with Paul Kinsey, 72, and his wife Opal, age 71. When Opal died on April 5, the cause was listed as a recently-discovered cancer. Paul Kinsey's health began deteriorating rapidly after his wife's death, but relatives attributed his lapse to grief and loneliness.

On September 9, 1986, Matajke acquired a new client, elderly Marion Doyle. Another cancer patient, Doyle survived nine days of nursing by Matajke, but her death was not ascribed to cancer. Rather, a police report suggested that the woman had committed suicide. A routine inventory, made by the executor of Doyle's estate, discovered several checks made out to Dorothy Matajke, totaling almost $4,000. There was something curious about Doyle's signature, and on a hunch, her body was exhumed for reexamination. Tissue samples showed sufficient drugs to cause a fatal overdose.

Meanwhile, Paul Kinsey's health continued to decline. The old man stubbornly refused to eat or take his medication, telling relatives that every meal or dose prepared by his "companion" left him deathly ill. Kinsey ordered Matajke out of his house on October 28, and three days later he was hospitalized in critical condition. Dorothy Matajke bullied her way past relatives and doctors to visit her ex-patient in the emergency room, and she was still by his side when detectives arrived to arrest her.

Initially, the "nurse" was charged with forgery and theft for looting Marion Doyle's bank account. Subsequent charges included felony possession of a firearm, and additional counts of forgery relating to checks written on Paul Kinsey's account. A search of Matajke's home yielded mislabeled bottles of drugs and tranquilizers, along with three bottles of arsenic-based ant poison, and more serious charges were added.

On November 24, she was accused of first-degree murder in the death of Marion Doyle and first-degree battery in the non-fatal poisoning of Paul Kinsey. Opal Kinsey's body was exhumed December 5, with the results of laboratory tests kept secret pending disposition of the standing charges. After Paul Kinsey died, on February 10, 1987, assault charges were replaced with another count of first-degree murder.

In June 1987, Matajke was convicted of Paul Kinsey's murder and sentenced to life. Two months later, in a negotiated plea bargain, she received another term of 60 years for killing Marion Doyle. Charges are pending in the case of Opal Kinsey, and new investigations are expected in the deaths of several patients "cared for" by Matajke in Iowa.

Mathurin, Jean-Thierry:
See Paulin, Thierry

Meadows, Johnny

Between October 1968 and June 1971, a series of sadistic murders terrorized the female population of Odessa, Texas, and surrounding towns. Today, despite conviction of a suspect, controversy still surrounds the case and several of the murders are officially unsolved.

The murder spree began October 19, 1968, when an Odessa barmaid—Linda Cougat—vanished from a local laundromat. Two months would pass before her violated body was discovered in a field northwest of town, hands bound behind her back with one of her own nylon stockings, the other wrapped tightly around her throat.

On November 5, 1968, motel owner Dorothy Smith was found shot to death in her apartment in Monahans, Texas, her hands bound with television cable. Eula

Miller was the next to die, found nude in her Odessa flat on July 16, 1970, a victim of multiple stab wounds. Nancy Miller was abducted from her home in Kermit on September 16, while her children slept peacefully in an adjoining room. Her skeletal remains would be discovered on an oil lease south of town, in June 1971.

The first victim of 1971 was Ruth Maynard, wife of an Odessa policeman. Reported missing on January 9, she was found February 15, a few miles from the site where Linda Cougat was dumped by her slayer in 1968. On June 17, after Gloria Green disappeared from her secretarial job in Kermit, Texas lawmen realized they had a crisis on their hands.

The case was broken in December, when Texan Johnny Meadows was jailed in Aztec, New Mexico, on unrelated charges. Meadows started telling tales of murder, and Ector County Sheriff A.M. Gambrel flew in from Texas to interrogate the suspect. Cash changed hands, $2,000 paid from Gambrel's pocket to the suspect's wife, and Meadows gave directions to a vacant lot in South Odessa, where investigators found the skeletal remains of Gloria Green beneath a rotting mattress.

In 1972, Meadows pled guilty to murdering Gloria Green and was sentenced to 99 years in prison. Deputies announced that he had also signed confessions in the deaths of Linda Cougat, Dorothy Smith, and Ruth Maynard. Charges were filed in the Cougat and Maynard cases, but both indictments were dismissed in the summer of 1973. Ten years later, when Meadows made his first bid for parole, ex-Sheriff Gambrel testified in opposition to the killer's release. Gambrel warned the parole board that Meadows would "kill within forty-eight hours of the time he's paroled." Meadows's application was predictably denied.

(In 1984, prolific author J.R. Nash examined the Odessa case in *Open Files,* declaring it "unsolved." Ignoring the conviction and confessions of incarcerated slayer Johnny Meadows, Nash attributes fourteen murders to the "Texas Strangler," roping in some obviously unrelated homicides from Dallas to increase the bodycount. Meadows victims Cougat and Maynard are included in the list of women slaughtered by "the most murderous sex fiend in modern Texas history.")

Menarik, Carl

A native of Vienna, born October 2, 1889, Menarik immigrated to New York in 1914, obtaining a job at the German Odd Fellows Home, in Yonkers, during July of that year. Using the name "Frederick Mors," Menarik worked for six months at the home, arousing no suspicions as he went about his duties. Patients came and went throughout his tenure, several leaving in a hearse, but they were old and no one gave a second thought to their demise before the early days of February 1915.

On the afternoon of February 2, "Mors" presented himself at the district attorney's office, dressed in a corduroy hunting outfit, complete with knee-pants and a feathered alpine cap. Approaching the desk sergeant, Menarik confessed to the murders of eight "superannuated octogenarians," killed in order to "make room for more inmates" at the home. A phone call confirmed the eight deaths—all listed as natural—and Menarik was taken into custody.

In jail, Menarik's story underwent a sudden shift. The homicides had not been his idea, he now proclaimed, but rather had been ordered by officials at the home, who described the elderly victims as "a lot of trouble and no good anyhow." On February 5, the home's superintendent and three more employees were clapped into jail as material witnesses, with the Odd Fellows lodge refusing to muster their bail.

Although authorities refused to order exhumation of remains, investigation seemed to bear out Carl Menarik's tale of inmates killed with chloroform and arsenic. Menarik had warned patient Elizabeth Houser of her impending death a day in advance, and a mortician recalled red markings—similar to chloroform burns—on the face of alleged victim Henry Horn. A teenage inmate of the home informed police about an errand she had run on January 4, delivering a bottle of chloroform from employee Max Ring—jailed as a material witness—to "Mors," in the room occupied by patient Ferdinand Scholz. Scholz had died the same day, and other inmates suspected "Mors" of sabotaging the painter's scaffold that dropped Jacob Groh to his death on December 14.

The list went on, but prosecution was deferred in favor of a psychiatric test. Described as "not well mentally," Menarik was committed to Poughkeepsie's Hudson River State Hospital for the Insane. His employer and co-workers were released, the case dismissed with a host of questions still unanswered. On May 10, 1916—a week before his scheduled deportation to Austria—Menarik escaped from the hospital in Poughkeepsie and disappeared. He was never recaptured, but authorities took the loss in stride, announcing that the fugitive was "not considered dangerous."

Michigan—Unsolved Murders

Between August 1982 and March 1983, residents of Battle Creek, Michigan, were stunned by the local murders of three young women. Authorities suggested possible Satanic motives in the case, and while no link with devil-worship cults was never proved, the mere suggestion was enough to spread a pall of fear in Battle Creek.

The first to die was 20-year-old Margaret Hume, an ex-cheerleader and National Honor Society member, found strangled in the closet of her own apartment on

August 18, 1982. She had been living on her own for just three months before she died, her body hidden by a pile of clothes and bedding.

Patricia Rosansky, age 17, was walking to school on February 3, 1983, when she disappeared within two blocks of campus. She was found outside town on April 6, her skull crushed, body concealed by leaves and branches in a shallow ravine. "Street talk" linked her murder with a local Satan cult, and while no charges have been filed, police admit their leading suspect is a self-styled Satanist who boasts of leading black masses around Kalamazoo.

On March 13, 17-year-old Karry Evans disappeared from rural Bellevue, 13 miles from Battle Creek. Last seen walking near her grandparents' home, she was found by mushroom hunters on May 10, strangled to death, her body concealed by brush in a swampy area south of town. Once again, there were rumors of demonic involvement, with Evans describing her own occult beliefs in letters to friends, allegedly sporting a jacket with the Satanic emblem "666."

To date, no suspects have been named or prosecuted for the crimes in Battle Creek. With passing time, it seems unlikely that the case will now be solved, but homicide detectives still invite new leads, in hopes that someone, somewhere, may provide a crucial piece of evidence to break the stalemate.

Miller, Benjamin Franklin

Between 1967 and 1971, black residents of Stamford, Connecticut, were intimidated by a string of murders claiming female victims, four of whom were strangled with their own brassieres. Police reported that some of the victims were junkies, and three were known prostitutes, but the killer's apparent selectivity did nothing to calm a community under siege. By the summer of 1971, black citizens were ready to accuse police of negligence—or worse—in their long-running search for an elusive strangler.

Rose Ellen Pazda, 29, had been the first to die, reported missing on August 4, 1967, her skeletal remains recovered during April 1969. Donna Roberts, age 22, was found on May 3, 1968, the day after her disappearance from Stamford. The third victim, 21-year-old Gloria Conn, was strangled to death on September 7, 1968, with her body recovered next day, 200 feet from the spot where Roberts was found. The killer took three years off before strangling 19-year-old Gail Thompson, on July 10, 1971. Six weeks later, on August 22, he returned to claim the life of 34-year-old Alma Henry, her body discarded like so much rubbish.

Thus far, all the victims had died or been found within a quarter-mile radius of the Riverbank-Roxbury Road overpass. Four of the five were from Stamford, with one reported missing from nearby Mount Vernon, New York, and police found evidence of a car backing into the places where bodies were found, indicating that the killer hauled his victims in the trunk.

Accumulated evidence put homicide investigators on the trail of Benjamin Miller, a Darien post office clerk and self-ordained street preacher who spent most of his time with black congregations after his own church expelled him. Described by his former pastor as "almost a fanatic," Miller had moved to Connecticut from Illinois at eighteen years of age, in 1948. Employed at the post office for ten years, he talked religion on the job but otherwise ignored his fellow workers, keeping to himself whenever possible.

Committed to Norwalk's Fairfield Hills Hospital on February 17, 1972, Miller found detectives waiting when he checked out a month later. Arrested on March 17, he was charged with all five of the Stamford "bra murders," his apprehension restoring a measure of peace to the troubled community.

Minow, Paul

An epileptic printer's apprentice, Paul Minow found it impossible to satisfy the demands of his mother and sister, with whom he resided in downtown Berlin. Together, they nagged him incessantly about his "laziness," provoking Minow to fits of rage directed at others. In July 1907, he exploded, briefly terrorizing the city with a series of attacks on young children. Selecting female victims, all below the age of five, Minow lured four into alleys and doorways, stabbing each repeatedly about the abdomen with scissors. Three of his victims died; a fourth survived to give police a vague description of the slayer.

After one attack, a note was found nearby, pinned to the seat of a public bench with a single sharp scissor blade. It read:

Away, away; in five minutes there will be a corpse. There is a child murderer in the neighborhood. Deliver this note to the police. I have killed children in Belforter, Preinzlauer, and Henserdorfer Streets.

Detectives questioned twenty suspects in the case, but Minow was not among them. Confined to an asylum at Herzberge after the final attack, he surprised investigators in November 1907, with his detailed confessions to the crimes.

Moore, Henry Lee

A lethal drifter prone to violent rages, Henry Moore was prosecuted in December 1912 for murdering his mother and maternal grandmother in Columbia, Missouri. Both his victims had been slaughtered with an ax, and while the crime was grim enough, it barely scratched the surface of a bloody rampage spanning eighteen months, five states, and more than twenty homicides.

Discovery of Henry's secret came about when lawmen in Villisca, Iowa, requested federal assistance in solution of a local massacre, in June of 1912. An unidentified assailant had employed an ax to slaughter J.B. Moore, four children, and a pair of female visitors, the Stillinger sisters; police had bodies in abundance, but they had no clues. A federal officer, M.W. McClaughry, was assigned to the case, and his investigation indicated that the crime in Iowa was not unique.

Nine months earlier, in September 1911, six victims had been slain in Colorado Springs; the victims there included H.C. Wayne, his wife and child, along with Mrs. A.J. Burnham and her children. October was a busy month, with triple murder wiping out the Dewson family in Monmouth, Illinois, rebounding into Ellsworth, Kansas, where the Showman family—five in all—were slaughtered in their home. On June 5, 1912—mere days before the carnage in Villisca, Rollin Hudson and his wife were murdered in Paola, Kansas. Axes had been used in every case. In no case had a suspect been identified, and rumors of "a romance angle" in the Hudson crime produced no leads.

McClaughry was convinced that he was dealing with a transient maniac, but clues were still in short supply. Hard work, coincidence, and luck eventually saved the day. McClaughry's father was the warden of the federal penitentiary at Leavenworth, a man with far-flung contacts in the prison system. When he heard about the case of Henry Moore, already serving life in the Missouri lockup, he informed his son. Comparison of *modus operandi* in the several cases, capped by interviews with Moore, inspired McClaughry to announce, on May 9, 1913, that the books were cleared on twenty-three Midwestern homicides.

Ironically, there was a ghoulish post-script in the case that launched McClaughry's own investigation. In September 1917, a minister, the Reverend Lynn George Kelly, was arrested for the murders at Villisca. Kelly signed confessions, indicating that the massacre was perpetrated in response to God's direction. Booming astral voices had directed Kelly to a rubbish heap, where he retrieved a cast-off ax, and on from there, until he reached the home of J.B. Moore. Obeying his instructions to "slay utterly," the pastor crept inside and killed eight persons as he wandered through the house.

But there were problems with the minister's confession. On the same day they were publicized, George Kelly told his wife the documents contained "pure fabrications." Granted, he had signed the statements, but he was not sure precisely why. Approaching trial, he publicly recanted, and his ramblings seemed to bolster pleas of mental illness. That November, members of a jury spent four and a half hours deliberating evidence before acquitting Rev. Kelly on all counts. Despite McClaughry's confidence in Henry Moore's participation, the Villisca case, officially, remains unsolved.

Mors, Frederick:
See Menarik, Carl

Murphy, Donald

Detroit police had fifteen unsolved homicides of women on the books when they arrested Donald Murphy, a 36-year-old ex-convict and unemployed construction worker, on December 15, 1980. Based on evidence in hand, they charged him with the deaths of prostitutes Cynthia Warren, beaten to death on October 23, and Cecilia Knott, stabbed and strangled two weeks later, on November 7. Officers were satisfied with his confession in those cases, but their suspect was not finished talking, yet.

To the chagrin of homicide investigators, Murphy also claimed three other victims for the year. Prostitute Jeanette Woods, age 24, had been raped, beaten and strangled on April 18, her throat slashed as a lethal afterthought. Two months later, on June 14, the body of 22-year-old Diane Burks was found in Detroit, hog-tied and strangled. On October 8, 26-year-old Betty Rembert was stabbed in the neck, finished off by crushing blows to the skull.

The problem was that officers already had a suspect in the last three slayings. Local athlete David Payton had confessed the murders, after 84 hours of police grilling, but now he was anxious to recant, charging third-degree tactics, and police were frankly embarrassed by Murphy's recital of intimate details in those crimes. A "compromise" was reached when murder charges against Payton were dismissed in March 1981, and Murphy pled guilty on two counts of murder (Warren and Knott) on July 27, 1982, receiving concurrent 30-year prison terms. Despite confessions from two separate suspects, the murders of Woods, Burks, and Rembert remain technically unsolved.

Nesset, Arnfinn

Norway's all-time record-holding killer was exposed in 1981 as a result of journalistic curiosity. The Orkdal Valley Nursing Home was opened during 1977, and its patients soon experienced a high rate of mortality. Considering their ages, this was not especially unusual; in early 1981, however, local journalists received a tip that hospital manager Arnfinn Nesset had ordered large quantities of curacit, a derivative of curare, the same poison used by South American Indians on the tips of their hunting arrows. Under questioning, Nesset first claimed he purchased the poison for use on a dog, later confessing to the murders of twenty-seven patients between May 1977 and November 1980.

At forty-six, Nesset had already cinched the Scandinavian record for mass murder, but he was not finished talking, yet. "I've killed so many I'm unable to remember them all," he told authorities, prompting police to request lists of patients who died in three institutions where Nesset had worked since 1962. In all, detectives were left with a list of sixty-two possible victims, but autopsies were useless, since curacit becomes increasingly difficult to trace with passage of time.

Nesset offered a variety of motives for the murders— mercy killing, schizophrenia, simple morbid pleasure in the act itself—which led defense attorneys to suggest that he was mentally unbalanced. Four psychiatrists examined the balding, bespectacled killer, each pronouncing him sane and fit for trial. Before his day in court, the suspect proved his sanity by suddenly recanting his confessions, leaving prosecutors in a quandary. He was finally charged with killing only 25 of the established Orkdal Valley victims; five counts of forgery and embezzlement were added, based upon the killer's misappropriation of some $1,800 from his victims.

Nesset pleaded innocent on all counts when his trial opened in October 1982. Five months later, on March 11, 1983, jurors convicted him on 22 counts of murder, one count of attempted murder, plus five counts of forgery and embezzlement. Nesset was acquitted on the three remaining murder charges, but it scarcely mattered. Judges were unmoved by the defense plea that Nesset considered himself a "demigod," holding the power of life and death over his elderly patients. Upon conviction, he drew the maximum sentence possible under Norwegian law: 21 years in prison, with a possibility of ten more years preventive detention.

Neu, Kenneth

A homosexual drifter, Kenneth Neu claimed his first victim on September 2, 1933, in the person of wealthy New Yorker Lawrence Shead. The men met in Times Square, and Shead followed Neu to the latter's hotel room. Once there, Shead was beaten to death with an electric iron, stripped of money and his suit, which Neu appropriated for his long flight southward, to New Orleans.

In the Crescent City, Neu attached himself to Sheffield Clark, a hardware store proprietor, threatening Clark with "exposure" as a homosexual if cash was not forthcoming. The merchant responded by reaching for his telephone, to call police, and Neu strangled him to death before looting the victim's home, departing in Clark's stolen car. Apprehended in New Jersey, the killer was still wearing Lawrence Shead's suit at the time of his arrest.

Tried and convicted of murder in December 1933, Kenneth Neu was sentenced to death. Appeals delayed the execution of his sentence, but the verdict was affirmed, and Neu mounted the scaffold on February 1, 1935. Before the trap was sprung, he treated witnesses to a spirited rendition of an original song composed especially for the occasion. Its title: "I'm Fit as a Fiddle and Ready to Hang."

New Castle, PA—
Unsolved Murders

While homicide detectives in Ohio stalked the Cleveland "torso killer" through the latter 1930s, they were periodically distracted by reports of unsolved slayings from the area of New Castle and West Pittsburgh, Pennsylvania. No solid link between the crime sprees was established, but coincidence of timing, the proximity of common railway lines, and the unanimous decapitation of victims in both states have produced some tantalizing theories. No two reports agree upon the number of New Castle victims, and several accounts make surprisingly detailed reference to non-existent crimes. A retrospective survey in the local paper, published in December 1971, refers to eleven victims slain between 1921 and 1940, but a detailed review of newspaper records reveals only five murders, spanning a period of fourteen years.

The first victim, a young man, was found in a marshy area between New Castle and West Pittsburgh—later dubbed the "murder swamp"—on October 6, 1925. Nude on discovery, the man had been dead at least three weeks when he was found, and discovery of his severed head on October 8 provided no clue to his identity. As with the other Pennsylvania victims, he remains unidentified.

On October 17, 1925, a headless male skeleton was found in the swamp. The matching skull was unearthed two days later, along with that of a woman, killed at least a year earlier. Neither victim was identified by authorities, and no trace of the woman's body was ever found.

The local "headless murders" were a fading memory by July 1, 1936, when a man's decapitated body turned up on a slag dump of the Pittsburgh & Lake Erie Railroad, at New Castle Junction. The victim's head was never found, and he remains anonymous. Newspapers spread beneath the body included issues from Pittsburgh and Cleveland, dating from July 1933.

On October 13, 1939, another headless, decomposing man was fished out of the swamp near West Pittsburgh. Charred newspapers surrounding the body included month-old copies from Youngstown, Ohio, and the victim's head was found nearby, in an abandoned box car, five days later.

Were the Pennsylvania crimes and Cleveland's murder spree connected? Did Ohio's "Mad Butcher" first try his hand in New Castle, taking a decade off before he resumed activities in Cleveland? Detective Peter Merylo, stalking the headhunter into retirement, blamed one man for both sets of murders, plus 20 to 30 more kills, nationwide. The final truth has managed to elude police for over half a century, and it may well lie buried in the Pennsylvania "murder swamp." (See also: "Mad Butcher of Kingsbury Run," Vol. 1)

"Occult" Murders—California

In February 1975, California's Department of Justice issued a confidential report stating that fourteen unsolved murders in the past three years had been committed by a single man. Six victims had been found near Santa Rosa, in Sonoma County; five were found in San Francisco, with one each in Redding, Marysville, and Monterey. The murders were distinguished from a host of other unsolved homicides by similar disposal of the bodies and the killer's fondness for retaining souvenirs.

The chain of homicides began on February 4, 1972, when Maureen Strong and Yvonne Weber, both twelve years old, vanished on their way home from a Santa Rosa skating rink. Their skeletons were found December 28, on an embankment near a rural road in eastern Sonoma County. The killer had removed the clothing and a single gold earring from each victim.

On March 4, 1972, Kim Allen, a 19-year-old co-ed, vanished while hitchhiking in Santa Rosa. Her nude body, strangled with clothesline, was found in a creek bed; there were superficial cuts on her chest, rope burns on her wrists and ankles. Once again, the clothing, handbag, and one gold earring were missing.

On November 21, 1972, 13-year-old Lori Kursa vanished from a Santa Rosa market. She was nude upon discovery, three weeks later, and the cause of death was listed as a broken neck. She still had wire loops in her ear lobes, but her earrings had been removed.

The killer shifted to San Francisco with spring, strangling Rosa Vasquez and dumping her nude body on May 29, 1973. Fifteen-year-old Yvonne Quilantang received similar treatment on June 9. Angela Thomas was found naked and dead July 2, but she had been smothered. On July 13, Nancy Gidley was snatched from a local motel and strangled, her nude body dumped in a high school parking lot.

The "occult" angle surfaced that same month, after Caroline Davis was kidnapped on July 15. A runaway from Shasta County, she was last seen thumbing for rides on Highway 101, near Santa Rosa. Poisoned with strychnine, she was found on July 31, at the precise spot where the first two victims were discovered seven months earlier. On the bank above her body, searchers found a strange design arranged from twigs, laid out to form two interlocking squares. An unnamed source described the sculpture as a witchy symbol understood to designate "the carrier of spirits."

On July 22, 1973, the nearly-nude body of Nancy Feusi was found near Redding, California, the cause of death obscured by decomposition. On November 4, the scene shifted back to San Francisco with discovery of Laura O'Dell's nude, strangled body. Therese Walsh, age 22, was hitching rides from Malibu to Garberville when she met her killer on December 22, 1973. Raped, hog-tied and strangled, she was dumped near the spot where Kim Allen was found in March 1972.

According to police, the same man murdered Brenda Merchant, at Marysville, by stabbing her to death on February 1, 1974, discarding her semi-nude corpse beside a rural road. On September 29, 14-year-old Donna Braun, nude and strangled, was found floating in the Salinas River near Monterey. And so, presumedly, the murders ceased.

A fifteenth victim, inadvertently omitted from the government's report, was Jeannette Kamahele, age 20, a co-ed who disappeared on April 25, 1972, while hitch-hiking near Santa Rosa. Her skeletal remains were finally unearthed on July 6, 1979, hog-tied in a shallow grave within 100 yards of Lori Kursa's final resting place.

The "occult" theory's chief proponent was Sergeant Erwin Carlstedt, of Sonoma County. Impressed by the sticks found at one murder scene, he also found significance in victims being dumped along the east side of a road. In passing, Carlstedt told associates that seven women killed in Washington, between January and July 1974, had been abducted in the waning (sacrificial) phase of the moon. The 1975 report suggested that the killer was "familiar with witchcraft or the occult, because of a witchcraft symbol found during the Caroline Davis case and the possible occult involvement in the missing females in the states of Oregon and Washington."

Unfortunately for the Carlstedt thesis, all the victims killed in Washington were ultimately linked to the "Ted" case, credited to Theodore Bundy. (Research into Bundy's movements has exonerated him from all involvement in the California murders.) Likewise, the reputed "witchcraft symbol" proved to be a piece of childish art, constructed by a small boy on vacation as a likeness of his family's car and trailer.

Slayer Harvey Carignan has been suggested as a suspect in the unsolved murders, based upon a traffic ticket he collected in Solano County, east of Santa Rosa, on June 20, 1973. Again, no solid evidence exists, and one week later Carignan was claiming victims in the state of Minnesota, leading to his ultimate arrest in September 1974. He was in jail when Donna Braun was murdered, and the other bodies showed no evidence of Carignan's traditional resort to beating with a hammer.

An intriguing theory published during 1986, by author Robert Graysmith, credits the elusive "Zodiac" with these and many other unsolved homicides. The point is moot, until such time as a solution is discovered. In the meantime, we can only say that one or more sadistic killers may be still at large within the Golden State.

(See also: "Astrological" Murders; Bundy, Theodore, Vol. 1; Carignan, Harvey; "Zodiac" Murders, Vol. 1)

Ogorzov, Paul

A German railway worker and loyal Nazi party member, Ogorzov earned local notoriety as the "S Bahn murderer" in World War II. Stalking female victims around Rummelsburg, on the Berlin line, he was a sadist who killed for sexual satisfaction, relishing the evident fear of his chosen prey. Between 1939 and 1941, he killed at least eight women, raping most of them before they were beaten to death with a length of lead cable. Twenty-eight years old when his trial opened on July 24, 1941, Ogorzov received no sympathy from his fellow Nazis. Anxious to put the scandal behind them and get on with the business of killing Jews, party leaders rushed through the proceedings in a single afternoon, sentencing Ogorzov to death. He was executed by a firing squad on July 26.

O'Neall, Darren Dee

Born in Albuquerque, New Mexico, on February 26, 1960, O'Neall grew up a drifter and pathological liar with a taste for violent sex. He traveled widely, favoring the West and avidly devouring the novels of best-selling Western writer Louis L'Amour. On the road, assuming various identities, O'Neall frequently lifted his latest alias from favorite L'Amour characters.

On March 28, 1987, 22-year-old Robin Smith left a Puyallup, Washington, tavern to attend a party with new acquaintance "Herb Johnson." She never came home, and police were alarmed when they found Johnson's car abandoned near Marysville, north of Seattle, on May 31. A search of the trunk turned up Robin's blood-stained jacket, plus several human teeth; a check on the vehicle's registration revealed it had been stolen two months earlier, in Nampa, Idaho.

The owner was a trucker, who recalled the thief in detail. Young and blond, with the word "JUNE" tattooed across the knuckles of his left hand, the drifter had been thumbing rides when the truck driver picked him up and offered him a place to spend the night. Next morning, he was gone, along with his benefactor's car and a Ruger .357 magnum revolver, stolen from the trucker's home.

The "JUNE" tattoo rang bells with law enforcement, leading to identification of the drifter as Darren O'Neall, a fugitive from child support payments after abandoning his wife and child six years earlier. His whereabouts was presently unknown, but officers suspected he was hunting other female victims.

On April 29, 1987, Wendy Aughe, 29, disappeared after leaving her beauty school night class to keep a date with the bartender from a neighborhood restaurant in Bellingham, Washington. It was the bartender's first day of work, and he never returned to pick up his paycheck, but fingerprints lifted from his job application identified the man as Darren O'Neall. Wendy's car turned up days later, outside a tavern in Eugene, Oregon, and federal warrants were issued charging O'Neall with unlawful flight to avoid prosecution for murder.

By that time, there were other warrants pending, including a federal charge of unlawful flight to avoid prosecution for sexual assault, in Colorado Springs, Colorado. A female victim there identified O'Neall as her assailant, and the list of charges grew longer when skeletal remains of Robin Smith were discovered on May 25, near Greenwater, Washington, north of Mt. Rainier.

On June 9, 1987, Lisa Szubert disappeared from a truck stop at Mountain Home, Idaho. Last seen with a young man bearing the familiar knuckle tattoo, she was found dead on June 13, southeast of La Grande, Oregon. A week later, O'Neall was linked with the bungled abduction of a woman in Burley, Idaho; his name was added to the FBI's "Most Wanted" list on June 25.

In flight, O'Neall was drawing attention from law enforcement agencies across the nation. Three women had been shot to death in Salt Lake City over the past year, each killed with the same small-caliber gun, and witnesses recalled seeing them last with a man bearing the "JUNE" tattoo on his knuckles. Speculative body-counts were climbing into double digits by the time FBI agents captured O'Neall in Florida, on February 3, 1988. He was returned to Washington for trial on murder charges, and the disposition of his case is pending.

"Orange Coast Killer, The"

The latter 1970s were witness to a sudden rash of random, homicidal violence in America, alerting criminologists to a disturbing increase in the incidence of serial murders. Some regions of the country—Texas, Florida, New York—seemed bent on hogging headlines for their local maniacs, but none could hold a candle to the battlefield of Southern California, where the "Hillside Strangler," "Freeway Killer," "Sunset Slayer," "Skid Row Slasher," and a host of others plied their trade. One such—the "Orange Coast Killer"—went his ghoulish counterparts one better, slipping out of newsprint into legend as the one who got away.

In retrospect, detectives would agree the terror dated back to August 2, 1977, when Jane Bennington was slain in Corona Del Mar. Attacked in her home, the 29-year-old was raped, then beaten to death with a blunt instrument. Her killer left no clues for the police, and in the gap of eighteen months before his next appearance, other homicides took precedence, demanding the attention of investigators.

The killer returned with a vengeance on April Fool's Day, 1979, raping Kimberly Rawlines in her Costa Mesa home before beating her to death. On May 14, Savannah Anderson, age 22, was assaulted and bludgeoned in Irvine. Ten days later, Kim Whitecotton, 20, survived an attack at her apartment, in Santa Ana

Heights, her graphic description of the incident spreading panic among her neighbors.

Overnight, there was a run on guns and guard dogs in the neighborhoods that seemed to mark the killer's chosen hunting ground. Publicity alerted women to the danger of an unlocked door or window, while composite sketches of the suspect—featuring a dark mustache and pock-marked cheeks—told women who to look for. Still, it seemed the slayer was invisible to everyone except his victims, free to come and go at will.

Jane Pettengill, age 24, was chosen on July 19, assaulted in her Costa Mesa home. She would survive, unlike her Costa Mesa neighbor, 30-year-old Marolyn Carleton, who was raped and bludgeoned on September 14. The killer moved to Tustin on the thirtieth, administering a near-fatal beating to Diana Green. A week later, he killed 24-year-old Debra Jean Kennedy in Tustin. On December 21, the slayer claimed his only teenage victim, battering Debra Lynn Senior in Costa Mesa, afterward raping her corpse.

A special task force stalked the killer through a maze of clues and useless "tips" from frightened members of the public, all in vain. As summer faded into autumn, slowly giving way to winter, it became apparent that their man was gone. This time, his disappearance was no ruse, no holiday. The Orange Coast Killer, for whatever reason, had retired. As far as homicide detectives know, their man is still at large.

Paulin, Thierry and Mathurin, Jean-Thierry

From 1984 through 1987, elderly Parisian women lived in terror of a savage killer whom they dubbed the "Monster of Montmartre." His targets were selected from the ranks of helpless senior citizens, the youngest 60 and the oldest 95. Attacked in their apartments, victims had been variously beaten, strangled, stabbed and smothered. One was nearly hacked in two, with 60 stab wounds, while another had been forced to swallow bleach. In every case, their humble dwellings had been ransacked, and the terror was escalating, three old women murdered in the final weekend of November 1987.

A survivor of November's rampage offered a description to police, resulting in the ultimate arrest of 24-year-old Thierry Paulin, on December 1. In custody, the suspect—a Guyana native and narcotics addict— cheerfully confessed to 21 sadistic slayings, naming a 22-year-old waiter, Jean-Thierry Mathurin, as his accomplice in some of the crimes. As outlined in the killer's statement, chosen victims would be followed home, accosted as they entered their apartments, tortured to reveal the hiding places of their meager cash or jewelry, and murdered in whatever fashion caught his fancy at the moment.

Paulin's fingerprints, on file from previous burglary and drug arrests, were matched to latent prints recovered from a number of the murder scenes, corroborating his confession. Mathurin, an immigrant of French Caribbean origin, was charged in nine of the slayings and bound over for trial. Since the abolition of capital punishment in France, the killers face a maximum penalty of life imprisonment.

Pennsylvania— Unsolved Murders

In a period of seven months, between November 1976 and June 1977, five young women were raped and murdered within a 25-mile radius of Washington, Pennsylvania, their killer striking with impunity and leaving homicide investigators at a loss for clues. Despite a fair description of the suspect, published in the form of artist's sketches, there were no arrests, and none are now anticipated in a case that terrorized the peaceful border region, holding women prisoners of fear inside their homes.

The first to die was 21-year-old Susan Rush, a native of Washington County, found strangled and locked in the trunk of her car on November 25, 1976. Detectives noted that her body had been "hastily clothed," her bra and panties left on the front seat, and a post-mortem examination confirmed that the victim was raped prior to death.

On February 13, 1977, 16-year-old Mary Gency was reported missing from her home in North Charleroi. She had gone out for a walk after supper and never returned, her body recovered three days later from the woods at Fallowfield Township. Gency was beaten to death with a blunt instrument, raped before death by an assailant the county coroner described as "a mad animal."

Debra Capiola, 17, was last seen alive on March 17, walking to meet her school bus in nearby Imperial, in Allegheny County. She never arrived at school, and searchers found her body in a wooded section of northwestern Washington County on March 22. Capiola had been raped before she was strangled with her own blue jeans, the pants left wrapped around her neck.

Two months later, on the afternoon of May 19, 18-year-old Brenda Ritter was found dead at South Strabane Township, in Washington County. Nude except for shoes and stockings, she had been raped, then strangled with a piece of her own clothing, tightened around her throat with a stick.

In June, the killer strayed from Pennsylvania, but he

did not travel far. His final victim was Roberta Elam, 26, a novice at Mount St. Joseph Mother House, in Oglebay Park, West Virginia, near Wheeling. Preparing to take her vows as a nun, Elam's career was cut short by a savage who raped and strangled her on June 13, dumping her corpse within 75 yards of the convent.

On the afternoon of June 15, authorities released a sketch of a long-haired suspect seen near the Ritter homicide scene, but none of the resultant tips proved fruitful. When the murder series ended, as mysteriously as it had begun, police could only speculate about the strangler's identity and whereabouts. Unless deceased or jailed on unrelated charges, he is still at large today.

Pinkerton, Jay Kelly

A native of Amarillo, Texas, born in 1969, Pinkerton had dropped out of school by age 17, to work as an apprentice butcher. On October 26, 1979, a prowler invaded the home of 30-year-old Sarah Lawrence, slashing her throat and stabbing her 30-odd times with a butcher knife, afterward raping her corpse and inflicting grisly post-mortem mutilations. Detectives followed a trail of footprints to Pinkerton's house, several blocks away, but he was released for lack of evidence after brief interrogation.

Six months later, on April 9, 1980, 25-year-old Sherry Welch, a former beauty queen, was murdered in the back room of an Amarillo furniture store that she managed. Police had no leads in the case, but they were still working the Lawrence homicide, studying bloody palmprints found on the victim's furniture. The prints were matched in late summer, and Pinkerton was arrested on September 26, charged with one count of first-degree murder.

Convicted of the Lawrence murder eight months

later, Pinkerton was sentenced to death on May 30, 1981. Indictments were returned in the Welch case on July 22 of that year, and Pinkerton celebrated the anniversary of his first murder trial with another conviction, drawing his second death sentence on May 13, 1982. Appeals won the killer three stays of execution, once coming within a half-hour of death before the Supreme Court intervened to save his life. A federal appeals court rejected Pinkerton's bid for a fourth stay, on May 14, 1986, and he was executed by lethal injection the following day.

Player, Michael

The life of homeless vagrants in Los Angeles has never been an easy one. Despite the pleasant climate, poverty and hunger take their toll, and random violence is a daily fact of life along "Skid Row." Since 1974, the drifter's plight has been further complicated by a succession of serial killers, preying on vagrants as the ideal "targets of opportunity." Easily reached and seldom missed in death, L.A.'s homeless rank low on the average homicide detective's list of priority victims. The appearance of another "Skid Row Slayer," in September 1986, provided Angelenos with an opportunity to act concerned while risking nothing of themselves.

The first to die, ironically, was not a transient. Visiting L.A. from San Diego, 54-year-old Rudolfo Roque was killed on the street by a gunman who stepped up behind him, firing a .22-caliber slug through the back of his head. The same weapon was used to kill 66-year-old Rick Stamps, a few days later, and the hunter claimed two victims on September 13: 31-year-old Rojello Sirven was killed outright, by a shot to the head, while a second victim, 47-year-old Joseph Griffin, lived until October 5. Michael Singer, age 66, was shot in the back of the head on September 20, and 36-year-old David Towns, another vagrant, was killed in his sleep three days later. September 30 marked another double-header, with victims Christopher Boyle, 25, and Leon Gaines, 56, murdered in separate attacks. Chang Kang, a 23-year-old Korean resident of Texas, was gunned down while visiting L.A. on October 7, and 44-year-old vagrant Wayne Ellis was killed in Athens Park the following day. That same afternoon, a surviving gunshot victim described his assailant as a youngish black man, offering police their first solid lead in the case.

Detectives were still beating the brush for a suspect on October 10, when a well-dressed black man checked into a Wilshire Boulevard hotel, paying in cash and signing the register as "Marcus Nisby." In his room, the guest removed his jacket, hung it in the closet, then lay down upon the bed and calmly shot himself to death. Upon discovery of his corpse, next day, a fingerprint comparison identified "Nisby" as 26-year-old Michael Player, convicted over the past two years on charges of theft, armed robbery, violating probation and carrying a concealed pistol. Player had been questioned as a suspect in the Roque murder and released for lack of evidence. A search of his belongings led police to name him as the Skid Row Slayer, and the case was closed in February 1987.

Poehlke, Norbert Hans

On May 3, 1984, a truck driver found the body of 47-year-old Siegfried Pfitzer, shot once in the head with a 9mm pistol, at a highway rest stop near Marbach, West Germany, not far from Stuttgart. Police soon determined that Pfitzer's missing car was used by the bandit who robbed a bank in Erbstetten, ten miles from

Marbach, on the same day, smashing the glass teller's cage with a sledge hammer to reach the money inside. In the wake of the robbery, Pfitzer's vehicle was abandoned less than a quarter-mile from the scene of the murder.

Seven months later, on December 21, 37-year-old Eugene Wethey was found shot to death at a rest stop near Nuremberg. On December 28, a hammer-wielding bandit used the dead man's car to flee a plundered bank in the village of Cleebroun, ten miles from Marbach. Police recognized the pattern, but it put them no closer to a suspect, and they could only wait while the killer plotted his next move.

On July 22, 1985, Wilfried Schneider, age 26, was found shot to death in a parking lot near his home, in the village of Beilstein-Schmidhausen. The murder weapon was identified as a Walther P5 pistol, routinely carried by many police officers, and authorities were not surprised when the dead man's car turned up at the scene of an attempted bank robbery in Spiegelberg, seven miles to the northwest. On that occasion, though, a quick-draw teller forced the thief to flee without his customary loot.

Two months later, on September 29, anti-terrorist officers were searching the Ludwigsburg railroad station for bombs when they found a police uniform in one of the lockers. The garments were traced to Chief Inspector Norbert Poehlke, a 14-year veteran of the Stuttgart constabulary, who claimed the uniform was left in Ludwigsburg for a quick change after a relative's funeral. Investigation revealed no recent deaths in Poehlke's family, but one of his daughters had died of cancer in March 1984, after a long siege that left the inspector with debts of some $400,000. Authorities now had their motive for robbery, and recent deviations in Poehlke's behavior indicated a potential for sudden, unpredictable violence.

The investigation was gathering steam when Poehlke requested sick leave on October 14, 1985. A week later, detectives stopped by his home to ask some questions, but they found only corpses. Poehlke's wife, Ingeborg, lay slumped in the bathroom, shot twice in the head, while his son Adrian had been shot once, in a bedroom.

Three days later, on October 23, Inspector Poehlke and his missing son, Gabriel, were found at the beach near Brindisi, in southern Italy. They were together in Poehlke's car, both shot with his Walther service pistol in an obvious murder-suicide. Ballistics tests confirmed that Poehlke's gun had also slain the first three victims in the murder series, and the case was closed.

Prince, Walter

On May 5, 1934, the body of Harriet Shaw, age 21, was found concealed in a thicket of shrubbery at Notts, near Retford, England. Last seen alive on May 2, the victim had been strangled by her assailant. On May 7, 32-year-old Walter Prince was arrested and charged with the crime before a local magistrate.

At his trial, Prince declared that the murder of Harriet Shaw was an act of revenge, committed after she infected him with venereal disease. Convicted on June 18, he was condemned to hang. After hearing the sentence pronounced, Prince startled his audience with an unexpected declaration. "I want to make a statement before I kick off," he declared, "and you can take it down if you want to. In 1928, I should have been strung up for the willful murder of Mr. Charles Armstrong, of Rusholme, Manchester. I will go for the two of them, and not sorry for the last one."

Another suspect, George Fratson, had been sentenced to hang for the Armstrong murder in July 1930, but he was reprieved on appeal. His record was cleared by Prince's confession, and the admitted slayer of two was "strung up" on schedule.

Quinn, Jane

Awakened by a gunshot in the pre-dawn hours of November 2, 1911, John Miller scrambled out of bed and rushed to the apartment of his landlord, whence the sound had emanated. On arrival at the scene, he found John Quinn, the landlord, lying in his bed, blood streaming from a fatal bullet wound. According to the dead man's wife, a prowler was responsible, though Miller saw no evidence of theft or any struggle. Jane Quinn declined to testify at the resulting inquest, and a Chicago coroner's jury deliberated for one hour before ordering her arrest on murder charges.

By that time, on November 10, police had learned a thing or two about the lethal Mrs. Quinn. They knew about her marriage to Canadian John McDonald, in October 1883, and his subsequent death—from "alcohol poisoning"—on September 28, 1901. A short month later, at Bass Lake, Michigan, the grieving widow had married Warren Thorpe—and he had later been shot to death in circumstances similar to those surrounding the Chicago case. Another death in bed—this time, involving Jane's own mother—had occurred a short time later, in the house once occupied by Warren Thorpe.

The evidence was overwhelming, and Jane Quinn was speedily convicted at her trial on murder charges, sentenced to a term of life imprisonment. If nothing else, the verdict may have spared some future victims from the clutches of a bona fide "black widow."

Quintiliano, Matthew

A 14-year veteran of the Stratford, Connecticut, police department, Quintiliano snapped one afternoon in May 1975, accosting his wife outside the Bridgeport hospital where she worked, shooting her eight times with a pistol. Arrested for murder (and fired from his job on the force), Quintiliano spent three years in custody before a panel of judges found him innocent by reason of insanity. After three months of treatment, staff psychiatrists ordered his release, describing Quintiliano as "no longer a danger to himself or others."

Remarried by 1983, Matthew had no more luck with his second fling at matrimony that he had the first time around. Served with divorce papers on February 11, he murdered his wife the next day and was arrested on February 16, faced with another count of first-degree murder. Held in lieu of $750,000 bond, he was indicted and convicted on the charge, confined to prison when psychiatrists agreed—this time—that he was sane.

Rand, Andre

Born Andre Rashan, in 1943, the "Pied Piper of Staten Island" employed various pseudonyms to cover his movements and criminal activities through the years. Between 1966 and '68, using the last name "Bruchette," he worked as a physical therapy aide at New York's Willowbrook State School—later renamed the Staten Island Development Center. On May 5, 1969, he was arrested in the South Bronx for kidnapping and attempting to rape a nine-year-old girl. Pleading guilty to a lesser charge of sexual abuse, he served sixteen months in prison, winning parole in January 1972. Back on the street, Rashan legally changed his name to

"Rand," logging three more arrests by the end of the decade for "minor" offenses, including burglary.

Along the way, his name was linked with disappearances of several children. Rand was working as a painter at a South Beach, Staten Island, apartment house when five-year-old Alice Pereira vanished from one of the flats in 1972, but officers were short on solid evidence required for an indictment. Nine years later, in July 1981, Rand was hauled in for questioning in the disappearance of seven-year-old Holly Hughes, from Port Richmond, and once more he was released for lack of evidence.

On January 9, 1983, Rand collected eleven children from West Brighton, loaded them into a van, and set off on a five-hour jaunt into Newark, neglecting to ask parental permission. They spent the day eating hamburgers and watching planes land at Newark airport, and while none of the children were harmed, Rand was arrested on charges of unlawful imprisonment, convicted in March and sentenced to ten months in jail. He was back on the street by August, listed as a suspect when ten-year-old Tiahese Jackson vanished on Staten Island.

No trace of the three missing girls had been found by July 9, 1987, when 12-year-old Jennifer Schweizer disappeared from her home at Westerleigh. A victim of Down's syndrome, Jennifer was traced to the grounds of the deserted Staten Island Development Center, where Rand had been living for several years in a makeshift shelter of his own design. Witnesses reported seeing Rand with Jennifer the day she disappeared, and after some preliminary questions, he was charged with her kidnapping on August 4, held without bail pending a psychiatric evaluation. Eight days later, Schweizer's body was unearthed from a shallow grave, within sight of Rand's lean-to, and a charge of murder in the first degree was added to his file.

Rijke, Sjef

Sjef Rijke seemed to have no luck at all with women. During January 1971, his 18-year-old fiancee, Willy Maas, experienced a week of racking stomach pains that climaxed in her death. The symptoms seemed to coincide with food poisoning, though friends and relatives could never be precise about the suspect dish. At Willy's funeral, in Utrecht, Holland, Sjef was visibly distraught.

His period of mourning was abbreviated by engagement to a female friend of several years, young Mientje Manders. Near the end of March, Sjef's second fiancee complained of nagging stomach pains that quickly proved debilitating. Rijke sat beside her bed and held her hand, tears streaming down his face when Manders died on April 2.

The authorities in Utrecht were concerned about the strange "coincidence," but Rijke seemed to have no motive for eliminating his fiancees. Flying in the face of grief, Sjef married only three weeks after Mientje's death. It was another star-crossed union, marred by Rijke's pathological jealousy; he quarreled bitterly with 18-year-old Maria, prompting her to leave him, filing for divorce six weeks after the wedding. Curious detectives asked about her health, and they discovered that Maria had been subject to repeated stomach aches throughout her short-lived marriage; change of domicile had cured the problem overnight.

A short time later, Sjef acquired a live-in lover who, in turn, began to suffer stomach problems. These were dutifully reported to her mother, who inquired about her diet. Sjef, the older woman learned, ate everything her daughter did, and seemed to feel no ill effects. It was discovered that his latest paramour was fond of eating peanut butter as a snack, between their normal meals, and samples from the jar were found to have a strange, metallic taste. Delivered to a chemist for analysis, the peanut butter was discovered to be laced with rat poison.

Still lacking any motive, homicide investigators searched for other suspects, grilling Rijke's cleaning lady. The investigation soon focused on Sjef, after a local merchant recalled selling him several boxes of poison in recent months. Under close questioning, Rijke broke down and confessed his crimes, describing the sadistic pleasure he obtained from watching women suffer. It was never his intention, he explained, to kill his fiancees; he simply loved to see them squirm.

Found legally sane by court psychiatrists, Rijke was tried for the murder of Willy Maas in January 1972. Upon conviction, he was sentenced to a double term of life imprisonment.

Rogers, David Keith

A navy veteran and father of two, born in 1947, Rogers moved to Bakersfield, California, at age 30, finding employment with the Kern County Sheriff's Department a year later. He spent five years on beats where prostitutes were numerous, and he was fired March 22, 1983, for taking nude photographs of a hooker in a local cemetery. On appeal, the state Civil Service Commission reduced his punishment to a 15-day suspension, and Rogers returned to duty in June 1983. (The prostitute in question failed to appear at this hearing, and she has not been seen since.) Assigned to the county jail, Rogers was accused of beating up an inmate in April 1984, but the charges were ultimately dismissed. He returned to active patrol in June 1986.

On February 21 of that year, the bullet-riddled body of Jeanine Benintende, a 21-year-old Los Angeles prostitute was fished out of a canal near Lamont, in Kern

County. The fatal bullets were identified as .38-caliber hollow-points, often used by police, and the same weapon was identified a year later, on February 8, 1987, when Tracy Clark, a pregnant 15-year-old hooker, was found in the same canal.

Arrested five days later, after background investigation revealed his "unusual interest" in prostitutes, Rogers admitted owning the murder weapon, reported stolen from a local tavern in 1982. Large quantities of pornography were discovered in Rogers's home, and detectives learned that he had once taken his teenage son on a tour of hooker-infested streets, to teach the boy that prostitutes were "scumbags." Prosecutors declared that the missing 1983 witness was "very much on the list" of potential victims, but Rogers was finally charged with two counts of homicide. Convicted on one count each of second-degree murder (Benintende) and first-degree (Clark), Rogers was sentenced to die on the latter charge.

Rogers, Dayton Leroy

The youngest of three children, Rogers was born in Moscow, Idaho, in 1954. His parents moved frequently, adopting four more children along the way, and Rogers turned to petty juvenile crime after losing his favored place as the baby of the family. In seventh grade, he was arrested for shooting a BB gun at passing cars, but serious violence was postponed until his late teens, with females singled out as his victims of preference.

On August 25, 1972, Rogers drove his 15-year-old girlfriend into the woods near Eugene, Oregon, for a sexual interlude, and wound up stabbing her in the abdomen with a hunting knife, telling her, "I just couldn't trust you anymore." Instantly remorseful, he first proposed marriage, then drove her to the hospital, where police were summoned. Pleading guilty to second-degree assault in February 1973, Rogers was sentenced to four years probation.

A year after his first escapade, on August 1, 1973, Rogers attacked two 15-year-old girls with a pop bottle, drawing charges of second- and third-degree assault. He was acquitted by reason of mental disease or defect—the Oregon equivalent of insanity—and was committed to a state hospital, winning release on December 12, 1974. In January 1976, he was indicted for first-degree rape in Clackamas County, but a jury found him innocent in May. While still awaiting trial, on February 24, he raped one high school girl and threatened another with a knife, apologizing afterward as if, in the words of one victim, "it was all some kind of game." Rogers pled innocent by reason of mental defect, and in August he was convicted on a reduced charge of coercion, drawing the five-year maximum jail term. The prosecutor referred to Rogers as "a murder case looking for a place to happen," but he still won parole after 17 months, hauled back for another ten on charges of parole violation.

In the predawn hours of August 7, 1987, Rogers was found in a Portland parking lot, crouching over the nude, mutilated body of prostitute Jennifer Smith. Witnesses gave chase at speeds topping 100 mph, recording his license number and a description of his pickup truck before Rogers gave them the slip. Arresting him at home, police found bloodstains in his truck, along with latent fingerprints from Smith. Witnesses fingered Rogers as the slasher, and several other prostitutes came forward, volunteering tales of brutal sex and torture at knifepoint, spanning the past year.

On August 31, with Rogers safe in jail, a woman's decomposing body was discovered on a sprawling timber farm near Molalla, in Clackamas County. Deputies were summoned, and by sundown on September 1, remains of four more victims were discovered. The body-count hit seven by September 5, each victim killed by multiple stab wounds, their nude bodies bearing the marks of torture and mutilation. The six identified victims included: Lisa Mock, age 23, a Portland prostitute and addict missing since July; another Portland junkie, 26-year old Maureen Hodges, who vanished around the same time; Christine Adams, 35, also of Portland; 26-year-old Nondace Cervantes, from Tempe, Arizona; Portland high school student Reatha Gayles, 16; and 21-year-old Cynthia DeVore, also from Portland.

A prime suspect in all seven murders, Rogers escaped indictment on grounds of insufficient evidence. Charged in the murder of Jennifer Smith, he went to trial in January 1988, with a lame plea of justifiable homicide. According to Rogers, Smith had disrobed before pulling a knife and attempting to rob him, thus compelling him to stab her eleven times in "self-defense." Jurors convicted him of aggravated murder on February 20, and Rogers was sentenced to life imprisonment, with a minimum of 30 years to serve before consideration for parole.

Ross, Michael B.

Born in Brooklyn, Connecticut, where his parents ran an egg farm, Ross concentrated on animal science in high school, moving on to Cornell University in 1977 and earning his bachelor's degree in 1981. After graduation, he worked briefly at an egg farm near Columbus, Ohio, but Ross had trouble keeping his mind on the chickens. Bicycling through LaSalle City, Illinois, on September 28, 1981, he kidnapped a 16-year-old girl and dragged her into the woods, gagging her with a handkerchief and belt before police arrived. Charged with unlawful restraint, Ross pled guilty the following day and paid a $500 fine, drawing two years probation before he returned to Connecticut.

On January 5, 1982, 17-year-old Tammy Williams disappeared in Brooklyn, while walking home from her boyfriend's house in broad daylight. Ross was not suspected in the case, but he had reason to be fearful, all the same. In February, he found employment at another Ohio egg farm, living peacefully for nearly three months before his next clash with the law.

On April 26, Ross turned up at a rural home in Licking County, asking to borrow a flashlight. His car had broken down, he said, and when Ross came to return the light, he also asked to use the telephone. Inside the house, he tried to choke his female benefactor—an off-duty policewoman—but she fought him off and gave a clear description to authorities, resulting in his swift arrest. Bailed out by his parents on May 11, Ross was sent home to Connecticut for 60 days of psychiatric study.

On June 15, 1982, Debra Taylor was riding with her husband when they ran out of gas near Danielson, Connecticut. They split up to find a filling station, and Debra disappeared, her skeletal remains discovered by a jogger on October 30. In the meantime, Michael Ross pled guilty to assault charges in Ohio, on August 4, paying a $1,000 fine and serving four months in jail before his release, on December 22.

In May 1983, Ross was hired by a Connecticut insurance company, his application falsely denying any criminal convictions, and his work record was satisfactory until early November. On November 16, 19-year-old Robin Stravinsky was reported missing in Norwich, Connecticut, her body found by joggers a week later, near a local hospital. Ross's employer was pleased to note an improvement in Michael's work through December and January, but by March 1984, the young man seemed to be entering another unexplained slump.

On April 22—Easter Sunday—14-year-old neighbors Leslie Shelley and April Brunais disappeared from Griswold, Connecticut, en route to a friend's house. Two months later, on June 13, Wendy Baribeault vanished in Lisbon, on a short walk to the neighborhood store. Her body, raped and strangled, was found on June 15, and witnesses recalled seeing a blue subcompact car near the scene.

Police began working their way through a computer listing of 2,000 sub-compact drivers, and they caught up with Ross on June 28. He swiftly confessed to the Baribeault murder, then directed authorities to a rural dump site, where the bodies of Leslie Shelley and April Brunais were recovered. On June 30, officers followed Ross's directions to the shallow grave of Tammy Williams, and by July 5 he was charged in a total of six homicides. Guilty pleas in the murders of Williams and Debra Taylor earned Ross a sentence of 120 years imprisonment. Convicted of four other slayings on June 26, 1987, he was sentenced to death ten days later.

Sach, Amelia and Walters, Annie

English born in 1873, Amelia Sach appeared to be a kindly soul who doted over children. So concerned was she about their welfare, that she opened up a "nursing home" in East Finchley, London, catering to unwed mothers in their hour of need. Sach's clients were recruited through an advertisement in the papers.

> ACCOUCHEMENT: Before and during, skilled nursing. Home comforts. Baby can remain.

That final sentence was the clincher, with Amelia promising to make arrangements for "adoption" . . . if an extra fee of twenty-five or fifty pounds was paid. In fact, the infants were delivered to her simple-minded sidekick, Annie Walters, for disposal, generally dispatched with chlordyne, their tiny corpses cast off in the Thames or buried in convenient garbage dumps.

In 1902, Amelia gave Walters the child of an unwed mother named Galley, instructing her to dispose of the baby as always. Ignoring the order, Annie took the infant home "for company," surprising her landlord (who was also a policeman). Walters explained that she was keeping the child as a favor to some friends, who lived in Kensington, but she appeared confused. While chatting with the landlord's wife, Annie referred to the baby as "a dear little girl," but the landlady, having recently changed the child's diaper, knew it to be a boy.

When Annie's tiny roommate died, a few days later, inconvenient questions were defrayed in deference to her grief. The tears seemed real enough, but two months later she produced another infant, this one also dying "accidentally" in its sleep. Interrogation of their suspect led detectives to the nursing home, and both women were sentenced to die on conviction of multiple murders.

As their hangman, H.A. Pierrepoint, noted in his diary: "These two women were baby farmers of the worst kind and were both repulsive in type. They had literally to be carried to the scaffold and protested to the end against their sentences."

Santo, Anthony

A triple killer by the tender age of fourteen years, Santo was jailed in Norwood, Massachusetts, during June 1908. Authorities from Brooklyn questioned him about the deaths of two young brothers, James and Frank Marino, murdered three months earlier, and

Santo readily confessed. A jack knife had been used on Frank, while James was beaten with a rock.

A sidelight of the questioning was Santo's startling confession to another homicide in Dedham, Massachusetts. Young Louise Staula was found dead in a field, on May 11, but the case had baffled local officers before they spoke with Santo. "When I saw her," he said, "I had a mad spell. I struck the girl once. Then I picked up a rock and she jumped when I threw it. When I struck her with the rock she fell. I thought she was dead. I started to pray to help her and make her get better."

The interrogation solved three crimes, but it would not result in Santo being sent to jail. According to investigators, recent illness had affected Santo's mind, and he was found incompetent for trial, confined to an asylum for the criminally insane.

Schaefer, Gary

A Vermont native and member of the fundamentalist Christadelphian Church, Schaefer first ran afoul of authority while serving in the Navy. Charged with arson and possession of illegal drugs, he responded with an insanity plea, but the Navy psychiatrists found him competent for trial. On discharge, he succeeded in convincing friends and relatives of his normality, but violent sexual obsessions simmered just below the surface of his quiet personality, the pressure mounting toward a detonation point.

In 1979, Schaefer kidnapped, raped and murdered 13-year-old Sherry Nastasia, whose family lived in a Springfield apartment complex managed by Schaefer's brother. Theresa Fenton suffered an identical fate in 1981, but 17-year-old Deana Buxton survived an attack in Brattleboro, during 1982. Her description focused police attention on Schaefer, but hard evidence was still lacking in early 1983, when the killer struck again.

On April 9 of that year, Schaefer abducted young Catherine Richards in Springfield, driving her to a remote location where she was forced to fellate him before he crushed her skull with a stone. The body was discovered at noon on April 10, and eyewitness descriptions of Catherine's abductor matched those of Deana Buxton's assailant the previous year. Police were working their way up to an arrest in September 1983, when the last victim's mother penned an open letter to Schaefer, accusing him of murder and challenging him to confess his sins, in accordance with the precepts of his church.

It was the final straw, and Schaefer cracked in custody, confessing on two counts of murder (Fenton and Richards), plus the rape of Deana Buxton. In December 1983, he pled guilty to kidnapping, sexual assault, and second-degree murder in the Richards case, with charges dismissed in the Fenton murder as part of a plea bargain. A month later, Schaefer was sentenced to a term of 30 years to life, his time to be served at the federal penitentiary in Leavenworth, Kansas.

Scieri, Antoinette

Little is known of Antoinette Scieri's early life, aside from the fact that she was born in Italy and emigrated to France as a child. In the early days of World War I, she worked at a casualty clearing station in Doullens, there beginning a long life of crime. She stole cash and jewelry from the wounded, also forging signatures on letters to their families, requesting money through the mail. Jailed for the theft of an officer's paybook in 1915, she was released the following year.

Celebrating her freedom, Antoinette married an Ital-

ian soldier named Salmon, bearing him two children
before he discovered her flagrant infidelity and left her
flat. Next, she took up with an alcoholic brute named
Joseph Rossignol, who beat her regularly. Several times
she had him jailed on charges of assault, but they were
always reconciled. She bore another child, outside of
wedlock, and in 1920 they moved to the village of St.
Gilles, in southern France. Billing herself as "Nurse
Scieri," Antoinette began shopping for elderly patients
who needed her care . . . at a price.

With Nurse Scieri on the scene, St. Gilles experienced a rash of sudden deaths among the elderly and
ailing. Antoinette lose five patients before the murder
machine hit high gear, in December 1924, and from that
point there was no turning back. On December 11, a
58-year-old spinster named Drouard died in Scieri's
care. Christmas Eve saw the death of Madame
Lachapelle, her final convulsions ascribed to "ptomaine
poisoning." When Lachapelle's husband collapsed two
days later, Antoinette blamed a heart attack, and a
friendly physician agreed.

Joe Rossignol welcomed the new year in typical
fashion, mauling his common-law wife in a drunken
rage, but this time he had gone too far. When
Antoinette served up a bowl of mussels, Rossignol consumed them greedily—and died two hours later. According to the testimony at her trial, Scieri watched his
death throes, then went out to celebrate her freedom
with a drunken orgy.

Nurse Scieri's next patients were Marie Martin, 67,
and her sister, Madame Doyer. When Antoinette prepared a pot of coffee, Madame Doyer found it bitter,
pouring hers down the sink when the nurse's back was
turned. Martin drank hers down and shortly died, a circumstance that started ripples of suspicion in St. Gilles.

The last to die was Madame Gouan-Criquet, an ailing
septuagenarian whose health declined rapidly under

Antoinette's "nursing." The victim's husband notified police of his suspicions, and a bottle was found beneath the dead woman's bed, containing a mixture of ether and the herbicide pyralion. The bodies of Joe Rossignol and several other victims were exhumed for autopsy, and all contained huge doses of pyralion.

In custody, Scieri openly confessed her crimes and tried to implicate a neighbor, who was later cleared by the police. On April 27, 1926, she was condemned to die upon conviction for a dozen homicides, the judge informing her: "You have been called a monster, but that expression is not strong enough. You are debauched. You are possessed of all the vices. You are also a drunkard, vicious, and a hypocrite. You have no shame. I do not believe judicial history contains the records of many criminals of your type."

Scieri shrugged and laughed as sentence was pronounced, aware that there had been no execution of a woman in France since the end of World War I. As expected, her death sentence was soon commuted to life imprisonment, and she subsequently died in jail.

Scully, Anthony

Known as "Jack" to his friends, Scully was a California native, born in 1944. A former policeman in Millbrae, he was working as an electrical contractor in Burlingame when he was arrested, on May 18, 1983, on charges of assaulting a prostitute. Accomplice Michael Shing, of Redwood City, made a statement to police that implicated Scully in a series of unsolved Bay Area murders.

Scully's victims included an Oakland prostitute and three hookers slain on the San Francisco peninsula. Three other victims—including a drug pusher, his prostitute girlfriend, and a teenage punk rocker—were found in Golden Gate Park, their bodies jammed into 55-gallon oil drums, on May 3, 1983. The drums had been cemented shut, but Scully had neglected to remove his fingerprints, and so the case was made. As police spokesmen told the press, "Right now we feel the motive was drugs. Probably, there were some sexual elements involved, too."

A San Mateo County jury convicted Scully of seven first-degree murders on June 4, 1986. Sentenced to life without parole, Scully shouted obscenities as deputies hustled him out of the courtroom to begin serving his time.

Seefeld, Adolf

An itinerant watchmaker in his native Germany, Seefeld was also a student of scripture, able to quote long Bible passages from memory. He preferred to sleep in the open, regardless of weather, and sometimes passed himself off as a witch to gullible peasants, professing ability to cast evil spells on their livestock. First charged with the murder of a young boy in 1908, Seefeld escaped conviction through lack of evidence, but spent nearly a quarter-century in prison on various convictions for child molestation. Committed to a mental home near Potsdam, he remained in custody for two years without speaking a word to attendants.

Seefeld did not always choose to murder his victims, once traveling with a kidnapped boy for three months and sparing his life. When he killed, the drifter's favorite weapon was a homemade poison, concocted from wild plants and fungi, that left his chosen targets in an attitude of peace, as if they were relaxing for a nap. Ironically, authorities recorded that his murder victims showed no signs of sexual abuse, while children he molested were allowed to live.

In custody, Seefeld confessed to a total of twelve murders. In some cases, names were unknown or forgotten, but Adolf remembered most of his children—or, at least, the ones he had dispatched in recent years. Eleven-year-old Kurz Gnirk was slain on April 16, 1933, followed by ten-year-old Ernest Tesdorf, on November 2. A bare five days later, Seefeld had murdered Wolfgang Metzdorf, age seven, rebounding on November 22 with the killing of ten-year-old Alfred Praetorius. Hans Korn, age 11, was killed on January 16, 1934, while two victims—six-year-old Edgar Diettrich and four-year-old Arthur Dinn—were found together at New Ruppin, on October 6. Seefeld's arrest followed the murder of a boy named Zimmerman, on February 23, 1935, and he was convicted at trial a year later, executed on May 23, 1936.

Siebert, Daniel Lee

Sherri Weathers, a hearing-impaired student at the Alabama Institute for the Deaf and Blind, in Talladega, had missed a week of classes without explanation when her counselor phoned the manager of her apartment building for help on February 24, 1986. Weathers did not answer her phone, and the school was concerned that something might be wrong. The manager used her pass key and found Sherri dead in her room, along with her two small sons—five-year-old Chad and four-year-old Joseph. The bodies were piled together on Sherri's bed and loosely covered with a blanket.

When police arrived, the manager directed them to another apartment, occupied by 33-year-old Linda Jarman, another student lately missing from the Institute. Inside, patrolmen found her nude and lifeless on the bed, a television set and the woman's car apparently stolen by her assailant.

Investigation revealed that an Institute art teacher, one "Daniel Spence," had expressed a romantic interest in Sherri Weathers. Missing from class since February 20, "Spence" had turned up at the school several months earlier, offering to teach for free in hopes of gaining a permanent job later on. Fingerprints from the Talladega murder scenes identified "Spence" as Daniel Siebert, convicted of a Las Vegas manslaughter in 1979, presently sought in San Francisco on charges of first-degree assault. Detectives also learned that Siebert had been dating Linda Odum, a 32-year-old cocktail waitress reported missing on February 24. (Her naked, decomposed remains were found outside of Talladega on March 30.) Independent evidence also linked Siebert with the strangulation of a prostitute in Calhoun County, found around the time he disappeared from Talladega.

Highway patrol officers found Linda Odum's car abandoned near Elizabethtown, Kentucky, on March 3, 1986, and Siebert's fingerprints were lifted from the vehicle. Over the next six months, sightings of the fugitive were reported from Ohio, New Jersey, Nevada, Southern California, and Montreal, Canada. The first solid lead was delivered on September 3, when a Las Vegas friend of Siebert's reported a telephone call from the fugitive. Police were ready when the next call came, and it was traced to a pay phone in Nashville, Tennessee. Employees at a nearby restaurant identified Siebert's mug shots, and he was arrested next morning, when he arrived to complete some work on the restaurant's sign.

In custody, Siebert readily confessed to five murders in Alabama and various others spanning the continent. How many? "Maybe a dozen," he said. "Maybe more. I try to put those things out of my mind." He killed for purposes of sex and robbery, being careful to murder his victims after a San Francisco hooker survived a throttling and filed charges against him. In addition to the Alabama cases, Siebert was charged with the 1985 murders of 28-year-old Gidget Castro and 23-year-old Nesia McElrath in Los Angeles, both previously attributed to the elusive "South Side Slayer." He was also charged in the 1986 strangulation of 57-year-old Beatrice McDougall, in Atlantic City, New Jersey, and authorities announced that they were checking other unsolved homicides in Arizona, California, Nevada and Florida.

On March 21, 1987, Siebert was convicted of Linda Jarman's murder in Talladega, receiving a sentence of death. Prosecution in other cases was held in abeyance, pending the outcome of his automatic appeal on the capital verdict.

Silva, Mauricio Rodriguez

Born with a cleft palate and chronic hormonal imbalance, Mauricio Silva started life with two strikes against him. Strike three was his temper, which led to the fatal shooting of a 16-year-old boy in 1978. Initially charged with murder, Silva struck a plea bargain for manslaughter and served five years in prison, including time added for his violent assault on a fellow inmate. Paroled on May 7, 1984, he wasted no time in killing again.

On May 18, while riding a bus in Los Angeles, Silva met 16-year-old Walter Sanders, somehow convincing the youth to join him on a drive through the barren Mojave Desert. Five miles east of Pearlblossom, they left the car and Silva took a shotgun with him, firing five rounds at close range to be certain the young man was dead.

On May 24, he picked up a teenaged hitchhiker, Monique Hilton, and drove into the desert east of

Palmdale, California, using the shotgun again in a ritualistic form of execution. Four days later, Silva switched to strangulation, invading the home of his own half-sister, 17-year-old Martha Kitzler, with whom he had stayed periodically since his parole. The crime led police to their man, and this time there would be no plea bargains as Silva faced three counts of first-degree murder.

Tried for his crimes in Los Angeles, Silva was convicted April 17, 1985, on two counts of first-degree murder (Sanders and Hilton), with one count of second-degree (Kitzler). Prosecutors sought the death penalty, while Silva's defender played on the theme of a traumatic childhood, describing the prisoner as a child of unfeeling parents, with "no house to call his home." After thirteen days of deliberation, the jury split seven to five in favor of execution, their deadlock leaving Silva with a mandatory sentence of life without parole.

Smith, George Joseph

An habitual criminal, born in January 1872, Smith was sentenced to eight years in a British reformatory at age nine. In 1896, he drew another year for receiving stolen goods, and was released in 1897. Smith celebrated the turn of the century with a two-year sentence for theft, hitting the streets again in October 1902. Discarding his first wife (and sometime criminal accomplice), Smith spent the next decade perfecting his technique as a matrimonial swindler. The risks were minimal, and they would be reduced to nothing, Smith decided, if his wives were not alive to testify against him.

Using the alias of "Williams," Smith married Beatrice Mundy in July 1912, a bigamous union made null and void by the fact he had never divorced his first wife. The honeymoon was still in progress when Smith called on Dr. F.A. French, insisting that his bride undergo treatment for "fits." Beatrice staunchly denied any symptoms of illness, but Dr. French was summoned to their residence three days later, by a note from Smith reading: "Come at once. I am afraid my wife is dead." French found Beatrice in the bathtub, her face partially submerged, and while he noted that the water was clear—rather than soapy—the doctor ignored his suspicions, certifying death by natural causes.

In October 1913, Smith spoke with an annuity insurance agent, discussing a planned investment of $2,500. Smith promised to have the money before his birthday, in January, and he promptly set about stalking a new victim to make up his cash shortage. He met Alice Burnham at Portsmouth, in November, and they were married days later, the bride taking out a $5,000 insurance policy on the afternoon before their wedding. Six weeks later, in Blackpool, Alice was "accidentally drowned" in the bathtub of their rented flat, and Smith collected her insurance money in time to follow through on his investment scheme.

In December 1914, posing as "Joseph Lloyd," Smith was married to Margaret Lofty, in Bath. They went to London the same day, and Smith returned from an early outing next day to find his bride dead in the bathtub. He was arrested on suspicion of murder when police learned his true identity, and they discovered Smith had also lied about his wife's lack of life insurance. He was expecting some $3,500 at the time of his arrest, for a total of $18,000 collected in the past two years.

The defense presented no evidence when Smith went to trial, charged with three counts of murder, in June 1915. As the prosecution rested its case, Smith rose and shouted, "I don't care whether you sentence me to death or not!" Convicted of all three "brides-in-the-bath" murders, he received the maximum penalty, and was hanged on August 13, 1915.

Solomon, Morris, Jr.

Born in 1944, Solomon was an ex-convict with a history of sexual assaults and violence, leading to his 1971 committal as a mentally disordered sex offender. Upon release from the state hospital as "cured," Solomon adopted the life-style of an itinerant handyman, repairing old homes around Sacramento, California, in exchange for free room and board. Along the way, he started killing women as a private form of sport.

According to authorities, the first to die was 22-year-old Yolanda Jackson, found inside the closet of a Sacramento home on June 18, 1986. A month later, 25-year-old Angela Polidore was found dead, buried beneath debris at another home where Solomon worked as a handyman. Suspected in both cases, he walked when authorities failed to come up with the evidence needed to win an indictment.

On March 19, 1987, the remains of Marie Apodoca, a teenage prostitute, were unearthed in the yard of a home in Sacramento's Oak Park district. Solomon had occupied the house until November 1986, and now detectives had their evidence in hand. More came on April 20, when Cherie Washington, age 26, was retrieved from a shallow grave in the same neighborhood. Solomon was taken into custody on April 22, after two more victims were discovered, buried at his current residence.

Investigators vowed to leave no stone unturned, procuring a military helicopter with infra-red scanners to canvas the neighborhood for graves. A seventh victim was uncovered on April 29, in the same yard where Marie Apodoca was found, and the search was called off a week later, after excavation of three other "hot spots" proved fruitless. Held without bond, the lethal handyman faced seven counts of murder in the first degree.

"Southside Slayer, The"— Los Angeles

Unidentified at this writing, the Southside Slayer of Los Angeles is credited with at least fourteen homicides between September 1983 and May 1987. At least three other victims are considered possible additions to the list, and three more managed to survive encounters with the stalker, offering police descriptions of a black man in his early thirties, sporting a mustache and baseball cap. The killer's chosen victims have been women, mostly black and mainly prostitutes, tortured with superficial cuts before they were strangled or stabbed to death in a grisly "pattern of overkill," their bodies dumped on residential streets, in alleyways and schoolyards.

Loletha Prevot was the first to die, discovered in Los Angeles on September 4, 1983. Four months passed before the killer struck again, on New Year's Day, dumping the corpse of Patricia Coleman in Inglewood. Another ten months slipped away before discovery of a third victim, Sheila Burton—alias Burris—on November 18, 1984.

The elusive slayer adopted a regular schedule in 1985, beginning with the murder of Frankie Bell on January 1. Patricia Dennis was the next to fall, her mutilated body recovered on February 11. The first victim for March was Sheily Wilson, murdered in Inglewood on the twentieth; three days later, the stalker claimed Lillian Stoval in Los Angeles. Number eight was Patsy

Webb, murdered on April 15, with Cathy Gustavson joining the list on July 28.

Thus far, the killer had missed only once, leaving one victim comatose after a vicious beating. On August 6, his next intended target managed to escape by leaping from his moving car. She offered homicide detectives a description and assisted in the preparation of a widely-published sketch, but officers appeared no closer to their suspect than they were in 1983.

Rebounding from his recent failure with another kill, the slayer dumped Gail Ficklin's body in Los Angeles on August 15. A twelve-week lull was broken on November 6, with Gayle Rouselle's murder in Gardena, and the killer returned the next day to slaughter Myrtle Collier in L.A. Nesia McElrath, 23, was found slain on December 19, and Elizabeth Landcraft's mutilated corpse was found on December 22, 1985. The day after Christmas, Gidget Castro's body was discarded in the City of Commerce.

The new year was five days old when Tammy Scretchings met her killer in Los Angeles, becoming number fourteen on the Southside Slayer's hit parade. On January 10, a 27-year-old prostitute was beaten and a male acquaintance stabbed when he attempted to restrain her violent customer. Their physical descriptions of the suspect tallied with reports from the survivor who escaped in August 1985.

The killer chalked up number sixteen, Lorna Reed, on February 11, 1986, discarding her corpse at San Dimas, twenty-five miles east of his usual hunting ground. Prostitute Verna Williams was found on May 26, her body slumped in the stairwell of a Los Angeles elementary school, and Trina Chaney joined the list November 3, in Watts. In January 1988, police announced that Carolyn Barney—killed May 29, 1987—was being added to the Southside list.

Three other victims have been unofficially connected

with the Southside Slayer, though detectives hesitate to make a positive I.D. Loretta Jones, a 22-year-old co-ed with no criminal record, was murdered and dumped in a Los Angeles alley on April 15, 1986. A white "Jane Doe," age 25 to 30, was discovered strangled in a garbage dumpster three weeks later. Finally, Canoscha Griffin, 22, was stabbed to death on the grounds of a local high school, her body discovered July 24.

By early 1988, police were backing off their initial body count, noting that defendant Charles Mosley had been convicted in one of the 1986 murders, while five more cases—involving victims Barney, Burris, Castro, Ficklin, and McElrath—were considered "closed" with the arrest of two other serial slayers. At the same time, identified suspects were cleared by police in the remaining fifteen cases, leaving at least one vicious stalker still at large. (See also: Siebert, Daniel Lee)

Spencer, Anthony

An illiterate Brooklynite, born in 1947, Spencer was arrested on an arson charge at age 13, committed to an institution for mental defectives after two months observation at Bellevue Hospital. Released in 1962, he continued therapy as an out-patient until April 1964. Two months later, on June 21, he was charged with raping a Bronx woman at knifepoint, released on $500 bond after formal indictments were handed down. On August 22, he assaulted Constance Thompson in an elevator, threatening to mutilate her infant son if she would not submit to rape. Interrupted by the building superintendent, Spencer fled on foot, but Thompson saw him on the street a month later, trailing him home and then calling police.

In custody, the 17-year-old rapist confessed to two

murders and ten sexual assaults. One victim, 29-year-old Charlotte Lipstick, had been raped and killed in her Brooklyn home on May 29, 1964. The other, Mary Payne, age 83, was murdered in the Bronx on Labor Day. Spencer's surviving victims included a five-year-old girl, but he could offer no motive for the crimes. "I don't know why I do it," he explained. "I get headaches, pass out, and I hear funny noises."

Indicted on two counts of murder, plus the rape of Constance Thompson, Spencer was returned to Bellevue for psychiatric evaluation. Pronounced sane by staff psychiatrists, he was ultimately convicted and sentenced to prison for life.

Spraggins, Jerry Jerome

There seemed to be a curse on the Cranetown Apartments, in Montclair, New Jersey—more specifically upon Apartment 31. In November 1981, tenant Lillian Harris, 83, died of an apparent heart attack while her apartment was being burglarized. Seventeen months later, on April 18, 1983, 51-year-old Joan Leight died under identical circumstances, at the same address. Her replacement as tenant in Apartment 31, 68-year-old Sarah McHale, was found dead in her living room September 2, smothered with a pillow. Police spokesmen made veiled references to "similarities" in the three deaths, refusing to offer more details for fear of jeopardizing their investigation.

On April 11, 1985, authorities in Essex County arrested 30-year-old Jerry Spraggins, a mechanic and dispatcher for a local taxi service, on charges of murdering Sarah McHale and Joan Leight. Also considered a prime suspect in the death of Lillian Harris, Spraggins escaped charges in that case through lack of conclusive evidence. Twice charged with criminal trespass and sexual assault at another Montclair apartment complex, in December 1984, the suspect had escaped with a $600 fine and two years probation after the judge suspended an 11-month jail term. Additional charges in the Cranetown Apartment cases included burglary, theft, and sexual assault.

Spraggins was ultimately convicted in the death of Sarah McHale, sentenced to a term of 30 years in prison. While the other crimes remain officially unsolved, Montclair authorities maintain a firm conviction of their suspect's guilt across the board. It is worth noting that the "Cranetown curse" was lifted when he went to jail.

Swango, Michael

Rated a genius in high school, with a tested IQ of 160, Swango graduated first in his class and was named "High School Student of the Year" by the National Merit Scholarship organization in 1975. By 1983, he had finished medical school and was serving his internship at Ohio State University, in Columbus. At least seven persons died under his care in that year, and hospital administrators were disturbed by reports from nurses who saw Swango injecting unknown chemicals into patient IV tubes, shortly before deaths were reported. Another patient, 19-year-old Cindy McGee, was recovering nicely from an automobile accident when Swango dropped by "to take blood samples," but she suffered a sudden, inexplicable relapse, and was soon pronounced dead. A survivor, rescued from the brink of death, told nurses, "A blond doctor put something in my IV and everything went black."

Intimidated by the prospect of lawsuits if Swango was dismissed, Ohio State administrators let him finish out the year, but he was not invited back to serve the normal five-year residency term. He *was* recommended for licensing as a physician, however, and moved on to Quincy, Illinois, where he joined the staff of Blessing Hospital, working around the emergency ward.

In short order, paramedics at Blessing began suffering attacks of violent nausea, invariably following a gift of snacks or beverages from smiling Dr. Swango. Suspicious, they placed Swango under unofficial surveillance, and one paramedic soon found quantities of ant poison in the doctor's gym bag. Police were notified, and Swango was charged with assault, a search of his home turning up stockpiles of acid, chemicals, and poisons, in addition to handwritten poison "recipes" and numerous items of occult paraphernalia.

As the investigation proceeded, authorities began exhuming Swango's unfortunate Ohio patients. At least one, Ricky DeLong, had apparently been suffocated, though Swango signed his death certificate with a notation of "natural causes." Convicted of assault in Quincy, during 1985, Swango was sentenced to five years in prison. No murder charges have yet been filed in Ohio, but on February 12, 1986—nearly a year after his conviction—Swango's license to practice medicine in that state was revoked. At this writing, he remains eligible to practice in Illinois upon release from jail.

Tahl, William Albert Autur

An American Eskimo, Tahl clashed with authority for the first time at age three, after deliberately hurling a brick through a window. More arrests followed, but his crimes remained petty until the spring of 1965, when unexpected violent urges surfaced at the age of twenty-seven.

On April Fool's Day, Tahl approached his man-and-wife employers, Mr. and Mrs. Victor Bowen, at the

Mission Bay Yacht Club in San Diego, California. Brandishing a shotgun, he demanded cash, and was indignantly refused. Impulsively, Tahl shot both victims, killing Mrs. Bowen instantly; her husband would survive just long enough to name the gunman for police.

Mere hours later, still on April 1, Tahl invaded a nearby apartment, threatening to stab a two-year-old child if the boy's teenaged mother did not submit to intercourse. Following the rape, he fled from California, giving San Diego officers the slip, and set his sights on Texas. In El Paso, Tahl acquired a bogus driver's license, draft card, and Social Security number in the name of "Arthur Spencer," moving on to Dallas as he searched for work.

In Dallas, Tahl made friends with Allen Wright, age 24, and shortly moved his few belongings into Wright's apartment. There, on April 26, a neighbor found Wright's body—naked, torn by knife wounds—and police began a search for "Arthur Spencer," on another count of murder.

Tahl, meanwhile, was hiding in Fort Worth. While there, he "found" a Social Security card in the name of "J.D. Baxter," usurping that identity as he evacuated Texas, homing on St. Louis. Back in Dallas, "Arthur Spencer" had been made as William Tahl, and federal warrants had begun to multiply on charges of unlawful flight. Tahl's name was added to the FBI's "Most Wanted" list on June 10, 1965.

Tahl's latest buddy, in St. Louis, was a teacher by the name of Marvin Thomas. After several meetings, Tahl moved into Thomas's apartment, watching from a distance as the FBI continued their pursuit across the great Southwest. Come autumn, William's cash and self-control evaporated simultaneously; on November 5 he bound his roommate, battered Thomas with a sock containing buckshot, and coerced the teacher into signing four $100 checks, made out to "J.D. Baxter." Leaving the apartment shortly after 1 a.m., Tahl had no way of knowing that a neighbor had already called police.

St. Louis officers arrived to rescue Thomas, listening as he related details of his ordeal. They were still on hand when Tahl returned, but they proved careless in allowing him to use the bathroom prior to making the arrest. Emerging with a pistol pointed at himself, Tahl threatened suicide, revealing his identity and startling police with details of his several homicides. An hour and twenty minutes passed before he finally surrendered and was carted off to jail, awaiting the arrival of the FBI.

Tannenbaum, Gloria

A peculiar chapter of Colorado's criminal history was closed on March 9, 1971, with the announcement that Gloria Tannenbaum, suspect in two deaths and one disappearance, had died in the state mental hospital at Pueblo. A suicide note was found at her bedside, and authorities concluded she had somehow managed to ingest a dose of cyanide—the same poison allegedly used to kill two of her victims in 1969.

Gloria Tannenbaum's publicized troubles began after Dr. Thomas Riha, 40-year-old professor of Russian history at Colorado University, vanished from his home near the Boulder campus on March 14, 1969. Within a short time, Tannenbaum was charged, both in Boulder and Denver, with four separate felony counts involving illegal disposal of Riha's property. Prior to her trial on one charge—that of forging his name on a $300 check—Gloria was pronounced insane by court psychiatrists and confined to the state hospital until such time as she recovered sufficiently to participate in her own defense.

In confinement, Tannenbaum boasted of influential

contacts and hinted at "secret assignments" performed on behalf of intelligence agencies. Outside her narrow world, the search for Dr. Riha's body yielded no results, but homicide detectives had begun suspecting Gloria in two more deaths. A couple of her neighbors, 78-year-old Gustav Ingwerson and Barbara Egbert, 51, had recently died of apparent cyanide poisoning. There was insufficient evidence for indictment, but police believed that Gloria had murdered both, perhaps because they had possessed some information on the Riha case.

The deaths and disappearance are officially unsolved, but Gloria appears to have claimed the last word on the case for herself. "It doesn't matter really," she wrote to her attorney on the last night of her life, "but I will tell you this. I didn't do Tom or Gus or Barb in. I went nuts with hurt over losing them. Everything that has made me feel good about myself has been taken away. Life is very cheap."

Taylor, Gary Addison

Michigan born in 1936, Gary Taylor spent his early years in Florida, launching his first attacks on women there, when he was in his teens. His standard M.O. involved loitering around bus stops after nightfall, waiting for solitary women to disembark, assaulting them with a hammer. Confined as a juvenile, Taylor returned to Michigan on release, in 1957, and there became notorious as the "Royal Oak Sniper," shooting women he found on the streets after dark. Thus far, none of his victims had died, and Taylor was shuttled from one psychiatric hospital to another over an eleven-year period, assaulting several Detroit women during ill-conceived furloughs. Despite his continuing violence and a self-proclaimed "compulsion to hurt women," Taylor was rated a safe bet for out-patient treatment, "as long as he reports in to receive medication." Tiring of the game in late 1973, he stopped showing up at the hospital, and authorities waited fourteen months before listing his disappearance with the National Crime Information Center in Washington, D.C.

By that time, Taylor had murdered at least four women in three different states. A pair of victims from Ohio—25-year-old Lee Fletcher and 23-year-old Deborah Heneman—were buried in Taylor's back yard before he abandoned his home in Onsted, Michigan, moving west to Seattle. There, on the night of November 27, he abducted and killed a young housewife, Vonnie Stuth. Officers traced him to Enumclaw, Washington, where he sat still for interrogation but refused to take a polygraph exam. In the absence of an NCIC listing, homicide investigators did not know he was a fugitive, and they were forced to set him free. By the time Michigan authorities plugged Taylor's name into the national computer, he had vanished again, bound for Texas.

On May 20, 1975, Taylor was picked up in Houston on a charge of sexual assault, swiftly confessing his role in four murders. Victims Fletcher and Heneman were unearthed in Michigan on May 22, and Taylor signed confessions in two other cases, including those of Houston victim Susan Jackson, 21, and Vonnie Stuth, found buried near his former home in Enumclaw. Further investigation cleared him of six other Washington murders, now blamed on Ted Bundy, but officers in Texas, Michigan, and California suspect him in as many as 20 unsolved homicides. Convicted on the four counts he confessed, Taylor was sentenced to a term of life imprisonment.

Terry, Michael

One evening in December 1985, Curtis Brown, a 21-year-old black man, left his home in Atlanta, Georgia, to purchase a package of cigarettes. Five hours later, when an unidentified corpse was discovered in Dean Rusk Park, no connection was made. Stripped of I.D., his pants pulled down, the victim had been shot several times in the head, and .38-caliber bullets were recovered in fair shape for ballistic identification.

Curtis Brown's body was not identified until four days later, when his girlfriend filed a missing person report with police. With confirmation in hand, detectives examined his final hours, tracing the victim as far as a neighborhood tavern. Employees remembered him there, on the night of his death, and they thought he had left with another black customer, known—for the sake of his 300 pounds—as "Big Mike."

From there, the trail went cold, and homicide detectives had no time to spare for chasing shadows. Six years earlier, Atlanta had been "honored" with the title of America's murder capital, boasting the nation's highest per capita homicide rate, and matters had scarcely improved in the meantime. Three sensational outbreaks of serial murder had captured the national spotlight from 1980 to 1984, and overworked police had many "ordinary" slayings on their hands, as well.

Ten months elapsed before authorities resigned themselves to yet another monster in their midst. In mid-October 1986, the decomposing body of a young black man was discovered in an abandoned building; he had been shot several times in the back of the head, the body left with pants pulled down around his knees. It took several days to identify the victim as Daryl Williams, a 21-year-old drifter from Ohio. Last seen alive

in a bar, on October 5, there was no trace of his movements from that night on.

Ballistics tests confirmed a link between the Williams murder weapon and victim George Willingham, a
local family man who left his home on an errand, October 5, and never returned. Found the next day in an
alley, he had been shot in the back of the head,
execution-style, with the same pistol used on Daryl
Williams.

The connection of two similar cases sent detectives
back to their files. In short order, they compiled a list
of further victims. Curtis Brown was added, on the basis of his killer's M.O., along with Richard Williams, of
South Carolina; Alvin George, 31, from Columbus,
Ohio; and 18-year-old Jason McColley, a native of Atlanta. The last three all had reputations as street hustlers
or male prostitutes; all had been slain execution-style,
with a pistol or knife, during the past year.

There were other striking similarities between the unsolved murders. Five of the six victims were found with
their pants down, apparently slain after sex. George and
McColley were murdered a month apart, but in the
same alley, each stabbed in the neck with a similar
knife. Two unrelated victims named Williams, the first
and last, had each been killed in abandoned buildings a
short distance apart. Richard Williams and Curtis
Brown had been shot with the same pistol, but *not* the
one used to kill Daryl Williams and George Willingham. Brown and Richard Williams had each suffered
post-mortem wounds from a short, sharp blade.

If further connections were needed, a witness recalled seeing Jason McColley with a hulk matching
"Big Mike's" description on the night he died. Renewed investigation led detectives to the rooming house
where Michael Terry had lived for the past year, collecting numerous guns and pawning a few when he ran
short of cash. Arrested at work, in a tire-capping shop,

Terry was relieved of a hidden .357 magnum and hauled in for questioning.

In his eventual confession, Terry stated that he met his several victims in saloons, adjourned to other sites for homosexual relations, after which the smaller men allegedly had threatened him with robbery or worse. The killings, he alleged, were simply self-defense. "I didn't want to hurt anyone," Terry insisted, "but they took advantage of me."

A jury thought otherwise, and on February 22, 1987, Michael Terry was convicted of murdering Richard Williams and Curtis Brown. He was sentenced to a term of life imprisonment without parole, four other cases held in reserve, against the possibility his sentence might be shortened on appeal.

Tholmer, Brandon

A native of Los Angeles, born in 1949, Tholmer was 26 years old at the time of his arrest for assaulting a police officer. A charge of rape was added, when his fingerprints were matched with those recovered from the apartment where a 79-year-old woman was attacked on October 22, 1975, and Tholmer later pled guilty to that crime, blaming his actions on an LSD "high." Suspected, but never charged, in a series of ten murders committed by the elusive "West Side Rapist," Tholmer spent three years in Patton State Hospital, undergoing treatment as a mentally disordered sex offender. Released in October 1979, he continued treatment as an out-patient at a rehabilitation center in suburban Silver Lake.

Memories of the West Side Rapist were revived from 1981 to '84, as homicide investigators probed the violent deaths of 32 elderly women around Los Angeles.

Eighty-year-old Rose Lederman was one of the first to die, her body discovered in her Silver Lake home, within walking distance of Tholmer's rehab center, on August 13, 1981. It was November 1984 when task force officers examined Tholmer's file and noted similarities between his old M.O. and the procedures of their latest maniac-at-large. Surveillance was initiated on November 6, and Tholmer was arrested one day later, poised outside the bedroom window of an 85-year-old paraplegic.

Evidence collected by authorities linked Tholmer to merchandise stolen from Rose Lederman in 1981, and one of his shoes matched a footprint found at the home of 69-year-old Wolloomooloo Woodcock, murdered in August 1982. Suspected of 34 slayings in all, strongly connected with 12 through circumstantial evidence, Tholmer was ultimately charged with only four. A jury convicted him on all counts—including charges of rape, sodomy, arson and burglary—on July 25, 1986. Sentenced to four consecutive terms of life imprisonment, he is unlikely to be prosecuted for numerous other suspected murders.

"Thrill Killings"—Texas

For seven months in 1984 and 1985, a gang of teen-aged gunmen roamed at will in Dallas, Texas, killing victims on the street. Police described the gang as "just a group of friends who liked to shoot people," and Investigator T.J. Barnes explained, "They were killing people because they didn't like their looks, or the way they looked at them."

The gang's first victim was 21-year-old John Hahn, gunned down on an East Dallas street without apparent motive, on December 7, 1984. Three months later, on

March 15, 1985, John Kane was shot and killed while chasing some youths who had pelted him with beer cans. Juan Cuevas, 20, died on April 6, the victim of another random, senseless shooting.

On June 7, 1985, police swept up five of the gang, ages 16 to 18, reporting that a 15-year-old suspect had escaped to Mexico. Charged with three counts of murder, two counts of aggravated assault, plus one count each of burglary, aggravated robbery and attempted murder, the unnamed teens were also suspected of four other East Dallas slayings.

Tison, Gary Gene and Greenawalt, Randy

In retrospect, considering the time he spent in jail, it seemed incredible that Gary Tison could command such loyalty from his family. Imprisoned at the age of 25 for robbery, he took advantage of a meeting with his wife to flee the county jail in Florence, Arizona. Recaptured and later paroled, Tison was charged with parole violation after passing a bad check in 1967. That April, en route to a court hearing, he overpowered a prison guard, handcuffed the officer, and shot him to death with his own service revolver.

Conviction of first-degree murder earned Tison a life sentence, but he wasted no time on self-pity. In prison, he quickly made friends with serial slayer Randy Greenawalt, serving life on conviction for one of his four random murders. (The victims were truckers, picked out, Randy said, because one of their kind "roughed him up" years before.) Proud of his "special" status as a multiple killer, Greenawalt fell into line with Tison's new plan of escape.

On July 30, 1978, Tison's son Ricky, 18, came to

visit his father at the state prison in Florence. They were chatting in the fenced picnic area when two more of the Tison boys—Raymond, 19, and Donald, 20—arrived with a basket of food for their father. Inside the lobby, one of the boys pulled a shotgun and covered the guards, demanding his father's release. Randy Greenawalt, meanwhile, had done his part by temporarily disabling the prison telephones and alarm system. Together, the five strolled so casually toward their getaway car that tower guards mistook them for departing visitors and let them go.

Next day, the fugitives were stranded with a blow-out when 24-year-old Marine Sgt. John Lyons stopped to help. Traveling from Yuma to Nebraska with his wife, their infant son and teenage niece, Lyons hated to see anyone stuck in the desert, but his act of charity resulted in disaster. Lyons, wife Donelda, and son Christopher were killed in the first blast of gunfire from Tison and Greenawalt. The sergeant's niece, Teresa Tyson, age 16, was wounded in the hip and left to die, discovered by a group of searchers after she had bled to death.

Scouring the countryside for Tison and company, authorities established a roadblock near Gary's home town of Casa Grande, Arizona. When the silver van approached, some hours later, it began to slow, the driver braking, but a blast of gunfire from the windows scattered offices as Tison and his gang swept past. A second roadblock waited five miles down the road, and this time deputies were ready, killing Donald Tison with their first barrage of fire. The battle raged for half an hour, Greenawalt and the surviving Tison boys surrendering as they ran out of ammunition, Gary taking off on foot across the desert.

Officers discovered that the van belonged to James and Margene Judge, a pair of newlyweds from Colorado. Never found, they were included in the list of murder victims charged to Greenawalt and the incarcerated Tison brothers. Gary Tison, meanwhile, managed to elude pursuit until the final week of August, when his bloated, decomposing corpse was found outside the tiny town of Chuichu, Arizona. Unwounded in the final shootout with police, he had apparently succumbed to thirst and desert heat.

Toronto—Unsolved Murders

Between May and July of 1982, Toronto citizens were terrorized by a series of brutal rape-assaults that left four young women dead and a fifth gravely injured. An editorial in the *Toronto Star* described the victims as "a cheerleader, a nanny, a mother and a bride-to-be." While angry women's groups attacked the notion that rape victims are invariably young and attractive, thus somehow "inviting" assault, local residents cringed from the published accounts of the crimes: pantyhose tied around one victim's throat; another's skull crushed with a brick; a third naked and floating face-down in the river.

The first to die, on May 28, was 19-year-old Jennifer Isford, battered and discarded on a lawn close by her parents' home. Four other attacks would follow in the next six weeks, climaxing with the July strangulation of 38-year-old Judy DeLisle. Police describe the crimes as "apparently unconnected," but locals remain unconvinced of the "coincidence." At this writing, the case remains unsolved, the killer (or killers) still at large.

Trueblood, Lydia

A classic "black widow," Lydia Trueblood would stop at nothing to collect the life insurance on her many mates. It took six years, and half a dozen victims, for detectives in a two-state killing zone to realize that sometimes arsenic—not diamonds—is a girl's best friend.

Lydia was born in Keytsville, sixty miles northeast of Kansas City, in the central flatlands of Missouri. Members of her family were friendly with another local clan, the Dooleys, and as time went by, young Robert Dooley fell in love with Lydia. She seemed to share his feelings, and when Lydia moved on to Twin Falls, Idaho, her would-be suitor followed close behind. They married there in 1912, and settled down to plan their future, with a sharp eye on security.

It was arranged for Robert and his brother, Edward, to secure a life insurance policy. In the event that either brother died, $1,000 would be paid to the surviving Dooley, with a like amount to Lydia. On August 9, 1915, Edward Dooley fell suddenly ill; his death, days later, was ascribed to typhoid, and his brother sadly split two thousand dollars with the grieving Lydia.

On August 10, while Edward clung to life and all around him prayed for recovery, a second life insurance policy was written in the names of Robert Dooley and his wife. Upon the death of either, the survivor would receive $2,000. "Typhoid fever" struck again in late September 1915, and by sundown on October 1, the widow Dooley had a decent nest egg in the making. Recently encumbered with a child, she cast about for remedies, and Providence was smiling. Barely six weeks passed before the infant "drank from a contaminated well" and died.

A mandatory period of mourning left the widow Dooley hungry for companionship. She found a viable solution in the person of William McHaffie, a waiter in her favorite Twin Falls restaurant. They wed in 1917, and he took out a $5,000 life insurance policy, with Lydia as beneficiary, before they pulled up stakes and moved to Hardin, in Montana. The marriage was a short one; "influenza" claimed McHaffie one year later, but his policy had lapsed because McHaffie failed to pay the second premium, and Lydia collected nothing for her pains.

She moved to Denver, where she married Harlan Lewis during May of 1919. They set up housekeeping at Billings, Montana, and Lewis purchased a $5,000 life insurance policy in June. Disaster struck in mid-July, a sudden case of "ptomaine poisoning" eliminating husband number three. This time, the check came through.

On August 10, the three-time widow married Edward Meyer in Pocatello, Idaho. She called herself "Anna McHaffie," but the change of name did not foreshadow any change in *modus operandi*. On August 11, Lydia applied for a $10,000 life insurance policy in Edward's name, but it was disapproved, for reasons never clarified. (In retrospect, perhaps the industry was waking up to Lydia's uncanny run of luck.) The Meyers settled on a ranch in the Snake River region, where Edward was taken ill on August 25. He was transported to the hospital, where doctors praised his chances of recovery, but on September 7 he was dead. Post-mortem tests discovered arsenic, but after brief preliminary questioning, detectives set the widow Meyer free.

She fled to California, seeking other prey and sanctuary while behind her, Idaho authorities were busy with petitions for the exhumation of her other victims. One by one, the test results were positive. The Dooley brothers had been murdered, as had Lydia's own child. Montana officers began to sniff around the Lewis and McHaffie cases, curious about the lethal widow's long run of coincidence.

While Twin Falls prosecutor Frank L. Stephen built a case, his quarry picked up husband number five, Paul Southard, in Los Angeles. They married in November 1920, and she tried to sell him on the notion of a life insurance policy, but he declined. A seaman in the navy, Southard saw no need for coverage beyond the normal government provisions. Southard had been transferred to Pearl Harbor shortly after wedding Lydia, and Honolulu officers were privileged to pick her up when warrants finally arrived from Idaho, on May 12, 1921. Returned to Boise for her trial, she drew a term of life imprisonment and subsequently died in jail.

Tuggle, Debra Sue

A former mental patient in Little Rock, Arkansas, Tuggle was arrested in March 1984 and charged with murdering four of her own children over the past decade. The first two victims—sons Thomas Bates, age two, and William Henry, 21 months—were suffocated at different times in 1974. Another son, nine-month-old Ronald Johnson, suffered a similar fate in 1976, while two-year-old Tomekia Paxton, the daughter of Tuggle's boyfriend, was deliberately drowned in 1982. Held on $750,000 bond pending trial and ultimate conviction on the outstanding murder counts, Tuggle was also suspected—but never charged—in the death of a fifth child. Coroner Steve Nawojczyk told newsmen that a faulty legal system had permitted Tuggle to remain at large for years, escaping prosecution in the string of homicides that claimed her children's lives. No motive was presented in the case.

Vermilyea, Louise

A "black widow" whose activities spanned the turn of the century, Louise Vermilyea came to grief when greed exceeded her discretion and she started reaching out to prey upon acquaintances, instead of relatives. At that, it took the death of a policeman in Chicago to alert authorities and raise suspicion over the peculiar fates experienced by several husbands, family members, and associates.

The officer in question, Arthur Bisonette, age 26, had been a boarder in Vermilyea's home when he fell ill and died in late October 1911. Homicide detectives grew suspicious after speaking with Bisonette's father, who also reported stomach pains after dining with his son at the boarding house. Louise Vermilyea, he recalled, had sprinkled "white pepper" over his food before it was served. An autopsy on Bisonette discovered arsenic, and Louise was taken into custody pending exhumation of other suspected victims.

The string of homicides apparently began in 1893, when Fred Brinkamp, Louise's first husband, died at his farm near Barrington, Illinois. He left his widow richer by $5,000, but at sixty years of age, Fred's death was not considered cause for any undue comment.

Soon, two daughters by the marriage—Cora Brinkamp, eight years old, and Florence, nearly five— were also dead. In January 1906, Lillian Brinkamp, Fred's 26-year-old granddaughter, died in Chicago, stricken by "acute nephritis." It began to seem that members of the Brinkamp tribe had stumbled on a previously undiscovered family curse.

Louise remarried, meanwhile, to one Charles Vermilyea, 59. By 1909 he was dead, another victim of sudden illness, leaving his widow $1,000 in cash. Harry Vermilyea, a step-son, dropped dead in Chicago after he quarreled with Louise over the sale of a house at Crys-

tal Lake, ten miles north of Chicago in McHenry
County. Once again, coincidence was blamed.

In 1910, Louise inherited $1,200 on the death of
Frank Brinkamp, her 23-year-old son from her first
marriage. On his death bed, Brinkamp informed his fiancee, Elizabeth Nolan, of belated suspicions involving
his mother, declaring that he was "going the way Dad
did."

Temporarily short of relatives, Louise began to practice on acquaintances. The first to die was Jason
Ruppert, a railroad fireman who became ill after dining
with Louise on January 15, 1910. Two days later, he
was dead, and others followed swiftly. Richard Smith, a
train conductor, rented rooms in the Vermilyea household, but he should have eaten elsewhere. Sudden illness struck him down a short time prior to Arthur
Bisonette's arrival on the scene, and other victims
might have fallen over time, had not Louise allowed the
elder Bisonette to get away.

While motive in the later homicides was never clear,
financial gain was obvious in the elimination of
Vermilyea's husbands and assorted offspring. Under-
taker E.N. Blocks, of Barrington, recalled that Louise
"actually seemed to enjoy working around bodies, and
while I never employed her, for a couple of years I
couldn't keep her out of the office. At every death she
would seem to hear of it just as soon as I and she
would reach the house only a little behind me."

While under house arrest, Louise Vermilyea deni-
grated the official efforts to indict her for a string of ten
known homicides. "They may go as far as they like,"
she said of police, "for I have nothing to fear. I simply
have been unfortunate in having people dying around
me." On the side, her tough facade was crumbling, and
on November 4 detectives rushed her to the hospital, a
victim of her own "white pepper." The authorities reported that Louise had been ingesting poison with her

meals since she was first confined at home, October 28. On November 9, she was reported as being near death, with valvular heart problems adding their punch to the poison. By December 9, she had been stricken with paralysis, described by her physicians as a permanent condition.

Villarreal, David

A homosexual drifter, 26-year-old David Villarreal was arrested in March 1981, after an informant tipped police to his involvement in a seven-year series of murders around Dallas and San Antonio, Texas. Picked up on March 10, Villarreal cheerfully directed police to the body of his latest victim, killed two days earlier, and tacked on confessions for crimes in which he was not yet a suspect.

According to statements recorded by Texas authorities, Villarreal claimed his first victim in San Antonio, during 1974. Moving to Dallas in late 1978 or early '79, he scored number two, hammering a middle-aged stranger to death. In March 1979, he had been held for questioning in the murder of Ernest Garcia—stabbed with an ice pick, then beaten with a board and concrete block—but he was finally released for lack of evidence. A month later, he staged a double event with the slayings of 30-year-old Charles Moya and 32-year-old Tony Gutierrez, dispatching both victims by slitting their throats.

More recently, in San Antonio, he had beaten 18-year-old Joe Duque to death on March 3, 1981. On March 8, he used a claw hammer to murder 72-year-old Robert Manley, the victim's body discovered on March 11 as a result of the killer's confession. Police reported that "sexual gratification was at least part of the motive" in Villarreal's San Antonio murders, while those committed in Dallas seemed purely mercenary, connected with various robberies.

Waldon, Billy Ray

Billy Waldon scarcely knew his mother. During 1957, at the tender age of five, he was delivered to his grandmother's care, and the older woman raised him as her own around Tahlequah, Oklahoma, teaching him the values that she hoped would guide his steps through life. Enlisting in the navy out of high school, Waldon had fourteen years of service behind him when he was discharged, as a first petty officer, in January 1985. One-quarter Cherokee, he was described by friends and neighbors as "a brilliant man" who "spent more time listening to others than talking about himself." If Waldon had a quirk, it was his fascination with the subject of AIDS, a compulsive quest for knowledge that encouraged some associates to think he might be homosexual.

The death of Waldon's grandmother, in 1985, appeared to be the trigger incident for an astounding, lethal shift in Billy's personality. A quiet, unassuming man by all accounts before her death, he changed dramatically in later weeks, like Mr. Hyde emerging from the passive Dr. Jekyll. With the change of seasons into autumn, Billy launched a one-man reign of terror that could claim four lives and leave at least eight other persons injured.

The rampage began in Tulsa, close to home. Police suspect that Waldon was the gunman who wounded an elderly man outside a neighborhood grocery store on October 10, 1985. The following day, they believe, he robbed three persons at a shopping mall, rebounding for an unsuccessful robbery attempt on October 15. Witnesses were hazy on descriptions of their assailant, but the crimes fit an emerging pattern, and there would be no doubt of Waldon's involvement in the next outbreak.

Laying off a month from his activities, the phantom gunman surfaced on November 15, firing a single shot that grazed 20-year-old Cynthia Bellinger's skull outside her parents' Tulsa home. Two days later, Annabelle Richmond, age 54, was cut down by four .25-caliber bullets outside her apartment. The shooting continued in Broken Arrow, on November 23, when Waldon confronted Frank Hensley and Tammie Tvedt in a parking lot, demanding cash, wounding them both when they refused to pay up.

The heat was on in Tulsa, and Waldon fled west, presumably to visit his ex-wife and their two small children in Gardenia, California. Drifting into San Diego, refreshing old memories of his navy days, Billy picked up his crime spree where he had left off in Tulsa. By mid-December, he would be suspected of three rapes, five robberies, two burglaries, and one count of receiving stolen property.

On December 7, a gunman invaded the home of 42-year-old Dawn Ellerman, shooting her in the neck with a .25-caliber pistol, beating her dogs and locking them inside a bathroom, then setting the house on fire before he fled with a personal computer and other valuables. Erin Ellerman, 13, came home from babysitting to find the house in flames, and she died in a futile attempt to save her mother's life.

Two weeks later, on December 20, a masked man tried to rob a San Diego woman in a parking lot. Foiled in the attempt, he fled on foot, veering through a yard where two men were working on a car. Frustrated again in his attempt to steal the vehicle, the gunman killed Charles Wells, 59, and critically wounded John Copeland, 36, with a spray of .25-caliber bullets. Eluding 150 officers in a seven-hour manhunt, the killer still left traces of himself behind. Police recovered the Ellerman computer in an abandoned car registered to Billy Waldon, along with Waldon's military passport and other pieces of I.D.

Communication with police in Tulsa matched the murder slugs from San Diego with the Oklahoma shootings. On January 3, 1986, a federal warrant charged Waldon with unlawful flight to avoid prosecution for murder, attempted murder, robbery, burglary, rape, and arson. His name was added to the FBI's "Most Wanted" list on April 23.

By that time, Billy had performed an eerie disappearing act. His latest stolen car, picked off a street December 20, had been discovered outside Tijuana on January 27. There was no other trace of the fugitive before June 16, when San Diego officers routinely stopped a car with a defective brake light. They had planned to let the driver off with a warning, but his face was familiar, and Waldon's use of the alias "Steven Midas" fooled no one at police headquarters.

Ordered to trial on multiple charges in San Diego, Waldon had truly run out of luck. Jailers discovered his effort to tunnel through a wall of his cell, and fellow inmates proved dangerous. On July 24, 1986, Waldon was severely beaten by cellmates, hospitalized for two days, after he refused their orders to kill another prisoner. The motive for the bungled contract? Jailers noted that the target was unpopular with other cons because of his attitude, which was "basically anti-social."

Walker, Clarence

A native of Tennessee, born February 25, 1929, Walker was convicted of manslaughter and sentenced to prison at age 14. Paroled after seven years, he adopted a rootless life-style, clashing repeatedly with the law in his travels and serving two prison terms in Ohio, on conviction for armed robbery and grand larceny. Before his ultimate arrest in 1965, authorities believe he claimed a minimum of fourteen victims—three in Cleveland, four in rural Michigan, another seven scattered over Illinois.

The crimes in Michigan were typical of Walker's style. On February 6, 1965, 37-year-old Mary Jones was reported missing in Benton Harbor, after a late night of bar-hopping. Nine days later, 19-year-old Delores Young was kidnapped off the street in Benton Harbor, her nude body found in the ruins of a burned-out house on February 16. Amelia Boyer, 60, was the next to go, abducted from a laundromat. On March 30, seven-year-old Diane Carter disappeared from the same neighborhood where Walker was residing, under the alias of "James Darnell."

On April 4, the mutilated remains of Jones, Boyer, and Carter were found together, in a secluded pine grove at Bainbridge Township. Body parts and articles of clothing taken from the corpses would be matched, in years to come, with other mutilation deaths in Cleveland. Mary Jones's severed skull was found on April 23, near the home of a man listed by "James Darnell" as a relative, but Walker left town before he could be questioned. Arrested weeks later in Chicago, he drew a term of 320 years in prison on conviction of rape, armed robbery, and assault with intent to murder.

In Michigan, authorities were hampered by the stubborn certainty that they were looking for a white man skilled in surgery. (Walker was black, with only minor public education.) As years went by, detectives tried to link their unsolved crimes with the activities of Albert DeSalvo, Richard Speck, and Antone Costa . . . all in vain. It would be summer 1970 before the homicides were linked to Walker, serving time in Illinois. The suspect has declined to talk with homicide investigators, and no charges have been filed in view of his existing sentence, but authorities in three states have closed the books on 14 murders, so convinced are they of Walker's guilt.

Walker, Gary Alan

Prior to embarkation on a spree of rape and murder, Gary Walker managed to compile a record of convictions spanning fifteen years, with charges that included auto theft, burglary, narcotics abuse and firearms violations. As Walker described his own life, "I haven't spent a full year out of jail since I was seventeen years old."

Nor was he any stranger to mental institutions. While confined in the Oklahoma state prison, between 1977 and 1980, Walker was sent to the state hospital at Vinita on three occasions. One psychiatric report indicates that he sometimes entered mental health facilities "to hide from law enforcement officers." Along the way, Walker had sampled therapy, drugs, and electric shock treatments. Released from a federal lockup on February 7, 1984, on charges of prison escape and firearms violations, Gary had spent the final months of his term at the Federal Medical Facility in Springfield, Missouri. According to the staff, Walker's dead brother had been "speaking" to him; diagnosed as paranoid and schizophrenic, he was still eligible for parole.

On May 7, 1984, Eddie Cash, age 63, was found dead at his home in Broken Arrow, Oklahoma, a suburb of Tulsa. His van was missing when the body was discovered, bludgeoned with a brick, the electric cord from a vacuum cleaner wrapped around his neck. That evening, 36-year-old Margaret Bell vanished, with her car, from a Porteau, Oklahoma, tavern. She was reported missing on May 8, but police had no reason to connect the crimes, so far.

On May 14, Jayne Hilburn, 35, was strangled in her home at Vinita, forty-five miles northeast of Tulsa; her classic black Camaro was reported stolen from the scene. Next day, a young woman in Oakhurst—a Tulsa suburb—accepted a ride from the bushy-haired driver of a black Camaro. He introduced himself as "Gary Edwards" before pulling a knife and demanding that she shed her pants. The woman managed to escape unharmed, and told her story to police.

Five days later, in Skiatook, another Tulsa suburb, the same man abducted a 17-year-old girl, raping her at knifepoint before she scrambled free of his Camaro. The car was found abandoned on May 22, indicating that the killer rapist might be searching for another set of wheels.

On May 23, 32-year-old Janet Jewell disappeared near Beggs, Oklahoma, en route to a job-hunting expedition in Tulsa. The next afternoon, Valerie Shaw-Hartzell, newscaster for a Tulsa radio station, vanished—along with her pickup truck—in the midst of her weekly shopping. On May 25, she was sighted at two different drive-up banks, in the company of an unidentified man, as she tried to cash personal checks. Unsuccessful in her first attempt, she obtained $500 at the second stop—and then vanished.

On May 26, a young woman was kidnapped at knifepoint from a bar in Vinita, the scene of Jayne Hilburn's murder. After being raped, she was released by her abductor and reported the crime to police. Her description of the rapist's pickup matched the missing radio announcer's vehicle, and its new driver was belatedly traced to a local motel, where he had registered as "Dana Ray."

The case "broke" on May 28, when agents of the Oklahoma State Bureau of Investigation announced that fingerprints recovered from Jayne Hilburn's Camaro had been positively identified. They belonged to ex-convict Gary Walker, now suspected in a string of violent crimes around the state. On May 29, surviving victims from Oakhurst, Skiatook, and Vinita chimed in with identifications of Walker's prison mug shots, and the hunt was on.

The next day, in Van Buren, Arkansas, a knife-wielding "madman" invaded a home and abducted two girls, taking them on a wild twenty-minute ride in their own car. He talked incessantly about the urgent need of finding "a deserted road," but the hostages escaped before he found a likely killing ground. On May 31, the girls identified Gary Walker as their abductor.

On the morning of June 2, Walker barged into another Van Buren home, threatening the female tenants with a pistol and escaping in their car. By noon, they had identified his photograph, and new alerts were issued in the Tulsa area, as homicide investigators braced themselves for Walker's possible return. That evening, a tip led officers to stake out a shabby mobile home, and Walker was captured at 10:45 p.m., approaching the trailer with two other men.

In custody, the transient slayer launched his marathon confession with a feeble plea for sympathy: "I'm sorry I killed five people, okay?" Over the next six days, Walker directed police to the bodies of missing victims Janet Jewell (near Beggs), Valerie Shaw-Hartzell (near Claremore, east of Tulsa), and Margaret Bell (in an old barn near Princeton, Kentucky). In 1985, Walker was convicted on five counts of murder and sentenced to die.

(An eerie reminder of Walker's case returned to haunt Oklahoma lawmen in 1986. On June 6, the lifeless body of Deronda Roy, age 24, was recovered from a rainswept forest between Claremore and Tulsa. Nude, except for stockings and the bra that had been used as a garrote, her corpse was bruised and marked with burns inflicted by a cigarette. The victim's last known companion had been Marshall Cummings, Jr., an ex-convict and one of the men arrested with Gary Walker on June 2, 1984. In early 1987, Cummings pled guilty to second-degree murder and was sentenced to 25 years in prison.)

Walters, Annie:
See Sach, Amelia

Whiteway, Alfred C.

A British serial slayer, 22-year-old Alfred Whiteway was arrested on July 1, 1953, on a charge of assaulting Patricia Birch in Windsor Park. The victim had been robbed of several shillings on June 12, after an attempted rape, and while Whiteway confessed the assault, he indignantly denied any intention of robbery. "I didn't want the money," he informed police. "She thrust it on me."

Whiteway's M.O. made him a prime suspect in the unsolved Teddington tow-path attacks, also committed during late May and early June. On May 24, 14-year-old Kathleen Ringham had survived the assault of a "man with a chopper," but 16-year-old Barbara Songhurst and 18-year-old Christine Reed were not so fortunate. Songhurst had been found in the Thames on June 1, with Reed fished out of the river five days later, their battered bodies bearing evidence of sexual assault.

On July 15, Whiteway pled guilty on two counts of assault, in the Birch and Ringham cases; a month later, he was charged with the murders of Songhurst and

Reed. His trial opened in Surrey on September 18, 1953, ending with his conviction and sentence of death on November 2.

Wille, John Francis

In early June 1985, 8-year-old Nichole Lapatta was reported missing from her home in Laplace, Louisiana, 40 miles from New Orleans. Searchers found her body—battered, raped, and strangled—on June 6, discarded in some nearby woods that had become a makeshift rubbish dump. A grisly bonus to their search was the discovery of another corpse—identified as Billy Phillips, 25, from Tickfaw—floating in the stagnant water of a local canal. Phillips had been stabbed at least 84 times, with his hands severed and his genitals mutilated by a maniacal killer.

A month later, on July 15, Frank Powe was thumbing rides near Bagdad, Florida, when a state trooper cautioned him against illegal hitchhiking. The warning didn't take, and the 26-year-old received a different sort of lesson that afternoon, when he was deliberately struck and killed by a hit-and-run driver.

Hours later, in Milton, Florida, sheriff's deputies were called to mediate a landlord-tenant dispute. John Wille and his girlfriend had missed several rent payments, and the landlord wanted them out. Persuaded by the sight of uniforms, Wille departed, but he crept back later and set fire to the landlord's mobile home, killing several pet dogs in the fire. Charged with first-degree arson, the 21-year-old suspect denied everything, but his girlfriend was already talking, unloading a tale of random murder spanning four states.

According to her story, Wille had given Frank Powe a lift out of Bagdad, later flying into a rage over Powe's flirtatious remarks to the woman. Beating Powe unconscious, Wille had thrown him in the pickup's bed and driven on for several miles before he stopped again, dumped Powe on the pavement and deliberately ran over his body.

Testimony from Wille's lover linked him to the Milton fire, and she described another case, years earlier, in which he burned another woman's home in retaliation for a police complaint. A phone call to LaPlace, Louisiana, confirmed the 1980 arson death of 78-year-old Ida Bodreaux, and police realized they had a serial killer on their hands. Charting Wille's travels between Louisiana and Florida, officers connected him with the murders of Nichole Lapatta and Billy Phillips, near LaPlace. Wille was also suspected in the murder of a Houston motorist, and in the case of Michael Foulk, a Pensacola cab driver abducted and dumped in a ditch near Fairhope, Alabama.

Breaking down in custody, Wille confessed to five of the murders, and then recanted everything, while agents of the FBI declared he might be linked with twice that many slayings. Indicted for Frank Powe's murder in September 1985, Wille pled guilty to escape the electric chair, receiving a sentence of life imprisonment with no parole for the first 25 years. Confined to a cell, he faced further indictments in the Foulk murder and at least two Louisiana cases.

Williams, George E.

A Chicago native, born in 1943, Williams watched his mother die in childbirth, later witnessing the murder of his infant brother by a sadistic step-mother. Convicted of armed robbery at age 18, he served time in state prison between 1961 and 1963, emerging to "go straight" as a security guard for a hospital in suburban

Oak Lawn. By 1980, his behavior on the job was classified as "erratic," and Williams was demoted to a post with the hospital's maintenance department, where he showed no improvement. Dismissed in 1983, he was embittered, hostile, seething with an urge to take revenge against society at large.

Police believe that Williams murdered seven women in the period between his firing and July of 1984, though he was only charged in two of the suspected homicides. The killer got careless on July 14, leaving his car near the home of 76-year-old Josephine McMullen, found tied to a kitchen chair in her Evergreen home, raped and strangled with a nylon stocking. Authorities learned that Williams had done some carpentry work for the victim, and discovery of his car nearby was the clincher. A warrant was issued for his arrest on July 15, and police tacked on the similar slaying of 76-year-old Dorothy Smith, raped, stabbed and strangled with a nylon stocking in her home, her body swaddled in a shower curtain. Five other area deaths fit a similar pattern, but there was insufficient evidence for an indictment.

The search for Williams went national on July 17, when Josephine McMullen's car was found in Indianapolis. Authorities thought he might be traveling to see his ex-wife, in Georgia, but Williams had actually run home to Chicago, seeking help from his family. Detectives were questioning his sister on July 20, when Williams appeared at the door and was taken into custody. Convicted on two counts of murder and rape, the defendant was sentenced to a term of life without parole.

Wolter, Michael

Twentieth-century German police are no strangers to serial murder. Since 1900, they have dealt with more compulsive killers than all their continental neighbors combined, a lethal phenomenon seemingly unrelated to historical phases of war and peace, depression or prosperity. Inevitably, such familiarity produces a degree of understanding, but authorities in Frankfurt were not ready for the series of attacks on females that began in spring of 1980 and continued for the next three years.

The first victim was Gabriele Roesner, age 25, a resident of Langen, ten miles southeast of Frankfurt am Main. On the night of May 7, 1980, while sleeping in her own bed, she was attacked and raped by an intruder, strangled with her own pajama bottoms. Homicide investigators typed the killer's blood from semen samples, but they had no other clues to his identity.

On June 14, Regina Barthel, a 14-year-old student in the town of Dietzenbach, near Langen, failed to make it home for dinner after strolling in the nearby forest. Searchers found her body late that night; she had been raped and stabbed to death.

October 21. In Offenbach, another town in the same general area, prostitute Annedore Ligeika was raped in her apartment, strangled with a pillow case. While semen samples matched the killer's blood type from the first two murders, there appeared to be no common pattern in the crimes.

On February 7, 1981, the murderer invaded Frankfurt proper, picking off Fatima Sonnenberg, another prostitute. Raped and stabbed to death at home, she was discovered by police after an anonymous caller—thought to be her pimp—reported the crime.

"Ordinary" crimes consumed the full attention of authorities until December 20, 1981, when 16-year-old Beatrix Scheible was raped and stabbed to death in a

Frankfurt park. Attacked on a short walk home from the movies, her body was still warm when discovered by officers on routine patrol.

The slayer shifted back to Dietzenbach on May 9, 1982, slaughtering young Regina Spielman in the same wooded area where Regina Barthel had been killed eleven months earlier. Picking flowers for her parents at the time she was attacked, the 17-year-old was raped and stabbed to death.

Eighteen months elapsed before the killer struck again. Police had finally agreed upon a pattern in the crimes, but now they feared the killer might have slipped away, perhaps to practice elsewhere. On the third day of November 1983, they greeted news from Babenhausen, south of Frankfurt, with the mixed emotions of dejection and relief.

The latest victim had been Ilke Rutsch, age 21, attacked and raped, then stabbed to death, while hiking in the woods near town. The killer stopped in Offenbach a second time, November 26, and claimed 22-year-old Simone Newin. Raped and strangled with her own sweat pants while running through the woods, she was found a short time later by other joggers. Three days later, the police got lucky. Walking home from work, a 19-year-old Frankfurt woman was accosted by a man who ripped her clothes off, threw her to the ground, and tried to rape her. Interrupted by a group of party-bound municipal employees, her assailant tried to flee, but he was overpowered and held for the police.

Confined initially on charges of assault and attempted rape, 25-year-old Michael Wolter was an electrician from Neu Isenburg, southeast of Frankfurt. A look at his record revealed two convictions for indecent exposure, in 1979 and 1982, but Wolter had escaped with payment of small fines on each occasion. This time, however, the charge was more serious. On

March 5, 1984, police announced Wolter's detailed confession to five of the serial slayings, with further interrogation in progress. The statements in hand were sufficient to earn him a sentence of life imprisonment.

BIBLIOGRAPHY

Abrahamson, David. *Confessions of Son of Sam*. New York: Columbia University Press, 1985.

Adam, H.L. *Trial of George Chapman*. London: William Hodge, 1930.

Allen, William. *Starkweather: The Story of a Mass Murderer*. Boston: Houghton Mifflin, 1967.

Altman, Jack, and Martin Ziporyn. *Born to Raise Hell: The Untold Story of Richard Speck*. New York: Grove, 1967.

Angelella, Michael. *Trail of Blood: A True Story*. New York: New American Library, 1979.

Bakos, Susan C. *Appointment for Murder*. New York: Putnam, 1988.

Berg, Karl. *The Sadist*. London: Heinemann, 1932.

Brussel, James A. *Casebook of a Crime Psychiatrist*. New York: Bernard Geis, 1968.

Bugliosi, Vincent, and Curt Gentry. *Helter Skelter.* New York: Norton, 1974.

Burn, Gordon. *Somebody's Husband, Somebody's Son.* New York: Viking, 1984.

Cahill, Tim. *Buried Dreams.* New York: Bantam, 1985.

Cheney, Margaret. *The Co-Ed Killer.* New York: Walker, 1976.

Clark, Tim, and John Penycate. *Psychopath.* London: Routledge & Kegan Paul, 1976.

Cray, Ed. *Burden of Proof.* New York: Macmillan, 1973.

Cross, Roger. *The Yorkshire Ripper.* London: Granada 1981.

Damio, Ward. *Urge to Kill.* New York: Pinnacle, 1974.

Damore, Leo. *In His Garden: The Anatomy of a Murderer.* New York: Arbor House, 1981.

Dettlinger, Chet, and Jeff Prugh. *The List.* Atlanta: Philmay, 1983.

Eggington, Joyce. *From Cradle to Grave: The Short Lives and Strange Deaths of Marybeth Tinning's Nine Children.* New York: William Morrow, 1989.

Elkind, Peter. *The Death Shift.* New York: Viking, 1989.

Emmons, Nuel, and Charles Manson. *Manson in His Own Words.* New York: Grove, 1986.

Fawkes, Sandy. *Killing Time*. London: Hamlyn, 1978.

Frank, Gerold. *The Boston Strangler*. New York: New American Library, 1967.

Freeman, Lucy. *"Before I Kill More ..."* New York: Crown, 1955.

Gaddis, Thomas E., and James O. Long. *Killer: A Journal of Murder*. New York: Macmillan, 1970.

Gibney, Bruce. *The Beauty Queen Killer*. New York: Pinnacle, 1984.

Godwin, George. *Peter Kurten: A Study in Sadism*. London: Acorn, 1938.

Godwin, John. *Murder USA*. New York: Ballantine, 1978.

Gollmar, Robert H. *Edward Gein*. New York: Charles Hallberg, 1981.

Graysmith, Robert. *Zodiac*. New York: St. Martin's, 1986.

Grombach, John V. *The Great Liquidator*. New York: Doubleday, 1980.

Gurwell, John K. *Mass Murder in Houston*. Houston: Cordovan Press, 1974.

Heimer, Mel. *The Cannibal: The Case of Albert Fish*. New York: Lyle Stuart, 1971.

Howard, Clark. *Zebra*. New York: Berkley, 1980.

Jones, Ann. *Women Who Kill.* New York: Holt, Rinehart and Winston, 1980.

Jouve, Nicole W. *"The Street Cleaner": The Yorkshire Ripper Case on Trial.* London: Marion Boyers, 1986.

Kennedy, Ludovic. *10 Rillington Place.* London: Gollancz, 1961.

Keyes, Edward. *The Michigan Murders.* New York: Pocket Books, 1976.

Kidder, Tracy. *The Road to Yuba City.* New York: Doubleday, 1974.

Klausner, Lawrence D. *Son of Sam.* New York: McGraw-Hill, 1981.

Kuncl, Tom, and Paul Einstein. *Ladies Who Kill.* New York: Pinnacle, 1985.

Langlois, Janet L. *Belle Gunness: The Lady Bluebeard.* Bloomington, IN: Indiana University Press, 1985.

Larsen, Richard W. *Bundy: The Deliberate Stranger.* Englewood Cliffs, NJ: Prentice-Hall, 1980.

Leith, Rod. *The Prostitute Murders: The People vs Richard Cottingham.* New York: Lyle Stuart, 1983.

Levin, Jack, and James Alan Fox. *Mass Murder: America's Growing Menace.* New York: Plenum, 1985.

Leyton, Elliott. *Compulsive Killers.* New York: New York University Press, 1986.

Linedecker, Clifford. *The Man Who Killed Boys*. New York: St. Martin's, 1980.

Linedecker, Clifford. *Thrill Killers*. New York: Paperjacks, 1987.

Livsey, Clara. *The Manson Women: A "Family" Portrait*. New York: Marek, 1980.

Lucas, Norman. *The Sex Killers*. London: W.H. Allen, 1974.

Lunde, Donald T., and Jefferson Morgan. *The Die Song: A Journey into the Mind of a Mass Murderer*. New York: W.W. Norton, 1980.

Marchbanks, David. *The Moors Murders*. London: Frewin, 1966.

Master, R.E.L., and Eduard Lea. *Perverse Crimes in History*. New York: Julian, 1963.

Masters, Brian. *Killing for Company*. London: Jonathan Cape, 1985.

McConnell, Brian. *Found Naked and Dead*. London: New English Library, 1974.

Meyer, Gerald. *The Memphis Murders*. New York: Seabury, 1974.

Michaud, Stephen, and Hugh Aynesworth. *The Only Living Witness*. New York: Simon and Schuster, 1983.

Moore, Kelly, and Dan Reed. *Deadly Medicine*. New York: St. Martin's, 1988.

Moser, Don, and Jerry Cohen. *The Pied Piper of Tucson.* New York: New American Library, 1967.

Nash, Jay Robert. *Bloodletters and Badmen.* New York: Evans, 1973.

Nash, Jay Robert. *Look for the Woman.* New York: Evans, 1981.

Nash, Jay Robert. *Murder, America.* New York: Simon and Schuster, 1980.

Neville, Richard and Julie Clark. *The Life and Crimes of Charles Sobhraj.* London: Jonathan Cape, 1979.

Newton, Michael. *Mass Murder.* New York: Garland, 1988.

Nickel, Steven. *Torso: The Story of Eliot Ness and the Search for a Psychopathic Killer.* Winston-Salem, NC: J.F. Blair, 1989.

Norris, Joel. *Serial Killers: The Growing Menace.* New York: Doubleday, 1988.

O'Brien, Darcy. *Two of a Kind: The Hillside Stranglers.* New York: New American Library, 1985.

Olsen, Jack. *The Man With the Candy: The Story of the Houston Mass Murders.* New York: Simon and Schuster, 1974.

Reinhardt, James M. *The Murderous Trail of Charles Starkweather.* Springfield, IL: C.C. Thomas, 1962.

Reinhardt, James M. *The Psychology of Strange Killers.* Springfield IL: C.C. Thomas, 1962.

Rule, Ann. *The I-5 Killer.* New York: New American Library, 1984.

Rule, Ann. *Lust Killer.* New York: New American Library, 1983.

Rule, Ann. *The Stranger Beside Me.* New York: New American Library, 1980.

Rule, Ann. *The Want-Ad Killer.* New York: New American Library, 1983.

Sanders, Ed. *The Family.* New York: Dutton, 1971.

Schechter, Harold. *Deviant: The Shocking True Story of the Original "Psycho."* New York: Pocket, 1989.

Schreiber, Flora R. *The Shoemaker: The Anatomy of a Psychotic.* New York: Simon & Schuster, 1983.

Schwartz, Ted. *The Hillside Strangler: A Murderer's Mind.* New York: Doubleday, 1981.

Sereny, Gitta. *The Case of Mary Bell.* London: Methuen, 1972.

Sifakis, Carl. *The Encyclopedia of American Crime.* New York: Facts on File, 1982.

Spinks, Sarah. *Cardiac Arrest: A True Account of Stolen Lives.* Toronto: Doubleday, 1985.

Sullivan, Terry and Peter Maiken. *Killer Clown.* New York: Grosset & Dunlap, 1983.

Terry, Maury. *The Ultimate Evil.* New York: Doubleday, 1987.

Thompson, Thomas. *Serpentine*. New York: Dell, 1979.

Tobias, Ronald. *They Shoot to Kill: A Psycho-Survey of Criminal Sniping*. Boulder, CO: Paladin, 1981.

Wagner, Margaret S. *The Monster of Dusseldorf*. London: Faber, 1932.

West, Donald. *Sacrifice Unto Me*. New York: Pyramid, 1974.

Wilcox, Robert K. *The Mysterious Deaths at Ann Arbor*. New York: Popular Library, 1977.

Williams, Emlyn. *Beyond Belief*. New York: Random House, 1967.

Wilson, Colin, and Patricia Putnam. *The Encyclopedia of Murder*. New York: Putnam, 1961.

Wilson, Colin, and Donald Seaman. *The Encyclopedia of Modern Murder, 1962–1982*. New York: Putnam, 1983.

Winn, Steven, and David Merrill. *Ted Bundy: The Killer Next Door*. New York: Bantam, 1980.

Yallop, David. *Deliver Us From Evil*. New York: Coward, McCann, 1982.

INDEX